IN THE NAME OF

ALLAH

THE ALL-COMPASSIONATE, ALL-MERCIFUL

Early Sources for Prophet Muhammad's Biography

- Title: *Early Sources for Prophet Muhammad's Biography*
- Author: Dr. Muhammad Saeed Mitwally ar-Rahawān
- English Edition 1 (2015)
- Layout Design: IIPH, Egypt Branch
- Cover Design: Samo Press Group, Beirut

Early Sources for Prophet Muhammad's Biography

A Source-Critical Study with Reference to MS. Berlin 9409, the So-Called "Tārīkh Ibn Abi Shaybah"

المصادر الأولى للسيرة النبوية

Dr. Muhammad Saeed Mitwally ar-Rahawān

الدار العالمية للكتاب الإسلامي

INTERNATIONAL ISLAMIC PUBLISHING HOUSE

King Fahd National Library Cataloging-in-Publication Data

ar-Rahawān, Muhammad Saeed Mitwally

Early Sources for Prophet Muhammad's Biography. / Dr. Muhammad Saeed Mitwally ar-Rahawān. — Riyadh, 2015

256 pp ; 24 cm

1- Prophet Muhammad 2- Biography of prophets
I- Muhammad Saeed Mitwally ar-Rahawān II- Title

239 dc

Legal Deposit no. **1436/907**
ISBN Hardcover: 978-603-501-277-5

International Islamic Publishing House (IIPH)
P.O. Box 55195 Riyadh 11534, Saudi Arabia
Tel: 966 11 4650818 / 4647213 — Fax: 966 11 4633489
E-mail: editorial@iiph.com — iiphsa@gmail.com
www.iiph.com | www.iiph.com.sa

Contents

Pronunciation and Transliteration Chart

Arabic script	Pronunciation	Trans-literated form
أ	short 'a', as in *cat*	a
آ — ى	longer 'a', as in *cab* (not as in *cake*)	ā
ب	/b/ as in *bell*, *rubber* and *tab*	b
ت	/t/ as in *tap*, *mustard* and *sit*	t
ة	takes the sound of the preceding diacritical mark sometimes ending in h (when in pausal form): ah, ih or ooh; or atu(n), ati(n) or ata(n) when uninterrupted	h or t (when followed by another Arabic word)
ث	/th/ as in *thing*, *maths* and *wealth*	th
ج	/j/ as in *jam*, *ajar* and *age*	j
ح	a 'harsher' sound than the English initial /h/, and may occur medially and in word-final position as well	ḥ
خ	as in *Bach* (in German); may occur initially and medially as well	kh
د	/d/ as in *do*, *muddy* and *red*	d
ذ	as in *this*, *father* and *smooth*	dh
ر	/r/ as in *raw*, *arid* and *war*; may also be a rolled 'r', as pronounced in Spanish	r
ز	/z/ as in *zoo*, *easy* and *gaze*	z

Arabic script	Pronunciation	Trans-literated form
س	/s/ as in *so*, *messy* and *grass*	s
ش	as in *ship*, *ashes* and *rush*	sh
ص	no close equivalent in English, but may be approximated by pronouncing it as /sw/ or /s/ farther back in the mouth	ṣ
ض	no close equivalent in English, but may be approximated by pronouncing it as /d/ farther back in the mouth	ḍ
ط	no close equivalent in English, but may be approximated by pronouncing it as /t/ farther back in the mouth	ṭ
ظ	no close equivalent in English, but may be approximated by pronouncing 'the' farther back in the mouth	ẓ
ع	no close equivalent in English: a guttur-al sound in the back of the throat	'
غ	no close equivalent in English, but may be closely approximated by pronouncing it like the French /r/ in 'rouge'	gh
ف	/f/ as in *fill*, *effort* and *muff*	f
ق	no close equivalent in English, but may be approximated by pronouncing it as /k/ farther back in the mouth	q
ك	/k/ as in *king*, *buckle* and *tack*	k
ل	/l/ as in *lap*, *halo*; in the word Allah, it becomes velarized as in *ball*	l
م	/m/ as in *men*, *simple* and *ram*	m
ن	/n/ as in *net*, *ant* and *can*	n

Arabic script	Pronunciation	Trans-literated form
ه – ـه – ـهـ	/h/ as in *hat*; unlike /h/ in English, in Arabic /h/ is pronounced in medial and word-final positions as well	h
و	as in *wet* and *away*	w
و	long 'u', as in *boot* and *too*	ū
ي	as in *yard* and *mayo*	y
ي	long 'e', as in *eat*, *beef* and *see*	ī
ء	glottal stop: may be closely approximated by pronouncing it like 't' in the Cockney English pronunciation of *butter*: *bu'er*, or the stop sound in *uh-oh!*	' (omitted in initial position)

Diphthongs

Arabic script	Pronunciation	Trans-literated form
أو، ـَو	long 'o', as in *owe boat* and *go*	au, aw
أي، ـَي	long 'a', as in *aid*, *rain* and *say*	ay, ai, ei

Diacritical marks (tashkeel)

Name of mark	Pronunciation	Trans-literated form
َ fatḥah	very short 'a' or schwa (unstressed vowel)	a
ِ kasrah	shorter version of ee or schwa (unstressed vowel)	i
ُ ḍammah	shorter version of oo	u
ّ shaddah	a doubled consonant is stressed in the word, and the length of the sound is also doubled	double letter
ْ sukoon	no vowel sound between consonants or at the end of a word	absence of vowel

Arabic honorific symbols

(سبحانه وتعالى)	*Subḥânahu wa Ta'âlâ*	The Exalted
(صلى الله عليه وسلم)	*ṣalla Allâhu 'alayhi wa sallam*	Blessings and peace be upon him
(عليه السلام)	*'alayhi as-salâm*	May peace be upon him
(رضي الله عنه)	*raḍiya Allâhu 'anhu*	May Allah be pleased with him
(رضي الله عنها)	*raḍiya Allâhu 'anhâ*	May Allah be pleased with her
(رضي الله عنهما)	*raḍiya Allâhu 'anhumâ*	May Allah be pleased with both of them
(رضي الله عنهم)	*raḍiya Allâhu 'anhum*	May Allah be pleased with all of them
(رضي الله عنهن)	*raḍiya Allâhu 'anhunna*	May Allah be pleased with all of them (females only)

Hadith grade terms

Sound:	*ṣaḥeeḥ*
Reliable:	*ḥasan*
Weak:	*ḍa'eef*
Odd:	*ghareeb*
Authentic:	includes sound, reliable, or any grade in between
Acceptable:	*sakat 'anhu;* the grader of the hadith did not comment on it, meaning that he found nothing unacceptable in it

Publisher's Note

All praise and thanks belong to Allah alone, the One, the Almighty and All-Merciful. Blessings and peace be upon Prophet Muhammad, the last of His messengers and prophets, and upon his family, his Companions and all those who follow in his footsteps until the end of time.

The life of the Prophet (ﷺ) has always been a source of great inspiration for the Muslims, but very few actually consider the extent of the research conducted by those who have delved deep into the various sources to reconstruct his life for us in the form of *sīrah*, or biography. In this commendable and in-depth study, the author explains that early Western researchers relied on the Qur'an and other Muslim sources for the biography of the Prophet (ﷺ), but that this approach received a setback when doubts were cast on the reliability of hadiths as a source of the Prophet's biography. Still, Western researchers gave Muslims many tools of critical analysis, which could then be applied to the current body of hadiths in order to paint a more complete and more accurate picture of the Prophet's life. Taking certain hadiths as examples, the author has applied some of those tools with insightful results. This book is a must-have for all students of Hadith as well as those who doubt the authenticity of the Hadith.

May Allah accept the efforts of all those who have contributed to the production of this book, and may it be acceptable to Him, *āmīn*.

Muhammad Abdul Mohsin Al-Tuwaijri
Managing Director
International Islamic Publishing House
Riyadh, Saudi Arabia

Quotations from the Qur'an

The *sūrah* (chapter)[1] and *āyah* (verse) numbers given in Qur'anic quotations are identical to those in the official Egyptian edition of the Qur'an. The sūrah number always comes first, followed by the āyah number. The translations of the verses have been taken from *The Qur'an*, translated by M. A. S. Abdel Haleem.

Arabic edition of the manuscript

For practical reasons, I relied solely upon MS. Berlin 9409 in editing the Arabic text of the manuscript. I tried to procure other copies of the manuscript, but I was unsuccessful. Another copy, which some thought could be found in aẓ-Ẓāhiriyah (Damascus), no longer exists; this was confirmed to me by the clerks and administrators of the Al-Asad National Library and aẓ-Ẓāhiriyah. Thus, I have relied on MS 9409 and on the edited edition of *Kitāb al-Muṣannaf* by Ibn Abi Shaybah, to which I have referred throughout this book as the *Muṣannaf*.[2]

Dedication

With genuine humility, I acknowledge Your aid and Your endless support for me, Allah (*Subḥānahu wa Ta'ālā*—Glorified and Exalted is He). If this work is worth dedicating, please bless it with Your acceptance.

Introduction

Early Western biographies of the Prophet of Islam (*ṣalla Allāhu ʻalayhi wa sallam*—blessings and peace be upon him), written during the first half of the nineteenth century, were largely based upon the Qur'an, as well as upon the late Muslim sources dating from the sixteenth century. From Gustav Weil[3] to William Muir, European writers proceeded on the assumption that if a certain amount of careful sifting was done, a considerable body of reliable tradition could be used for biographical purposes.

During the twentieth century, a corpus of major biographical sources, compiled between the end of the second and the end of the third Islamic centuries, became available. Such sources included al-Wāqidi's *Maghāzi*, Ibn Saʻd's *aṭ-Ṭabaqāt* and aṭ-Ṭabari's *Tārīkh* (History). Many Western biographers realized that:

> [T]here were contradictions in the sources, traces of legends, exaggerations, and many kinds of biases, but they were, nonetheless, convinced that a critical mind would be able to reconstruct what really happened.[4]

A more critical perspective within the academic study of the Prophet's life was set in motion with the publication in 1890 of Ignác Goldziher's *Muhammedanische Studien*, which had a considerable impact on Western study of the Hadith (the collected statements and actions of Prophet Muhammad [ﷺ] that with the Qur'an form the basis of Islamic law). As a result of Goldziher's research, many scholars began to view Muslim sources as increasingly controversial.

Doubts were further intensified with Joseph Schacht's publication of *The Origins of Muhammadan Jurisprudence*, an extremely influential book. He argued that many of the legal maxims contained in the hadiths (statements or actions of Prophet Muhammad [ﷺ] that were remembered and recorded by his Companions and followers) discuss issues that could only have become problems long after the Prophet (ﷺ) had died. Thus, he concluded that these hadiths could not have been sayings of the Prophet (ﷺ) and that they must have been 'created' at a later date and attributed to him.[5] Schacht also wrote some articles in which he tried to apply his methods to historical materials.[6]

After the publication of Schacht's work, Western scholars adopted different views concerning the authenticity and reliability of early Muslim biographical sources. Some, such as William Montgomery Watt, believed that the narrations had historical value despite their 'tendentious shaping' (or partisan influences on them).[7] Others, such as Michael Cook, Patricia Crone[8] and Maxime Rodinson,[9] tried to reconstruct the early history of Islam using non-Muslim sources. A third group, which included John Wansbrough, felt that the available sources justified nothing more than an approach based on literary criticism.

Consequently, at least in the West, critical evaluation of the sources of the Prophet's biography is the norm. According to Western scholars, one cannot write a complete historical biography of the Prophet (ﷺ) without being accused of using the sources uncritically, yet when one is consistent in using the sources as critically as suggested, one cannot write such a biography at all.

The aim of this study is to prove that applying Western critical analysis to the available Muslim sources can take us back to early, reliable information about the Prophet (ﷺ). This hypothesis is based on three insights:

1. The issue of historical traditions is blurred by a number of biases that are dominant in Western scholarship. According to some Western scholars, biographical materials are of an exegetical character; in other words, they were fabricated to explain the Qur'an, to support the creation of Islamic theology, or to form legal precedents. However, all these biases are based on theoretical discussions, and most of them lack in-depth and direct investigation of biographical sources.
2. A considerable number of early biographical and Hadith compilations have been discovered and edited in the last few decades. Such sources were not available in the first half of the twentieth century. They include the two *Muṣannafs* of 'Abdur-Razzāq and Ibn Abi Shaybah, 'Umar ibn Shabbah's *Tārīkh al-Madīnah*, al-Fākihi's *Akhbār Makkah*, and the *Tafsīr* (Qur'anic exegesis) of 'Abdur-Razzāq aṣ-Ṣan'āni.
3. Notable and influential advancements in the field of Hadith methodology have been achieved during the last few years. For example, analysis of the *sanad* (or *isnād*, pl. *asānīd*, meaning the chain of narration) of single traditions, a method developed by G. H. A. Juynboll, has proven to be a powerful research tool. Moreover, the advancement of source criticism based on isnād-cum-*matn* analysis (study of the isnād alongside the *matn*, or body of the hadith) has achieved considerable progress by combining the

investigation of asānīd with literary analysis and by involving the use of an exhaustive corpus of sources.[10]

These methodological advancements, along with the discovery of new sources, should prompt further discussions on the origin and development of early Muslim biographical sources. This topic is the focal point of this book.

Identifying the main questions of the study and detailing the research methodology

The main concern of this book is the origin and development of early biographical sources about the life of Muhammad, the Prophet of Islam (ﷺ). We will examine traditions from the first two Islamic centuries, with an emphasis on those of Iraqi origin.

The main new source used is a manuscript known as MS. Berlin 9409, which contains the text of *Kitāb at-Tārīkh* by Abu Bakr 'Abdullāh ibn Muhammad ibn Abi Shaybah al-'Absi (159-235 AH/ 775-849 CE), who is usually referred to as Ibn Abi Shaybah.[11]

According to Schützinger, who published a brief description of the manuscript in 1979,[12] there is no doubt that it is correctly attributed to Ibn Abi Shaybah. Schützinger also affirms that the manuscript does not constitute a part of Ibn Abi Shaybah's famous *Muṣannaf*, although Schützinger did not have access to a complete version of this text.

His study was written more than 30 years ago; since then, new sources have been published, allowing us to revise some of his conclusions. Knowing that Ibn Abi Shaybah is the compiler and transmitter of the material contained in the manuscript does not tell us whether the material is reliable, though. In Chapter Two, we will address the material's origin and reliability by using the source-critical approach to ask and answer the following questions:

- What are Ibn Abi Shaybah's sources?
- Are they real sources?
- Did Ibn Abi Shaybah actually receive the material from the people he cites as his sources?

In order to date the material more accurately, this study applies the method of isnād-cum-matn analysis on single traditions. Thus, the most important question is:

What is the development and origin of the material about the life of the Prophet (ﷺ) as transmitted by Ibn Abi Shaybah?

Chapter Three of this study will compare some of Ibn Abi Shaybah's sources to those of his Iraqi contemporaries, in order to track the development of this material in the first two Islamic centuries.

Ibn Abi Shaybah is an Iraqi scholar who studied with Iraqi teachers mostly; in contrast, most standard sources of the Prophet's biography are based on traditions from the *Ḥijāz* (the Western region of the Arabian Peninsula, which includes Makkah and Madinah). In Chapter Four, we will compare the different origins of the biographical material. Such a comparison necessitates a further evaluation of Ibn Abi Shaybah's traditions (or those of his sources) against those of Ḥijāzi origin, for example, against Ibn Hishām, Ibn Is-ḥāq, 'Abdur-Razzāq, and Ma'mar az-Zuhri. Thus, this chapter also discusses the origin of the Prophet's biographical sources.

In short, this study tries to answer three main questions:

1. To what extent are Ibn Abi Shaybah's sources reliable?
2. How did his materials develop over the first two Islamic centuries?
3. What are the origins of the standard biographical sources of the Prophet's life?

This book consists of an introduction, four chapters, a conclusion and three appendices.

Chapter One sheds light on the history of Western research in the nineteenth and twentieth centuries as well as on the origin and development of early Muslim biographical sources of Prophet Muhammad (ﷺ).

Chapter Two tackles the edited source of the study (MS. Berlin 9409, the so-called *Kitāb at-Tārīkh* of Ibn Abi Shaybah); it also elaborates on the life of its author and demonstrates his authorship of the manuscript as well as the reliability of his sources. This chapter is mainly concerned with answering a number of preliminary questions, such as:

- Does MS. Berlin 9409 really contain the work of Ibn Abi Shaybah?
- Is it truly the *Kitāb at-Tārīkh*, as claimed by some Western scholars?
- To what extent can the reliability of Ibn Abi Shaybah's sources be ascertained?

Chapter Three touches specifically upon the main discussion by examining some of Ibn Abi Shaybah's reports, as transmitted in MS. Berlin 9409, to determine the development of the author's materials and the history of their transmission during the first two Islamic centuries. These reports are compared to other variants in the Iraqi and Ḥijāzi sources by means of isnād-cum-matn analysis.

Chapter Four introduces an answer to the question of the origins of standard material of the Prophet's biography, by comparing Ibn Abi Shaybah's materials to the Ḥijāzi sources.

The thesis also contains three appendices. Appendix 1 includes charts used for analyzing isnād bundles that are discussed in Chapters Three and Four, Appendix 2 contains images of the original folios of MS. Berlin 9409, and Appendix 3 contains the Arabic text of the traditions discussed in Chapters Three and Four.

I am deeply thankful to Prof. Dr. Bruce Jones, Professor of Religious Studies, California State University of Bakersfield (CSUB), whose generous assistance helped me to procure all of the sources and references used in this work. Also, I greatly appreciate the assistance of Mrs. Ellen Elsabagh in proofreading and editing my English as well as providing valuable insights regarding the work.

Finally, I would like to express my gratitude to the members and trustees of the Islamic Center of San Joaquin Valley in Bakersfield, California, who hosted me during my stay in the United States, where I completed this work.

Chapter One

Early biographical sources of the Prophet's life used in nineteenth and twentieth century research

1.1 Introduction

The main intent of this chapter is to review the history of nineteenth and twentieth century Western research into the origin and development of early Muslim biographical sources about the life of Prophet Muhammad (ﷺ). This review will clarify the point at which the investigation begins and the problem it attempts to solve. Therefore, this chapter covers the following topics:

- Early research: from the first half of the nineteenth century to the publication of Goldziher's *Muhammadinsche Studien* in 1890;
- The beginning of the Western criticism of early classical Muslim sources, which commences with Goldziher;
- Research from the era following Goldziher, during which scholars reacted differently to his theories;
- Schacht's theory on the subject of legal and biographical traditions, which marks the beginning of contemporary Western criticism of the Hadith;
- Research from the era following Schacht, including contemporary studies, which represents the research context of our study;
- A review of the current status of the issue of related resources in the West;
- A conclusion outlining the main points of the history of the problem.

1.2 Early research

The academic study of the life of the Prophet of Islam (ﷺ) began in the West during the first half of the nineteenth century. In 1843, Gustav Weil published the first Western scholarly biography of Prophet Muhammad (ﷺ);[1] it was based on the Qur'an and on Islamic sources dating from the sixteenth century onwards. Weil's work is considered to be the first scholarly attempt because he applied the historical method to biographical sources, even though he did not delve deeply into them during the course of his investigation. As Arthur Jeffery notes, "He founded and applied the method."[2]

In 1864, Weil introduced the first German translation of Ibn Hishām's recension[3] of Ibn Is-ḥāq's *Sīrah*.[4] In addition, he wrote a history of the early caliphs of Islam[5] by referencing some sources that had not been used before his time; he also wrote a history of the Muslims.[6] In writing the biography of the Prophet (ﷺ), Weil relied on two major sources: the Qur'an and the Hadith. About the Qur'an, Weil states, "It is [in] a highly poetical garb full of legends which was calculated to attack and captivate the imaginative minds of the Arabs."[7]

Weil's biography of the Prophet (ﷺ) clearly contains traces of hostile Orientalist attitudes, and he reiterates the medieval Western allegations that the Qur'an was borrowed from Judeo-Christian scripture. He applied *Historiche-Kritische* (historical criticism) to the Qur'an, using a method that proposed a four-period dating system and that was later adopted in Theodor Nöldeke's better-known chronology *Geschichte des Qorans*, published in 1860.

Although he relies on the Hadith literature for his biography of the Prophet (ﷺ), Weil notes that in the second century AH/ eighth century CE, an immense number of fictitious traditions became prevalent. He comments:

> Reliance upon oral traditions at a time when they were transmitted by memory alone, produced every day divisions among the scholars of Islam, which opened up a wide field of fabrication and distortion.[8]

Although he regards the traditions as "numerous and some of them so contradictory, that no historian or biographer has been able to admit them all,"[9] he concedes that proper criticism may be worked out. He remarks:

> In order to make [these reports] in some degree complete, we were obliged to draw from various sources as it was only in this way that the unity and roundness could be obtained.

Weil claims that Muslim criticism of the Hadith is unreliable, so he based his biography mainly on the Qur'an and on later Islamic sources from the sixteenth century onwards, after making criticism that was not fully evolved.

In 1847 in Paris, Causin de Perceval published his three-volume *Essai sur l'Historie des Arabes*, which contains an account of the life and work of the

Prophet of Islam (ﷺ). He apparently wrote it quite independently of Weil. Arthur Jeffery said about it, "While not of any great value in itself, it is of real importance for the mass of material from Arabic sources that it brings together."[10] Causin de Perceval relied primarily on assembling original sources, without conducting scientific criticism.

Western research in the first half of the nineteenth century was distinguished by a need for editing and unearthing more Arabic manuscripts about the life of the Prophet (ﷺ). Ferdinand Wüstenfeld (d. 1899), one of those who participated extensively in editing Arabic manuscripts, made three contributions within the field.

1. He wrote a biography of the Prophet (ﷺ) that relied mainly on Arabic sources.[11]
2. He edited a number of Arabic sources, including Ibn Hishām's *Sīrat an-Nabi* in 1859.[12]
3. His masterly studies—which include *Genealogische Tabellen der Arabishcen Stamme und Familien*, *Chariken der Stadt Mekka*, *Das Gebiet von Medina*, and *die Geschichtsreiber der Araber und Ihre Werke*—illuminated much of the early history of Islam.

Wüstenfeld relied extensively on Arabic sources. When he published his German work *Arabic Historians* in 1882, he mentioned 27 names before Ibn Isḥāq as earlier sources of Islamic history. These were individuals who lived during the first century and the early half of the second century AH.[13]

Aloys Sprenger's *The Life of Mohammed from Original Sources*,[14] a meagre sketch of the life of the Prophet of Islam (ﷺ) up to his migration to Madinah, appeared in 1851. Sprenger later expanded his biography of the Prophet (ﷺ) in his *Das Leben und die Lehre des Mohammad.*[15] Sprenger's works relied on early and later Arabic sources that were extant in manuscript form in European and Indian libraries at his time. Sprenger is also credited with the earliest discovery of Muhammad ibn 'Amr al-Wāqidi's *Kitāb al-Maghāzi.* He succeeded in examining a portion of the long volume of *Tārīkh aṭ-Ṭabari,* beginning with the birth of the Prophet (ﷺ) and ending with the Battle of the Trench, which took place five years before the Prophet's death.

Although Sprenger relied on original sources, his approach to the life of the Prophet (ﷺ) retained subjective attitudes and hostile medieval European legends, clinging to pathological interpretations as the key to understanding the Prophet's personality. Sprenger presents these interpretations in both *Life of Mohammed* and *Das Leben*; he emphasizes them even more in *Mohammed und der Koran: eine*

Psychologische Studie.[16] Arthur Jeffery notes that this pathological approach was not convincing and was subject to sharp criticism from Sprenger's contemporaries.[17] Muir characterizes Sprenger's work as 'marked by a love of paradox and tendency to strike out theories based on too slender ground.'[18] Hirshfeld remarks, "He is mistaken in attributing a large share in the creation of Islam to [the Prophet's] nerves."[19]

Sprenger divided his source materials into the following five classifications:

1. the Qur'an,
2. biographies of the Prophet (ﷺ),
3. the Sunnah (the precedent, practice and collected sayings of Prophet Muhammad [ﷺ] that together with the Qur'an forms the basis of Islamic law),
4. commentaries on the Qur'an, and
5. original documents compiled by the collectors of traditions.

In 1856, Muir published his *Life of Mahomet*,[20] which is regarded as one of the most influential nineteenth century Western biographies of the Prophet of Islam (ﷺ). In writing this biography, Muir relied on biographical literature in the Arabic, Persian and Urdu languages. In his introduction, there is a statement about the principles he applied in his criticism of the sources.[21] In it, he makes a distinction between the two main sources from which he drew his materials, namely the Qur'an and the Hadith; he also mentions the two minor sources he used: contemporary documents and Arabic poetry.[22] About the Qur'an, Muir says:

> [It] consists exclusively of the revelations or commands which [Mohammad] professed from time to time through Gabriel, as a message direct from God; and which, under an alleged divine direction, he delivered to those about him.[23]

Muir's conclusion about the Qur'an is to "hold it to be surely Mohammad's words, as the Muslims hold it to be the word of God." Regarding his other source, Muir states that the Hadith:

> consists of the sayings of the friends and followers of the Prophet, handed down by a real or supposed chain of narrators to the period when they were collected, recorded, and classified.[24]

As for the transmission history of the Hadith, Muir is convinced that "traditions were handed down orally and, moreover, were affected by bias and prejudice."[25] To form an adequate understanding of both the value and shortcomings of traditions, Muir proposes that:

The reader should possess an outline of the historical aspect of the empire of Islam from the death of the Prophet to the period at which our written authorities commence.[26]

The historical review that Muir provides, however, relies mostly on traditions, which would seem to point to a circularity in his method. In any case, he affirms that:

> although the features of the Prophet were magnified into majestic and supernatural dimensions, yet the character of his friends and followers, and the general events of early Islam, were undoubtedly preserved with tolerable accuracy and thus a broad basis of historical truth was maintained.[27]

Muir believes that historical reality lies in Muslim sources, but he doubts the standards by which early Muslims criticized the hadiths. He describes what he sees as three shortcomings of classical Muslim criticism:

1. Each tradition was regarded as 'a unity to be accepted or rejected as a whole.' Therefore, "the power of eradicating interpolated words or of excluding the erroneous traditions was thus renounced."[28]
2. Their exclusively oral character 'deprives early tradition of check against error and fabrication.'[29]
3. The Muslims rely on the isnād for verification of the hadiths. Muir remarks, "Early Muslim tradition was confined to the names responsible for it not to the subject matter."[30] Moreover, the political element in the history of the Muslims 'extinguished free inquiry and real criticism.'[31] Muslim sources rest their authority on the memory of those who handed them down and who retained convictions and prejudices of their own. The same applies to the general collections of hadiths, which 'were made under similar influence.'[32]

One can easily see that most of Muir's premises are generalized observations that lack solid proof or even extensive study of biographical or legal traditions. Fabrication did spread among early traditions, a fact which was ascertained by classical Muslim critics, but it was not the only phenomenon.

Moreover, Muir suggests relying on only a few early biographical sources whom he deems 'worthy of attention', namely Ibn Is-ḥāq, Ibn Hishām, al-Wāqidi, Ibn Sa'd and aṭ-Ṭabari.[33] He adds to these sources 'traditions in general collections of the earliest traditionists, Bukhari, Muslim, and at-Tirmidhi.'[34] Later compilations, in Muir's view, do not have any original or independent authority. He states, "They do not allow any historical weight whatsoever,"[35] and he asks:

whether these collections contain any authentic elements of the life of Mohammad and, if so, how and to what extent these have become commingled with adventitious or erroneous materials...[36]

To answer these questions, Muir proposes an internal examination of traditions, based on three points upon which the probable accuracy of any tradition can be determined. Accordingly, critics should evaluate each tradition by answering the following three questions:[37]

1. Did a bias exist in the mind of the nation at large concerning the subject narrated?
2. Are there any traces of special interest, prejudice or design on the part of the narrator?
3. Did the narrator actually have the opportunity to know these facts?

Next, a critic should test the traditions by means of 'internal criticism,' which, according to Muir, 'relies on the investigation of the period to which a tradition purports to refer and then the subject which it treats.'[38] He also notes, "The value of evidence depends upon the degree to which the facts were noticed by the time of their occurrence."[39]

After the publication of Muir's book, reliance on Arabic sources was intensified in the works of Nöldeke[40] and Julius Wellhausen.[41] Nöldeke relied on the popular original sources, while Wellhausen provided an abridged translation of the complete copy of al-Wāqidi's *al-Maghāzi*. Thus, in the course of the nineteenth century and the beginning of the twentieth century, manuscripts of earlier sources about the biography of the Prophet (ﷺ) were edited. Besides al-Wāqidi's work, Ibn Hishām's *Sīrah,* aṭ-Ṭabari's *Tārīkh* and Ibn Sa'd's *aṭ-Ṭabaqāt,* along with the Qur'an and Bukhari's collection of hadiths, became the standard sources for Western biographies of the Prophet (ﷺ).

The period from Weil to Muir is mainly distinguished by its recourse to original sources in Arabic, accompanied by an increased interest in unearthing the original sources. These early writers were not satisfied with later authorities; they succeeded in bringing to light all the earliest documents. During this period, European writers worked on the assumption that if a certain amount of careful sifting was done, one could find a considerable body of reliable traditions upon which biographies could be based.[42] Western biographers realized, of course, that there were contradictions and many kinds of biases; nonetheless, they were convinced that a critical mind would be able to reconstruct what had actually happened.[43]

1.3 The beginning of criticism

This optimistic stance—that a critical mind could rely on the early Arabic sources to reconstruct biographies—received its first blow in 1890 when Ignác Goldziher, a Hungarian Orientalist and the Secretary of the Hebrew congregation in the Hungarian city of Pecs, published the second part of his *Muhammedanische Studien*.[44] This work is generally considered, at least in the West, to be the first milestone in the Western efforts to depict the earliest history of the Hadith, which is one of the two major sources of the Prophet's biography.[45]

According to Goldziher, hadiths (on both historical and legal matters) were invented as needed in order to document the different views espoused by various scholars.[46] To him, they reflected attitudes and viewpoints obtained in the second and third Islamic centuries and had little to tell us about the early part of the first century, to which they allegedly belonged. This argument instantly gained wide acceptance among the Western scholars and has remained their established thesis ever since.[47] In Goldziher's view, Muslim sources do not faithfully transmit historical information; they are literary creations based on a transmission history (isnād) whose validity remains doubtful. According to him, they are 'primarily documents which show how the oldest teachers of Islam set out to teach, in the spirit of their teacher.'[48] He also believed that, "These literary creations do not belong to the time of the Prophet but are invented by philologists and antiquarians of the second century."[49]

Goldziher was not interested in reconstructing the history of Islam; he was more interested in the hadiths that reflected the problems of the era after the Prophet's death.[50] His primary theory about the early Muslim sources consists of two major propositions.

- The first proposition, based on a number of his observations regarding the early history of Islam, is that these sources are generally unreliable.
- The second proposition concerns the dating of traditions; he tried to date traditions by relying on the content of the hadiths. He elaborated on his efforts in his article "Uber die Entwicklung des *Hadith*," published in 1890 in the second volume of his *Muhammedanische Studien.* Goldziher's method of dating Muslim sources relies on two principles.

1. According to Goldziher's first principle, most of the materials available in canonical collections and early sources of the early history of Islam are actually of late origin; they reflect issues that did not emerge in the Islamic

community until it reached more mature stages of development.[51] Thus he argues that the bulk of traditions concerning the Prophet (ﷺ), and most reports on the Companions, do not have any worth as historical sources for the time about which they purport to inform us.[52]

2. Goldziher's second principle relies on a number of rudimentary assumptions that were summarized by Motzki[53] as follows:
   a. Anachronisms indicate a late origin of the text.[54]
   b. Traditions showing secondary development in an issue are more recent than those with less developed content.[55]
   c. A tradition can be accepted as having an early origin if it shows early Muslims and the Prophet (ﷺ) in an unfavourable light.[56]
   d. Reproaches between two opposing parties probably have a historical kernel.

Based on his theories about the origin and dating of traditions, Goldziher concluded that historians could not use the Hadith as a source for the time period at the beginning of Islam. For later periods, they could use as sources those few traditions that were proven to have a late origin.[57] He also refrained from using biographical traditions to give a sketch of the Prophet's life; he restricted his presentation to the Qur'an only.

Goldziher's treatment of biographical and historical reports is certainly more critical than that of Weil, Sprenger and Muir. However, by being too quick to dismiss as inauthentic or fabricated those reports which do not fit into his pre-constructed theories, he leaves himself open to criticism. Most of this criticism relates to inconsistencies that can be found in his arguments. What follows is a brief elaboration of some of the critical points raised against Goldziher.[58]

He argued that it was impossible to distinguish genuine from fictitious reports about the Prophet's time, but he did not explain what new criteria made it possible to draw such distinctions when it came to the later period.[59]

Goldziher's argument that a number of hadiths are not genuine, and that they reflect later developments within the Islamic society, does not support the conclusion that this is true for all hadiths. This apparent generalization lacks any substantial proof.[60]

Moreover, Goldziher's conclusions are based merely on the limited sample of traditions that he collected, many of which have sources that are not even accepted by the Muslims. His reliance on Shiite[61] (as opposed to Sunni) sources makes his argument indefensible. Motzki remarks that Goldziher did not formulate his general dating of the Hadith as a universal statement; it was only a partial generalization about the vast stock of hadiths.[62] In other words, he accepted that some authentic hadiths do go back to the first half of the first Islamic century, but he did not concern himself with them, thus presenting an epistemological problem.[63] Motzki points out the result of Goldziher's assumptions:

> If we have to do with a tradition which is not clearly a late fabrication—which is most frequently the case—thus into which category must we place it? If Goldziher's general dating is correct, thus for statistical reasons, we have to conclude, indeed it is safer to answer, that the tradition is late or not authentic, for the probability of coming across an early and possibly authentic hadith is not large.[64]

As a result of his evaluation of the sources, Goldziher was left with almost nothing about the first century and little that is definite about the first half of the second century.

Even though his conclusions were mainly based on legal traditions, they affected the Western study of biographical traditions relating to the Prophet (ﷺ). After Goldziher, Western scholars dealt with hadiths—at least the legal materials—more critically and cautiously. Nevertheless, a few scholars, such as J. W. Fück, explicitly rejected Goldziher's scepticism and provided a critical response to his thesis.

1.4 Post-Goldziher: Exegetical and dogmatic origin of sources

During the late nineteenth and early twentieth centuries, there were a number of small, popular works based largely on the work of Goldziher. The best known among them are:

- Johnstone's *Muhammad and His Power*
- Sell's *The Life of Mohammed*
- Wollaston's *Muhammad, His Life and Doctrines*
- Albert Fua's *La vie et la Morale de Mahomet*
- Reiner's *Muhammad und der Islam*
- Reckendorf's *Muhammed und die Seinen*

As a result of Goldziher's influence, some of the biographies published during the first half of the twentieth century contained introductions or postscripts pointing out the precarious or doubtful value of the sīrah and *maghāzi* material,[65] although the authors were forced to rely heavily upon this material.

After Goldziher's study of the Hadith, scholars formed three major groups.

1. The first group felt that he corroborated their view that the majority of traditions circulating in the third century AH were not genuine hadiths and did not contain even a kernel of historical relevance. These scholars included, for instance, Theodor Nöldeke[66] and Carl Heinrich Becker.[67] This opinion is no different from that of the critical Muslim Hadith scholars of the classical era, in the sense that they too rejected large numbers of traditions; however, there are differences in the methods that various scholars apply in determining whether a given hadith is genuine.
2. The second group adopted a more radical position, developing Goldziher's principle that the Hadith must be generally considered false.

   Leon Caetani and Henri Lammens held the opinion that almost all traditions about the Prophet's life were apocryphal (well known but probably untrue).[68] In 1910, Lammens published his *Qoran et Tradition*, presenting for the first time the thesis that the material which constitutes the biography of Prophet Muhammad (ﷺ) has an exegetical character and owes its existence to the efforts of the Muslims of the first two Islamic centuries to understand and explain the Qur'an.[69] In this article, Lammens goes further than Goldziher by assuming that the traditions are simply elaborations of some phrases or words in the Qur'an; he argues that they have no independent authority and thus cannot be used as independent sources for biographical purposes.

   In a similar manner, Wensinck in 1932 applied Goldziher's thesis to dogmatic traditions and reached the conclusion that traditions about the basic tenets of Islam reflect the development of Muslim dogma going back no earlier than the end of the Umayyad period.[70]

   Richard Bell based his work entirely on the Qur'an, taking no account of the Hadith or sīrah; he thought that the Qur'an itself contains the main principles needed to guide one through the maze of traditions.[71]
3. A third group, with J. W. Fück the most prominent among them, rejected Goldziher's theory and criticized the sceptical approach. In 1939, Fück published *Die Rolle des Traditionalismus im Islam* [The role of traditionalism in Islam], which is a commendable summary of the less skeptical approach to Muslim sources. He explicitly criticizes Goldziher, although without mentioning his name, saying:

If the Islamic critique of traditions did not succeed on either internal or external grounds in excluding all the spurious elements of tradition, it would be an inaccurate generalization, however, if one were to deny to it all confidence on that account...[72]

Fück's thesis was that the historical investigation of Qur'anic exegesis and the administration of law merely formed different aspects of an activity whose real focus was quite naturally the historical Prophet (ﷺ).[73] He thus argued that Islamic Hadith criticism appeared at the beginning of the Abbasid period and started with 'an examination of the trustworthiness of individual authorities.'[74]

The subsequent increase in the number of Hadith transmitters led to the emergence of the 'bibliographical literature on the traditions' in the second century by such scholars as al-Wāqidi, Ibn Is-ḥāq, Ibn Sa'd and Khalīfah ibn Khayyāṭ.[75] The definitive consolidation of the authority of the Sunnah started under the leadership of Aḥmad ibn Ḥanbal, who provided a defence against the Mutazilite views.[76] Fück points out that at the time of this split in the Muslim community, there were indications of attempts to prove the authenticity of traditions. He comments:

The fact that no traditions reflecting an anti-Mu'tazilite point of view were accepted in the canonical collections is splendid testimony to the honesty of the traditionists.[77]

Nonetheless, Fück argues, there were many obstacles hindering the Muslim critics from purging all traditions containing spurious elements, such as the practice of incorrectly connecting narrators to the Companions by dating the transmitters inaccurately and the use of collective asānīd, which formed an obstacle to critical activity.[78] Added to these complications was the Muslim scholars' belief in the uprightness of the Companions and their reliance on the younger transmitters among them.[79]

Fück offers an explanation for the contradictions found in Muslim traditions by affirming that a comparison of pre-canonical sources with the canonical collections can solve the problem by identifying the prototype as well as the individuals responsible for changes to it. He affirms that these changes were highlighted by early classical critics,[80] and he states that contradictions found in Muslim traditions did not necessarily reflect later developments or political arguments in the third century, as Goldziher claimed.[81]

For example, in commenting on the hadith about saddling camels to go to three mosques only,[82] which was held by Goldziher to be a fabrication by az-Zuhri, Fück argues that it is certainly not tenable on chronological grounds.[83] According to Fück, dating Muslim sources is demonstrated by reference to external evidence, such as the science of language, which blossomed independently of the religious disciplines.[84] Fück refers directly to original Muslim sources in outlining the origin and development of early Muslim sources and in explaining the role of the Hadith in early and late Islamic periods.

Overall, Fück represents a less skeptical attitude towards Muslim sources, one which is closer to the classical Muslim perspective; however, his attitude did not prevail in Western circles. After a lapse of 60 years since Goldziher's seminal study of Hadith, Joseph Schacht launched the second fierce attack in the West against the authenticity of the Hadith.

1.5 Joseph Schacht, and the response to his *Origins of Muhammadan Jurisprudence*

Although Schacht's verdict about the Hadith (like that of Goldziher) resulted from a study of hadiths concerning legal matters, he claimed that his conclusion was also applicable to maghāzi materials. In several publications, Schacht advocated the thesis that none of the corpus of traditions from or about the Prophet (ﷺ) or the Companions is genuine. In 1949, introducing the first article devoted to the issue, he wrote:

> We must… abandon the gratuitous assumptions that there existed originally an authentic core of information going back to the time of the Prophet.[85]

When Schacht published his *Origins of Muhammadan Jurisprudence,* it immediately met with immense approval. The only Western scholars who offered any serious criticism of Schacht's views were N. J. Coulson (in his *A History of Islamic Law*), John Fück,[86] and Guillaume (in his review).[87]

The reactions to Schacht's theories on the Hadith were as enthusiastic as those evoked by the arguments of Goldziher. Schacht's *Origins* was praised as thorough, methodologically sound, and highly original. Thus, Schacht's ideas influenced Western scholarship on the Hadith for a long time, and new studies written since then could not ignore his views. Indeed, much subsequent research is derivative of Schacht's thesis.

After Schacht, Western researchers on the biographical sources concerning the early history of Islam can be divided into three main groups.

1. The first group, which emerged in the early decades after the publication of Schacht's *Origins*, flatly rejected Schacht's views. Muslim scholars acquainted with Western research were strongly represented in this group, but it also contained a few non-Muslims.[88]
2. The second group agreed with Schacht on the main points of his thesis. They focused increasingly on the impossibility of reconstructing the past (or at least the past that was intended by the authors and collectors of the traditional material) from traditional sources. Some of these scholars, like John Wansbrough, were convinced that only literary criticism of the sources was possible;[89] others, like Michael Cook and Patricia Crone,[90] as well as A. Mingana and Maxime Rodinson,[91] dispensed with the idea of relying upon Muslim sources for the reconstruction of the early history of Islam.
3. The third group consisted of scholars who accepted some but not all of Schacht's opinions concerning the Hadith and who tried to moderate points that they considered to be too extreme or too generalized. This produced two different approaches:
   - Some scholars sought to draw distinctions among hadiths that were ignored by Schacht. Some biographers of the Prophet (ﷺ) who were contemporaneous with Schacht, such as William Montgomery Watt, admitted an apparent distinction between legal and historical traditions and therefore argued that Schacht's findings were only applicable to the former.[92]
   - Other more recent scholars have drawn a distinction between the content and the form of traditions. They accept Schacht's claim that many of the traditions in the form in which they are now found in Hadith collections are late, but they have distinguished this from the claim that such hadiths are not from the Prophet (ﷺ) in terms of origin. To this subgroup belong N. Coulson, G. H. A. Juynboll, John Burton and David Powers.

Scholars of the second group attempted to use Schacht's method, and in checking his results, they developed it further. These scholars, who continue to develop and publish their research up to the present day, are optimistic that a reconstruction of the Prophet's life is possible if the dispute over the reliability of the source materials can be solved through use of a better methodology. Gregor Schoeler,[93] Joseph van

Ess and Harald Motzki belong to this group. They introduced developments in the sphere of methodologies and their application to biographical sources.

What follows then is an elaboration, in historical sequence, of the three major approaches (associated with the three groups mentioned above) with reference to their impact on the study of biographical sources of the Prophet (ﷺ).

The specialists of sīrah and maghāzi who came a few years after the publication of Schacht's *Origins* were not very impressed by his arguments. J. W. Fück (in 1953)[94] and A. Guillaume (in 1954),[95] both experts on Ibn Is-ḥāq's *Sīrah*, confirmed that Schacht's conclusions cannot be reconciled with evidence from this work, which dates to an earlier time than that of the legal sources used by Schacht. Fück concludes that Schacht's dating of traditions with the help of the *argumentum e silentio*[96] procedure is not compelling, and that it is refutable in a number of cases through material in Ibn Is-ḥāq's *Sīrah.*[97] Fück puts Schacht's theory on a level with Lammens' theses about the *Sīrah*, stating:

> It too rests on the inadmissible generalization of individual observations and fails… because of its incompatibility with the sources.[98]

In the same year as Fück's criticism, and a few years after the appearance of Schacht's book, William Montgomery Watt published the most exhaustive biographical study of Prophet Muhammad (ﷺ) to be written in the second half of the twentieth century by a non-Muslim scholar. He disputed the idea that Schacht's findings were applicable to sīrah materials. He rejected Schacht's theory in the sphere of Islamic history, remarking:

> The personality of the Prophet made such an impression on his followers that we cannot believe the picture of him given in tradition is purely late development.[99]

Watt's *Muhammad at Mecca* and his *Muhammad at Medina* are based on a qualified acceptance of the main Arabic sources. These sources consist of the Qur'an as well as historical works of the third and fourth centuries AH. He relies on the *Sīrah* of Ibn Hishām (d. 218 AH/ 833 CE), the section of the *Annals* of aṭ-Ṭabari (d. 316 AH/ 922 CE) that deals with the life of the Prophet (ﷺ), the *Maghāzi* of al-Wāqidi (d. 207 AH/ 822 CE), and *aṭ-Ṭabaqāt* of Ibn Sa'd (d. 230 AH/ 845 CE). He also relies on traditions from the sound collections of Imam Bukhari and Imam Muslim, and on the *Musnad* (a hadith collection arranged by narrator) of Aḥmad ibn Ḥanbal. He does not rely much on later sources.[100]

Watt justifies his reliance on Muslim sources (regardless of the conclusions of Goldziher and Schacht, and their enormous impact on Hadith-based studies) by drawing a distinction between legal and historical traditions. He affirms that

Goldziher's and Schacht's conclusions are 'mainly applicable to legal traditions, though by no means entirely so.'[101] He was satisfied that there was 'tendentious shaping' of historical reports, but he was convinced that with a critical mind, it was still possible to find out what really happened. Therefore, in dealing with the sources, Watt proceeds on the basis that traditional accounts should generally be accepted. He explains that they are:

> …received with care and as far as possible corrected, where tendentious shaping is suspected, and are only to be rejected outright where there is internal contradiction.[102]

According to Watt, tendential (or controversial) shaping of sources is discerned through the identification of the alleged motives behind incidents; therefore, his position is far less skeptical about Muslim sources.

In the 1970s and 1980s, several studies on the Prophet of Islam (ﷺ) were published. Their authors accepted Goldziher's and Schacht's views but in a more consistent manner. They refused to use hadiths as a source for a historical reconstruction of the time of the Prophet (ﷺ) and the first Islamic century, and they raised several doubts about the traditional biographical sources. W. Raven summarizes these doubts as follows:

- Hardly any sīrah text can be dated back to the first century of Islam.
- The various versions of a text often show discrepancies in both chronology and content.
- The later the sources are, the more they claim to know about the time of the Prophet (ﷺ).
- Non-Islamic sources are often at variance with Islamic sources.[103]

Rudi Paret and Maxime Rodinson[104] also accepted Schacht's position. The introduction of Rodinson's book reveals the profound influence in the West of Goldziher and Schacht's criticism of the Hadith:

> A biography of Muhammad limited only to absolutely unquestioned facts could amount to no more than a few dry pages. Yet it is possible to present a probable, and now and then, a highly probable picture of what that must have been like; to do so, one must use some information from sources whose veracity cannot be proven.[105]

Rodinson's serious doubts regarding early Arabic sources are shown throughout his biography. He often uses phrases like 'seemingly,' 'it was said,' and 'as was recounted later.'[106] Rodinson's confidence in Goldziher and Schacht is indicated by his doubting the possibility of finding a certain criterion for verifying Muslim sources; he states, "Though these are the sources, it must be admitted that they are far from being certain historical facts."[107] Rodinson raises the problem that "any scientific study demands a critical study towards source material," without outlining this proposed source criticism and how it might be conducted.

Scepticism regarding Muslim biographical sources reached its climax in 1952 when Regis Blachère published his *La Problème de Mahomet*,[108] in which he writes:

> The Prophet's early life can only be sketched, and that faintly in large brush strokes, while any attempt to go further must result in hagiography or romance, which we already have in the standard Muslim sources.[109]

This skeptical tendency emerged from extreme interpretations of Goldziher's theories and developed into two major approaches; the first was the application of Biblical literary criticism to Muslim sources, whereas the other relied on non-Muslim sources for reconstructing early Islamic history.

1.6 Literary and Biblical criticism of historical traditions

The historico-literary method of criticism, which emerged in the eighteenth and nineteenth centuries, emphatically raises questions of interpretation and relevance. This is because it is concerned with such problems as authorship, reliability of sources, and the process of transmission and editing. Although it was originally used in the field of Biblical scholarship, Western scholars have also applied it to early biographical sources of the Prophet (ﷺ).

This method found great impetus in the writings of John Wansbrough, who argues for a critical assessment of the value of sources from a literary point of view. Wansbrough introduced his literary analysis of Muslim sources in two major works:

- *Qur'anic Studies: Sources and Methods of Scriptural Interpretation*, written between 1962 and 1972, published in 1977.
- *The Sectarian Milieu: Content and Composition of Islamic Salvation History*, written between 1973 and 1977, published in 1978.

Andrew Rippin remarks, "Both books fit together quite logically, although it should be noted that there is some progression of thought between the two works."[110]

Qur'anic Studies deals primarily with the formation of the Qur'an, along with the witness of exegetical writings. *The Sectarian Milieu* further develops the theme of the evolution of Islam, beginning with the traditional biographies of the Prophet (ﷺ)—sīrah and maghāzi—and then working through the process of the theological elaboration of Islam as a religious community, examining questions of authority, identity and epistemology.[111] According to Wansbrough:

> Neither the Qur'an nor Islam is a product of Muhammad or even Arabia. During the early Arab expansion beyond Arabia, there is no evidence that the conquerors were Muslims. Almost 200 years later 'early' Muslim literature began to be written by the Mesopotamian clerical elite.[112]

The implication is that a secular society discovered and adopted a new movement that, although it was neither Jewish nor Christian, was nevertheless a product of the Judeo-Christian milieu. According to this notion, the movement and its history were soon 'Arabicized', but the Qur'an took somewhat longer to be canonized—this did not happen until about 800 CE.[113] Therefore, Wansbrough sees Iraq, not the Ḥijāz, as the birthplace of Islam.

In *The Sectarian Milieu,* Wansbrough labels the entire corpus of early Islamic sources, including tafsīr, sīrah and theological writing, as 'salvation history.' In his view, all these sources are trying to prove that the sequence of worldly events centred around the time of Muhammad (ﷺ) was directed by God. Thus, the events in this salvation history did not really occur, and since they are only literary fiction, such sources should be approached with caution. According to Wansbrough, the biography of the Prophet (ﷺ) does not represent the history of Islam but only represents the events of this literary salvation history. Specifically, he states:

> Its narrative techniques are exegetical in which serial or isolated Qur'anic extracts provide the framework for a longer narrative; parabolic, in which the narrative itself is the source for frequent allusion to logia [not verbatim but in terms of diction and imagery];[114] and paraphrastic, in which logia are presented in the form of anecdotes replete with scriptural keywords. In this way, salvation history was produced.[115]

Wansbrough sees some 23 topics in this literature, all of which are derived from a Judeo-Christian milieu.[116] A written source, according to Wansbrough, cannot tell us:

> What really happened, but only what the author thought had happened or wanted to believe had happened or wanted others to believe had happened.

Therefore, the key factor in the use of a written text is the motivation of the writer.[117] The authenticity of a literary source should be ascertained by cross-checking its contents against external evidence;[118] since external evidence is needed to corroborate Muslim literary accounts, the lack of such corroboration is an important argument against their reliability. This approach, according to J. Koren and Y. D. Nevo, is open to *argumentum e silentio.*[119] Authenticity, according to Wansbrough, "can be as much as a result of [successful] narrative techniques as of veracity."[120]

Wansbrough constructs a historical and thematic classification system for the chronological development of tafsīr, through a literary analysis of a multitude of early pre-aṭ-Ṭabari works. His scheme suggests the following historical sequence:

- narrative,
- legal,
- textual,
- rhetorical,
- allegorical.[121]

For biographical traditions, Wansbrough compares both Ibn Is-ḥāq and al-Wāqidi with Bukhari, and he postulates:

> [A] development from loosely structural narrative to concise exemplum… [which] illustrates perfectly the stylistic difference between seera and sunna, between the mythic and the normative preoccupations (Geistesbeschäflungen) of early Muslim literature.[122]

The historical and literary analysis of early biographical sources by other scholars has led to the conclusion that, in fact, the reverse took place. In other words, the biographical writers were forced to build up the narrative as a whole from many discrete and sometimes conflicting reports about what had happened. Thus, Wansbrough's theory is undermined by the work of those, including G. Schoeler[123] and M. Lecker,[124] who convincingly argue that an extensive comparison will lead to the conclusion that the variation among the scholars derives from their reliance upon distinct sources from the first to the seventh centuries.

The theory of literary criticism of sources was continued by Andrew Rippin, who focused on *asbāb an-nuzūl* (reasons for revelation) in his *The Functions of Asbab an-Nuzul in Qur'anic Exegesis*, which was published in 1988. Rippin's point of departure is that the primary purpose of these materials is not in fact concerned with deriving laws from the Qur'an; rather, the asbāb provide an interpretation of a verse with a broad narrative framework. Therefore, according to Rippin, asbāb material is essentially storytelling.[125]

Recently in the field of sīrah, Wansbrough's approach has been championed by Uri Rubin who, in 1995, wrote his study of the Prophet (ﷺ).[126] This study provides a textual analysis of the story of the Prophet's emergence in Makkah, as documented by early Islamic tradition. In his biography, Rubin does not seek to judge the historical value of the events described; rather, his intent is to observe their textual dynamics and to examine the traditions as a reflection of the self-image of early medieval Islamic society.

According to Rubin, Muslims sought to provide their Prophet (ﷺ) with a biography no less sacred than that of any prophet of the Jews and the Christians. They adopted and borrowed stories and aspects of the biographies of previous monotheistic religions, namely Judaism and Christianity. They proceeded through five major themes: attestation, preparation, revelation, persecution, and salvation. These themes were, thus, adapted to specific Arabian conditions as well as to Qur'anic models that were cited to legitimize these themes in Islamic terms.[127]

In his review of Rubin's study, Mahmood Ibrahim asks whether the Muslim community really needed that 'legitimacy' after they had devastated the Byzantines and the Sassanids. "Were not their victory and other achievements enough to give them the self-confidence for which Rubin claims they were searching?"[128]

Although Rubin criticizes Goldziher and Schacht, his study is nonetheless mainly based upon the premise that Muslim sources cannot be trusted for the reconstruction of early Islamic history, which is a continuation of their essential assumption.

1.7 Reliance on non-Muslim sources

In 1980, Patricia Crone and Michael Cook published their *Hagarism*, in which the radically skeptical views of Schacht are clearly manifested. Crone and Cook reject the validity of early Islamic materials, attempting to reconstruct the history of Islam from non-Muslim sources instead. Although they successfully draw attention to problems involved in the study of Islam, they are not able to go beyond the limitations inherent in the sources, for they are all of questionable historical authenticity and are based on polemics. Crone and Cook, moreover, do not provide or even mention a consistent method for authenticating biographical sources before basing their reconstruction on them.

In her *Slaves on Horses,* Crone maintains the same hostile attitude towards early Arabic sources, while nonetheless justifying her trust in the prosopographical[129] elements found in *Hagarism*. Crone claims a 'total lack of continuity, between the contemporary Greek, Roman, and Sassanian sources about Syria and Arabia and later Islamic traditions.'[130]

In *Meccan Trade and the Rise of Islam*, Crone develops the theory that there is a striking growth in early Muslim biographical sources at the hands of early collectors. To prove this hypothesis, Crone compares Ibn Is-ḥāq to al-Wāqidi and perceives a 'steady growth of the information'[131] as narrated by the storytellers. She notes, for example:

> If one storyteller should happen to mention a raid, the next storyteller knows the date of this raid, while the third knows everything that an audience might wish to hear about it.[132]

Crone also points out that al-Wāqidi always gives precise dates, locations, and names, whereas Ibn Is-ḥāq does not. From this observation, she concludes that such detailed information was unknown to Ibn Is-ḥāq, and thus its value is doubtful in the extreme.[133]

Similarly, in his work *Early Muslim Dogma*, Michael Cook, building on Schacht's work, examines the growth and especially the spread of asānīd occasioned by 'the pressure [to emphasize upon]… elegance [over stating the]… truth.' He provides detailed examples to illustrate the various mechanisms that could be involved in the spread of asānīd,[134] and he concludes that the spread of asānīd is inadmissible as proof of authenticity. His point of departure is that the traditions must be dated by criteria external to the isnād itself.[135]

There are, however, two points of criticism raised against Crone and Cook's argument.

1. The results of their comparison between Ibn Is-ḥāq and al-Wāqidi are contested by scholars such as Lecker, on the same grounds by which he critiqued Wansbrough.[136]
2. They face a severe problem by relying predominantly on sources external to the Muslim community because these sources themselves lack any definite authenticity.

Still, Crone and Cook are not the only ones calling for revised methodological approaches to the recovery of the Islamic past. M. R. Waldmann rejects the validity of early Islamic materials in much the same manner and on similar grounds. Waldmann argues for the use of historical narrations—not mainly to reconstruct the past but to identify the claimed author or compiler of the source.[137]

Waldmann's methodological approach adopts Mary Louise Pratt's *Speech Act Theory* of linguistics and literary discourse and applies it to Muslim sources by analyzing the narrative character of specific passages from the surviving portion of *Tārīkh al-Bayhaqi*.[138]

According to Waldmann, speech act theory maintains that al-Bayhaqi's work, regarded as a 'natural narrative', provides direct evidence of the personality, cultural formation, and mental processes of the author himself—but only indirect and dubiously reliable information about the historical events it purports to relate. Though Waldmann does not apply this approach to sīrah materials, his work shows how the writings of Goldziher and Schacht had an immeasurable impact on the possibility of relying on Muslim sources.

Today, therefore, scholars in the West face a critical impasse over the use of sources in composing a biography of the Prophet of Islam (ﷺ). Notably, Motzki writes:

> At present the study of Prophet Muhammad is obviously caught in a dilemma. On the one hand, it is not possible to write a historical biography of the Prophet without being accused of using the sources uncritically, while on the other hand, when using the sources critically, it is simply not possible to write such a biography... Are we faced with a hopeless situation?[139]

Still, there is reason to believe that a solution is possible. According to Motzki, such optimism is nurtured by the observation that the dispute over the reliability of sīrah materials is blurred by several shortcomings, which may be summarized as follows:

1. Systematic source-critical studies concerning the Prophet's life are almost nonexistent.
2. Methods which have been used, or could be used, to assess the reliability of biographical sources have been in very short supply.
3. Consequently, the dispute over the reliability of biographical traditions has taken place on a rather abstract level, and mostly not on the basis of the biographical traditions themselves.[140]

In fact, recent research on the biographical sources of the Prophet's life has focused on improving research methodologies, but usually without actually applying these methodologies to historical traditions. This study hopes to address this gap.

1.8 Recent methodological advances and their impact on studies of sīrah

In the last three decades, there has been considerable progress in the Western study of Hadith, due primarily to the recent unearthing of a great number of new sources as well as to developments in methodology.[141] Specifically, pre-canonical collections such as the *Muṣannaf* of 'Abdur-Razzāq, the *Muṣannaf* of Ibn Abi Shaybah, 'Umar ibn Shabbah's *Tārīkh al-Madīnah*, and many others have proved to be of prime importance.[142] Moreover, the new sources confirm that the earliest available source is not, as was once assumed, Bukhari.[143]

In the sphere of methodology, two main developments have occurred as a consequence of applying source criticism to Hadith.

First, the need for more accurate methods of checking the reliability and delineating specific dates of traditions led to the emergence of sanad analysis of single traditions, which proved to be a powerful research tool. This methodology, which will be explained below, is credited to G. H. A. Juynboll and Joseph van Ess.

Second was the emergence of a type of source criticism known as isnād-cum-matn analysis, which combines the investigation of asānīd with literary analysis and, moreover, involves the use of an exhaustive corpus of sources. Schoeler first elaborated on this method and applied it to two of his case studies in *Character und Authentie der Muslimischen Überlieferung*, and Harald Motzki and G. H. A. Juynboll recently applied this method.

To illustrate the process, the following subsections delineate the main outlines of source criticism, sanad analysis of single traditions, and isnād-cum-matn analysis, as well as the significant impact they have had in the last three decades on the study of the biographical sources of the Prophet's life.

1.8.1 The source criticism approach

The source criticism approach, as Motzki remarks, became well-known in modern Western Islamic Studies after the work of Julius Wellhausen.[144] It aims at eliciting development of the historical sources from the material included in available works.[145] Primarily, it attempts to check the authenticity, originality, and correctness of what a source purports to be or is thought to inform us about. Using this methodology, historians ask the following questions:

- How far away from each other, in time and place, are the event and its source?
- Are the date and place of origin that the source claims for itself correct?[146]

Even though reliance on the isnād for establishing the authenticity of resources runs the risk of overestimating its historical value, such an approach has produced fruitful results, particularly when applied to tafsīr.[147] In 1956, Fuat Sezgin published his work *Bukharinin Kaynaklarihakkinda Arştumarlar* [Research on the personage of Bukhari],[148] in which he investigated the feasibility of reconstituting an assortment of early works on the basis of later compilations. He also applied this method in his work *Geschichte der Arabischen Schriftrums*. In a 1991 treatise, Motzki addressed the source-analytical and tradition-historical approaches in order to ascertain their applicability to legal traditions.[149]

1.8.2 *Sanad* analysis of single traditions

Among the scholars who were convinced of the importance and usefulness of asānīd for historical research was Aloys Sprenger, as shown in his nineteenth century *Das Leben und die Lehre des Mohammad.*[150] Sanad analysis was first developed in Western scholarship with Schacht, after whom scholars began to develop different theories about asānīd. Joseph van Ess worked on this method in research published in 1975;[151] he was followed by G. H. A. Juynboll, who fully developed the sanad analysis of single traditions in his book *Muslim Tradition*[152] and in other essays and lectures on the subject.[153] The following is a review of Juynboll's development of the method, beginning with his views on the origin of Muslim sources.

In Juynboll's article "A Tentative Chronology of the Origins of Muslim Tradition,"[154] he returns to the pre-Schachtian view that the beginnings of the Hadith originate in the time of the Prophet (ﷺ).[155] He assumes that at first, storytellers who were motivated by pious concerns spread edifying tales about the lives and virtues of the Prophet (ﷺ) and of the first Muslims, and that more formal and standardized transmission began only at the end of the first century AH/ seventh century CE, not before 670 or 805 CE.

Juynboll derives this hypothesis from biographical traditions about the origin of the isnād, from the beginnings of transmission criticism, and from the introduction of hadiths into certain regions.[156] This reveals that Juynboll (like

Goldziher but in contrast to Schacht) was convinced that formal hadiths from the Prophet (ﷺ) were already being circulated in the last two decades of the first century AH.[157] He also agreed with Goldziher that, apart from exceptional cases, it would be possible to identify genuine hadiths of the Prophet (ﷺ).[158] In his *Muslim Tradition,* Juynboll is still reserved and cautious with respect to the benefits of using common links for identifying genuine asānīd. He states:

> […] it is mostly impossible to prove with incontrovertible certainty that asāneed are not invented in their entirety. Thus, the common link, if there is one, is often only a useful tool from which to distill an approximate chronology and possible provenance of the Hadith.[159]

In his article "Some Isnad-Analytical Methods," published six years later, Juynboll attaches much more value to the common link for the purpose of dating. He argues that it is the common link that is responsible for the wording of the hadith, at least for the form of the text found in Hadith collections today. In his view, if there is no common link for a hadith—in other words, if there is only one transmitter at each level of the isnād, making what Juynboll calls a 'single strand'—then it is not possible to claim authenticity for this strand, because the absence of a common link in an isnād signifies that the hadith was produced either by later Hadith collectors or by their own teachers.[160]

He goes on to argue that a single strand must continue to be considered 'unhistorical' unless new sources reveal that at least one of its transmitters had indeed passed the tradition to more people and thus had become a historical common link.[161]

Sometimes a tradition includes a common link in the chain, and there are other single strands traced back to the Prophet (ﷺ) that run parallel to this common link. Juynboll calls these strands 'dives' and states that the deeper the dive under the common link, the more recent the date of origin for that particular strand.[162]

Though Juynboll's method proved to be an effective tool for researching historical traditions, Western scholars reacted to it with reservations. Motzki and others re-examine the conclusions that Juynboll reached by applying this method. In his article "Dating Muslim Traditions: A Survey," Motzki identifies three major problems challenging the sanad analysis of single traditions (or more precisely, relying mainly on this method alone for studying hadiths) as applied by Juynboll.[163]

1. The first critique is that the assumption that the common link is the originator of the tradition, and that "the single strand from the common

link down to the Prophet (ﷺ) is 'a path invented by the common link' are problematic generalizations."[164] Motzki provides a different explanation for the phenomena of common links and single strands. He argues that a common link is the first systematic collector and 'scholarly transmitter' of the tradition. In his view, the fact that only one strand survived does not mean that only one ever existed; there could be other strands that were not recorded by the collector.[165]

Additionally, Motzki argues that the explanation of the common link as being a result of forgery has several shortcomings. The first shortcoming is that there is no indication that any forgery of asānīd developed in this way. Secondly, the assumption of forgery seems manufactured, because it is possible for other theoretical methods to be applied.[166]

2. The second problem in Juynboll's thesis is that his division between historical and 'unhistorical' common links is impractical. Juynboll states:

The more transmission lines there are coming together in a certain transmitter [...], the more that moment of transmission has a claim of historicity.[167]

Motzki, on the other hand, affirms that if one takes seriously Juynboll's general rule, then most of the traditions dealt with in his article must be considered unhistorical. Juynboll's conditions for traditions to be accepted as historical make too great a demand on the scanty sources available to be useful in practice.

3. The third problem is Juynboll's use of *argumentum e silentio* in claiming that the 'diving single strands' are fabricated by the authors of Hadith collections. This argument labels as fabrications the asānīd which contain the names of early collectors for whom Hadith compilations are available, such as Mālik or 'Abdur-Razzāq, or those richly documented in the collections of their pupils, such as Ibn 'Uyaynah in al-Ḥumaydi, or Shu'bah in *aṭ-Ṭayālisi*, but which are only found in later canonical Hadith collections.[168]

This conclusion, as Motzki comments, is based on the assumption that the earlier compilations contain the complete or exhaustive transmitted material of the persons in question. For the second and third centuries, at least, this seems unlikely.[169] Therefore, Juynboll's application of sanad analysis was based on dubious assumptions. However, the method proved to be a more effective research tool when combined with related matn investigation, a method which has flourished recently in some Western studies.

1.8.3 *Isnād*-cum-*matn* analysis

This method combines the use of Juynboll's sanad analysis of single traditions with an analytical comparison of the body of the texts (the *mutūn*, *pl.* of matn) attached to their asānīd, in order to provide more accurate information on their transmission history and dating. Three prominent Western scholars utilized this method in recent Hadith studies: Schoeler, Motzki and Juynboll. In recent years, Motzki and Schoeler have been very active in this area of research, producing many significant publications, as the following section shows.

1.9 The current state of Western research

In the West, current research on the sources of information on the life of Prophet Muhammad (ﷺ) is characterized by two groups of researchers, each of which stands directly opposed to the other. G. Schoeler remarks:

> The one group advocates somewhat aggressively the conviction that all transmitted traditions because of great inner contradictions, legendary form and so forth, are to be rejected.[170]

Despite all these defects, the other group of researchers believe that the Islamic transmission has a genuine core at least, which can be recognized by using the appropriate source-critical methods.[171] Certainly, the difficulty lies in finding criteria for differentiating the genuine from the false.

In the spring of 1997, a colloquium on the life of Prophet Muhammad (ﷺ), held in Nijmegen (the Netherlands) under the direction of Motzki, brought together prominent representatives of both groups.[172] Following that, in 2002, Gregor Schoeler received a grant from the Swiss National Fund for a three-year research project designed to break the deadlock between the two opposing groups.[173] Schoeler states:

> The idea of the project was connected to the conviction that neither the extensive trust in the Muslim transmission, represented by scholars such as F. Sezgin and [not quite so extremely] W. M. Watt, nor the total rejection of the traditional material, as it is endorsed by Wansbrough, Crone and Cook, is successful; rather a middle way must be found.[174]

The project resulted in research by Gregor Schoeler on the traditions narrated by the *tābiʿī* ʿUrwah ibn az-Zubayr.[175] All the corpus comprising ʿUrwah's traditions in major Hadith collections, as well as historical and legal exegetical works of the third century and later, were to be collected to encompass the entire framework of the

Prophet's life. The thematically related traditions would be systematically compiled and organized. The original versions spread by 'Urwah would be reconstructed by comparing those transmitted by his son Hishām to those transmitted through az-Zuhri. This procedure uncovered "from the structure [abridgements and additions] and the wording of the text in the best case of certainty a common archetype."[176] Schoeler achieved two positive results through this method; he proved that the two texts were independently transmitted and that they had one common archetype. The contents of these hadiths were then condensed and coherently paraphrased.

1.10 Conclusion

Interest in the West in the biography of Prophet Muhammad (ﷺ) started in the early seventeenth century at the latest. Genuine academic and scholarly studies of this subject started in the mid-nineteenth century. A prerequisite was the blossoming of the study of history in general and the growing interest in other cultures, which was encouraged by the colonial expansion of the European powers. Interest in Muslim sources about the biography of the Prophet (ﷺ) was intensified by the development of Christian theology, the appearance of historical critical studies on the life of Jesus (*'alayhi as-salām*—peace be upon him), and the rise of a source-critical approach to Biblical studies.

The period from Weil (1843) to Muir (1856) is mainly distinguished by recourse to Arabic original sources. European writers were not satisfied with late authorities; they succeeded in bringing to light some of the earlier documents. During this period, they proceeded on the assumption that if a certain amount of careful sifting was done, they could find a considerable body of tradition that could be relied on for biographical purposes.

This optimistic stance received its first blow in 1890 when Ignác Goldziher published the second part of his *Muhammedanische Studien,* which is regarded, at least in the West, as the first milestone in Western efforts to depict the earliest history of Hadith (one of the two major sources of the Prophet's biography). During the late nineteenth and early twentieth centuries, Western biographers relied on Muslim sources in writing the biography of the Prophet (ﷺ), although a number of smaller popular works are largely based on the work of Goldziher.

Radical skepticism was not given new impetus until 60 years after Goldziher's seminal study of the Hadith had been published, when Joseph Schacht advocated in several publications the thesis that none of the corpus of traditions from the Prophet (ﷺ) and the Companions was genuine. Although his verdict, like that of

Goldziher, resulted from a study of legal hadiths, Schacht claimed that his thesis was applicable to early Muslim traditions in general, and he attempted to prove this with reference to some maghāzi material. Schacht's thesis has had a great impact on Western research from the second half of the nineteenth century up to the present time.

Three major attitudes toward biographical sources developed immediately after Schacht.

- Some Western biographers, such as William Montgomery Watt, were willing to generally accept the content of traditions unless an obvious bias could be detected on the part of the narrator.
- Others, such as Michael Cook, Patricia Crone and Maxime Rodinson, tried to reconstruct the early history of Islam using non-Muslim sources.
- A third group, which included Wansbrough, was only content with the literary criticism of available sources.

Consequently, there is no doubt that Schacht's confident standpoint found favour with many other Western researchers, including Wildman, Jacob Lassner, Alin Luther, Fred Donner and many others.

Therefore, the biographical study of Prophet Muhammad (ﷺ) in the West was caught between two extremes: using what scholars regarded as 'unhistorical' sources or being unable to write a biography at all.[177] Recent Western work on early Islamic traditions has increasingly focused on the impossibility of reconstructing the past from traditional sources. Thus, scholars in Western academia are faced with a critical situation regarding the issue of the sources. A myriad of questions regarding the origin, provenance, and authenticity of early biographical traditions still needs to be answered.

In summary, current Western research is characterized by two groups of researchers, who stand directly opposed to one another. One group holds that it is impossible to reconstruct the life of the Prophet (ﷺ) from existing Muslim sources, while the other maintains a more optimistic view about the results that may be obtained using source-critical methods. So far, this has resulted in Schoeler's project to construct a new biography of the Prophet (ﷺ) based on 'Urwah's corpus of traditions. Although this project helped to solve the dilemma concerning the way that Muslim biographical sources are used in Western scholarship, its scope is limited to the corpus of traditions narrated through 'Urwah.

Chapter Two

MS. Berlin 9409 (the so-called *Kitāb at-Tārīkh* of Abu Bakr 'Abdullāh ibn Muhammad ibn Abi Shaybah [159-235 AH/ 775-849 CE]): A newly-unearthed early source for the biography of Prophet Muhammad (ﷺ)

2.1 Introduction

The core intent of this chapter is to shed light on MS. Berlin 9409 (the so-called *Kitāb at-Tārīkh* of Ibn Abi Shaybah) and its author. We will also examine the authorship of the manuscript and the reliability of the sources of its compiler. Thus, this chapter will be concerned with answering a number of preliminary questions, such as:

1. Whether or not MS. Berlin 9409 really contains the work of Abu Bakr 'Abdullāh ibn Muhammad ibn Abi Shaybah;
2. Whether the manuscript contains the well-known book *at-Tārīkh*, as claimed by some Western scholars; and
3. To what extent we can ascertain the reliability of the sources used by its author.

Therefore, this chapter comprises the following subsections:

- Preliminary remarks on the biographical sources of the life of Prophet Muhammad (ﷺ).
- A detailed description of MS. Berlin 9409, elaborating on its format and content.
- The authorship of the manuscript.

- The relationship between MS. Berlin 9409 and Ibn Abi Shaybah's *Kitāb at-Tārīkh*.
- The reliability of Ibn Abi Shaybah's sources as maintained in MS. Berlin 9409. This assessment will be conducted by means of source criticism based on the analysis of asānīd.
- The author and his work in light of the Muslim biographical sources; here, we will compare the information included in Muslim biographical sources about the author with the results obtained from source analysis of the materials at hand.

2.2 Biographical sources of the life of Prophet Muhammad (ﷺ)

'Tārīkh' is the most common Arabic word for 'history', in the sense of an ordered account of actual events. The word was in use by the middle of the second century AH/ eighth century CE, when it first appeared in the titles of works recounting past events.[1] By the late third century AH/ ninth century CE, tārīkh had become the most common word for this genre of writing. When the word is attached to literary compositions, it denotes a chronologically ordered account of events. The word was rapidly extended to include any record of events or persons, no matter how it was organized; for instance, by the middle of the third century AH/ ninth century CE, Imam Bukhari (d. 257 AH/ 871 CE) wrote *at-Tārīkh al-Kabīr*, an alphabetically arranged dictionary of Hadith transmitters, which contains very few dates.[2]

The bulk of early Arabic historical texts have not come to us in their original form but are preserved only in citations and paraphrases within compilations that were assembled between the mid-third century AH/ ninth century CE and the fourth century AH/ tenth century CE.[3]

The earliest biographies of the Prophet (ﷺ) took the name 'maghāzi'. Prior to the time of the work ascribed to al-Wāqidi (d. 207 AH/ 823 CE), this term signified, in particular, the expeditions and raids organized by Prophet Muhammad (ﷺ) from Madinah.[4]

Sīrah, *sīrah rasūl Allāh* (sīrah of the Messenger of Allah), or *as-sīrat an-nabawiyah* (sīrah of the Prophet) have been the most widely used names for the traditional accounts of the Prophet's life.[5] Martin Hinds argues that the biographical material on the Prophet (ﷺ) was transmitted during the first two centuries of Islam exclusively under the name maghāzi, whereas the term sīrah was applied only since Ibn Hishām (d. 218 AH/ 833 CE or 213 AH/ 828 CE).[6] This view has been challenged by Maher Jarrar, though; he claims that maghāzi is only part of the sīrah, the designation being used occasionally as *pars pro toto* (taking a part for the whole), and that the biography was already called sīrah by az-Zuhri (d. 124 AH/ 742 CE), who was a central figure in the transmission of materials on the Prophet (ﷺ).[7]

In addition to al-Wāqidi's *Kitāb al-Maghāzi* and Ibn Is-ḥāq's *Sīrah*, there were some other well-known works that no longer exist in their original form, such as those by 'Urwah ibn az-Zubayr (d. 94 AH/ 714 CE), az-Zuhri (d. 124 AH/ 758 CE) and Mūsā ibn 'Uqbah (d. 141 AH/ 758 CE). After Ibn Is-ḥāq, Ma'mar ibn Rāshid (d. 154 AH/ 770 CE) composed a limited but interesting maghāzi collection;[8] it is preserved in the *Muṣannaf* of 'Abdur-Razzāq aṣ-Ṣan'āni (d. 211 AH/ 826 CE).[9] Several other Hadith compilations, especially those in the category of muṣannaf, such as that written by Abu Bakr ibn Abi Shaybah (d. 235 AH/ 848 CE), included sections on maghāzi.[10] Ibn Abi Shaybah's section on maghāzi is larger and more homogeneous than other materials of similar works, and he is reported to also have a separate compilation of similar content titled *Kitāb at-Tārīkh*. There is, however, a controversy over the existence and the nature of the materials included in this book, which is the subject of the present study.

According to Sezgin[11] and Brockelmann,[12] the book is extant in manuscript form in Berlin MS. 9409, which is now in the possession of Berlin's *Preussischer Kulturbesitz*. It is also claimed that another copy—transmitted by al-Khaṭīb al-Baghdādi, Abu Bakr Aḥmad ibn 'Ali (d. 463 AH/ 1071 CE)—exists in al-Maktabat aẓ-Ẓāhiriyah of Damascus (Dimashq, Group 18/ no. 127).[13]

In 1974, Heinrich Schützinger examined MS. Berlin 9409 and described it in detail.[14] Schützinger, along with Sprenger,[15] Ahlwardt and Brockelmann, concluded that the work goes back to Ibn Abi Shaybah. They differed on whether it embodies a part of the so-called *Kitāb at-Tārīkh* or is identical to the maghāzi section contained within the *Muṣannaf.* Ahlwardt and Brockelmann supported the former conclusion without thoroughly investigating the issue. They relied solely on Ibn an-Nadīm's conclusion that the *Tārīkh* is a well-known book of Ibn Abi Shaybah and on the fact that the manuscript included content on the history of Islam.[16] Sprenger, after consulting portions of the *Muṣannaf,* doubted this conclusion.[17] Schützinger concluded that MS. Berlin 9409 is not a part of the *Muṣannaf* of Ibn Abi Shaybah,[18] but he did not consult any complete text of *Muṣannaf,* and his argument is not compelling.

Therefore, we are faced with two major problems regarding the source of our study.

1. Does MS. Berlin 9409 comprise, in part or in its entirety, the so-called *Kitāb at-Tārīkh,* or is it only a copy of the maghāzi section of the *Muṣannaf*? In the decades since Schützinger's study, new sources—especially the *Muṣannaf*—have been published, allowing us to revise some of his conclusions. In this context, it becomes essential to edit Berlin MS. 9409 before we can reconsider any of Schützinger's conclusions.[19] This is the reason for providing an edition of the manuscript, which, as far as I know, has not been edited previously.[20] By editing this work, we will be able to compare its traditions to the *Muṣannaf*, to other books authored by Ibn Abi Shaybah, and to other compilations of Hadith and sīrah.
2. Even if it is established that Ibn Abi Shaybah is the actual compiler and transmitter of the work, this does not give any indication about the reliability of his materials. Thus, the current study should ask about the sources Ibn Abi Shaybah used in the manuscript: did he really have access to the sources he claimed, and if so, did he receive all his material from them?

To answer these questions, we will investigate by using source criticism, a method of studying historical accounts that is employed in Western studies of Islamic sources. Source criticism endeavours to extract earlier sources from compilations we have on hand that are not preserved as separate works. It focuses on the material of certain transmitters, rather than on Hadith clusters dealing with specific topics.[21] Sebastian Günther defines source criticism as follows:

> Source criticism aims to determine those literary sources which as basic elements, make up the mosaic of the finished compilation in order to clarify their origin and the time when they came into being and to draw precise conclusions as to their nature, the ways and terms of their transmission and their value as sources of the literary work in question and finally to verify and evaluate the most important of these older literary materials as well as the individuals involved in their transmission.[22]

Although source criticism runs the risk of overestimating the value of asānīd, there is a reason to support its application to the current study. As we discussed in Chapter One, severe Western scepticism about asānīd first emerged after the works of Goldziher and Schacht; before this, Western scholars relied on Muslim sources supported by chains of authority, and they used them widely in their biographies about the Prophet of Islam (ﷺ). The source-critical studies by Horst,[23] G. Stauth,[24]

Fuat Sezgin,[25] Gregor Schoeler,[26] Motzki,[27] Manfred Fleischhammer,[28] Sebastian Günther,[29] and many others all suggest that Goldziher and Schacht viewed the isnād too sceptically due to generalizations based on single observations. Contrary to Goldziher and Schacht, these Western scholars examined asānīd in the realm of historical, exegetical and legal traditions, and they produced fruitful results, which encourage optimism regarding the possibility of reconstructing Muslim sources.[30] Moreover, some recently discovered materials concerning early Islam, such as those in Nabia Abbott's study of early Islamic historiography and Hadith literature,[31] as well as newly-undertaken investigations of the period, like Harald Motzki's work on the development of early Makkan jurisprudence,[32] are leading to wider acceptance of the value of asānīd.

There are three reasons for choosing MS. Berlin 9409 as the experimental material for this study.

1. Its structure of transmission is, at first glance, more homogenous (having the same type of material, namely historical accounts) than the maghāzi sections of other muṣannaf works like that of 'Abdur-Razzāq, which contains the transmissions of just one compiler: his teacher, Ma'mar ibn Rāshid.
2. The number of transmissions included in MS. Berlin 9409 is comparatively wider than those included in other compilations of Hadith such as the collections of Bukhari and Muslim.
3. The fact that Ibn Abi Shaybah was an Iraqi who studied mostly with Iraqi teachers makes his materials of particular interest because the standard sources of the Prophet's biography are based on traditions from the Ḥijāz. Studying an Iraqi source enables us to compare Ibn Abi Shaybah's materials (or those of his sources) with those of other contemporary and earlier Iraqi scholars as well as those of Ḥijāzi origin, such as the transmissions from Ibn Is-ḥāq to Ibn Hishām, and from az-Zuhri to Ma'mar to 'Abdur-Razzāq. This comparison will be conducted in Chapter Three.

2.3 Description of MS. Berlin 9409

Among the Arabic manuscripts from the old *Preussische Staatsbibliothek*, whose possessions were transferred to the *Preussischer Kulturbesitz* in Berlin, Germany, there is a manuscript bearing the number Berlin 9409 (Sprenger 104).[33] According to Brockelmann[34] and Fuat Sezgin,[35] it contains the work of Abu Bakr 'Abdullāh ibn Muhammad ibn Abi Shaybah. According to them, it includes a compilation of the *riwāyāt* (transmissions) of historical content on the beginnings of Islam, and it is written in readable black Naskh handwriting.[36] According to Schützinger, it was written in 1250 AH/ 1834 CE.

It consists of 224 pages (113 folios) according to the pagination made by Sprenger, who did not count the two blank pages in the middle of the work (after page 54). Ahlwardt counted it as 226 pages; he included the two blank ones.[37] Each page contains 19 lines. It has some copying errors and some missing words, especially on pages 50 (hadith no. 117), 206 (hadith no. 520), 212 (hadith no. 529), 214 (hadith no. 536), 216 (hadith no. 538), 219 (hadith no. 540), 222 (hadith no. 545), and 224 (hadith no. 551). We were able to detect the missing words and phrases by referring to the complete edited edition of Ibn Abi Shaybah's *Muṣannaf*.

Sprenger's handwriting appears on the manuscript. He writes:

> The part of the mosannaf of Ibn Abi Shaybah, which contains the biography of Mohammad. The full name of the author is Abu Bakr 'Abd Allah ibn Aby Shaybah 'Absy, he was a pupil of Waky' and one of the teachers of Bokhary. [He] died in 235 [AH].

Sprenger, who was probably acquainted with Indian manuscripts of the complete text of the *Muṣannaf*, used the manuscript 21 times for his *Das Leben und die Lehre des Mohammad*. In eight places, he quotes longer or shorter Arabic citations accompanied by their English translations. Sprenger's handwriting appears in the first 86 pages of the manuscript, sometimes correcting errors or providing explanations for difficult terms and phrases. His comments are written in English, and the corrections appear in Arabic.

The manuscript does not have a title or even a list of *samā'āt* (records of transmission lines, starting with the compiler and ending with the scribe who wrote the manuscript by hand and received permission to transmit it) or transmitters who received it from the original compiler (in this case, Ibn Abi Shaybah himself).

It starts with an Arabic sentence that can be translated as, "This is the end of *Kitāb al-Awā'il*.[38] Praise is due to Allah alone, and prayers of Allah be upon Muhammad (ﷺ) and his family."

Thus, it begins with the concluding lines of the chapter of *al-Awā'il*. This is an indication that this particular chapter preceded the one concerning the maghāzi within this particular copy of the *Muṣannaf*. In the published version of the *Muṣannaf*, the chapter containing Ibn Abi Shaybah's legal responses to Abu Ḥaneefah falls between that of *al-Awā'il* and the maghāzi, so this copy is different from the standard copies of the *Muṣannaf*. Such differences may be due to a copyist's error or to a re-ordering of chapters by a later compiler.

2.4 Authorship of MS. Berlin 9409

In terms of internal criticism, historians and critics usually differentiate between authenticity and authorship. Authenticity, according to Lucey, refers to all possible information on the origin of a report, including the date of composition or production, the place of composition and whether a source is the original manuscript.[39] Authorship is a more restrictive term referring to whether or not ascribing a text to a particular author is credible.

In the present case, we are interested in determining whether Ibn Abi Shaybah is the author and compiler of the manuscript at hand. This crucial question was convincingly answered in the affirmative by Sprenger, Ahlwardt, Brockelmann and Schützinger. Brockelmann relied on the confirmation in bibliographical sources like Ibn an-Nadīm's *al-Fihrist*, and Sprenger relied on a complete or partial copy of the *Muṣannaf*.

Schützinger added that the name Ibn Abi Shaybah was mentioned in a number of traditions and titles.[40] He also pointed out that 61 out of 76 teachers mentioned in MS. Berlin 9409 are proven, through reference to biographical sources, to have been Ibn Abi Shaybah's teachers.[41] Schützinger reviewed the traditions of Ibn Abi Shaybah that were recorded in Muslim's *Jāmi'* and found that Muslim received 1,304 reports directly from him. Schützinger then confirmed that the sources for Ibn Abi Shaybah's hadiths in Muslim's *Jāmi'* match those in the manuscript. Schützinger even attested that a number of reports in the manuscript were quoted exactly, with their respective asānīd and mutūn, in Muslim's *al-Jāmi'*.

The following is a summary of the conclusions drawn by Schützinger and others on the authorship of MS. Berlin 9409:

1. The asānīd and texts maintained in the manuscript are completely retained in the other copies of the complete *Muṣannaf,* which is certainly attributed to Ibn Abi Shaybah.
2. The sources from which Ibn Abi Shaybah received his accounts in MS. Berlin 9409 are well known to have been his teachers; this is attested by biographical sources.[42]
3. An examination of other newly-unearthed and independent works of Ibn Abi Shaybah, such as *Kitāb al-Adab*[43] and *Kitāb al-Īmān*,[44] established that of all the teachers named by Ibn Abi Shaybah in MS. Berlin 9409, only six do not appear in those two books. When the search is extended further to include the six canonical books of Hadith, this number is reduced to five.

This last conclusion is not applicable to the overall materials of the entire manuscript, though. The concluding seven pages of *Kitāb al-Awā'il,* which come at the very beginning of MS. Berlin 9409, list 17 accounts. A cursory look indicates that they were not originally related by Ibn Abi Shaybah, the original compiler of the work. They were most probably added by one of the later transmitters of the manuscript, namely Abul-Qāsim Maslamah ibn al-Qāsim ibn Ibrāhīm al-Andalusi al-Qurṭubi (d. 353 AH/ 964 CE),[45] who, according to the edited version of the *Muṣannaf,* received the section concerning *al-Awā'il.*[46] By reviewing the paths of transmission through which *Kitāb al-Awā'il* was received, we will have a clear vision for judging the origin of those 17 traditions with which MS. Berlin 9409 commences.

The transmission path starts with Abul-Qāsim Maslamah ibn al-Qāsim, who received 95% (300 out of the 317 accounts that represent the entire book of *al-Awā'il*) from Aḥmad ibn Muhammad ibn al-Jahm al-Māliki[47] in Baghdad in Rabī' I, 324 AH/ 936 CE. Aḥmad ibn Muhammad received the materials in 290 AH/ 903 CE from Muhammad ibn 'Abdūs ibn Kāmil as-Sarrāj (d. 293 AH/ 906 CE)[48] by means of the transmission method called *'arḍ*, in which a student recites the material to the teacher while the rest of the students follow along in their copies. Muhammad ibn 'Abdūs was, in turn, one of the students of Ibn Abi Shaybah.[49] The remaining 17 traditions, which represent about 5% of *Kitāb al-Awā'il*, are transmitted by Maslamah ibn al-Qāsim from seven different sources:

1. Ya'qūb ibn Is-ḥāq ibn Ibrāhīm ibn Yazīd ibn Ḥajar al-Qurayshi al-'Asqalāni (224-320 AH/ 839-932 CE);[50] Maslamah supposedly travelled to 'Asqalān to receive hadiths from him. Ya'qūb provides only two hadiths: one that he received from Ṣāliḥ ibn Aḥmad ibn Muhammad ibn Ḥanbal (203-264 AH/ 818-878 CE),[51] and the other received through Abu Mūsā.[52] There is no mention of Ibn Abi Shaybah in either of these two reports, or even of any of his teachers. In addition, the reports are not found to be attributed to or received by him in any of the available, published Hadith compilations.
2. Abu Ja'far Aḥmad ibn Ibrāhīm ibn 'Abdullāh ibn Muhammad ibn Yaḥyā al-Mu'āfiri al-Miṣri; Maslamah travelled to Fustat, Egypt, where Abu Ja'far dictated a number of records to him from a book he had, at the mosque of 'Amr ibn al-'Āṣ in the month of Dhul-Qa'dah, 322 AH / 934 CE. There is only one hadith in *Kitāb al-Awā'il* transmitted through this authority.[53] If one checks the chain of authorities and reviews other books of hadiths, it is evident that this hadith is not Ibn Abi Shaybah's.

3. Muhammad ibn al-Ḥasan al-Hamadāni[54] related two traditions contained in MS. Berlin 9409, one through Abu Bakr Yaḥyā ibn Ja'far ibn Abi Ṭālib[55] and the other through Ja'far ibn Aḥmad al-Hamadāni.[56] Neither of them belongs to Ibn Abi Shaybah.
4. Abu 'Ali 'Abdullāh ibn Muhammad ibn Abi Rajā' az-Zayyāt al-Māliki; Maslamah might have travelled to Makkah and received hadiths from him by dictation from memory. Abu 'Ali received the two traditions introduced in MS. 9409 from Abu Ḥārithah Aḥmad ibn Ibrāhīm al-Ghassāni, whom he visited in Ramallah in 277 AH/ 891 CE.[57] The traditions introduced to MS. 9409 from this path do not belong to Ibn Abi Shaybah or to any of his sources.
5. Ibn al-Washā' Abul-'Abbās Aḥmad ibn 'Īsā; Maslamah read for him a number of hadiths that he received through different narrators, none of whose traditions seem to be Ibn Abi Shaybah's.[58]
6. Muhammad ibn 'Abdullāh ibn Muhammad ibn Yūsuf al-Makki al-Baghdādi; Maslamah received one hadith from him.[59]
7. Abu 'Ali al-Ḥasan ibn Manṣūr al-Baghdādi; Maslamah received one hadith from him.[60]

If we review the paths of transmission of the first 17 reports of MS. Berlin 9409, it becomes evident that they are not Ibn Abi Shaybah's, nor do they come from any of his well-known sources. We reach this conclusion because:

- Ibn Abi Shaybah's name is not mentioned in any of them.
- Not one of Ibn Abi Shaybah's direct sources, whose materials were maintained in the *Muṣannaf* or his other books, are included in these 17 traditions.
- Comparing the traditions with other external sources, whether Iraqi or Ḥijāzi, shows that no source ascribed any of those traditions to Ibn Abi Shaybah or claimed that they were transmitted through him.

Therefore, *Kitāb al-Awā'il* was most probably transmitted separately, as was the case with most of Ibn Abi Shaybah's books. The final form of the book was made by Maslamah ibn al-Qāsim after 324 AH/ 936 CE. Maslamah not only introduced the compilation of Ibn Abi Shaybah but also added reports that he himself received through other sources. This explains why he put those 17 accounts under a separate title to show that they are the concluding materials of the chapter of *al-Awā'il*, which preceded that of maghāzi within the *Muṣannaf*. It also explains why the order of the books in MS. Berlin 9409 is different from the standard organization of the text.

2.5 MS. Berlin 9409 and the *Kitāb at-Tārīkh*

After the question of the authorship of MS. Berlin 9409 has been answered, there is another crucial question, which has not yet been settled by the scholars who have studied the manuscript. Does the work contains *Kitāb at-Tārīkh* (the Book of History) by Ibn Abi Shaybah, or is it merely a copy of the maghāzi section of the *Muṣannaf*?

Before answering this question, we should elaborate on the contents of the work. The manuscript contains 551 accounts, supported by chains of authority, about the early history of Islam.61 It includes 42 chapters of varying lengths; the shortest is only three lines, and the longest is 26 pages.

The manuscript starts with the period before the Prophet's birth and ends with the death of 'Umar ibn al-Khaṭṭāb (*raḍiya Allāhu 'anhu*—may Allah be pleased with him), the second caliph after the Prophet (ﷺ).[62] In other words, the book does not end with the death of the Prophet (ﷺ); it includes traditions in sequence about the two Caliphs (Abu Bakr and 'Umar) who succeeded him. Quite apart from their inherent interest, the presence of these traditions in this context, as Zaman remarks, is significant as an indication that the scope of early works of maghāzi was not necessarily limited to the career of the Prophet (ﷺ).[63]

The manuscript generally follows a chronological sequence. It starts with 'the affair of the elephant'[64] immediately before the birth of the Prophet (ﷺ) and shows considerable interest in the Makkan period of his life. The earliest sections of the manuscript comprise thematically grouped traditions in the following order:

1. The portents of his prophethood;[65]
2. The beginning of his mission;[66]
3. His persecution in Makkah;[67]
4. The night journey and heavenly ascension (*al-isrā wal-mi'rāj*);[68] and
5. The conversion of some of those who were later to become his prominent Companions.[69]

Traditions about the migration of certain persecuted Muslims from Makkah to Abyssinia, and about the occasion when one of these Muslims was questioned about Islam in the court of the ruler there,[70] are reported after traditions about the letters regarding the Prophet's migration to Madinah [even though they happened earlier].[71] Traditions about the letters that the Prophet (ﷺ) is supposed to have written to Chosroes II, Caesar and other foreign rulers to summon them to Islam come between the account of the conversion of prominent Companions and the traditions regarding Abyssinia.[72] This may be explained by the presupposition that the epistles directed by the Prophet (ﷺ) to kings and rulers marked a new stage in his mission in the form of inter-state relationships. This is correlated to the migration to Abyssinia, which marked the beginning of this new trend in the Prophet's career.

Ibn Abi Shaybah starts discussing the Prophet's military campaigns by giving different views on the number of Muslims who participated in the Battle of Badr.[73] He lists each campaign in chronological sequence, starting with Badr[74] and continuing with Uḥud,[75] al-Khandaq (the Trench),[76] Banu Qurayẓah,[77] Banu al-Muṣṭaliq,[78] Banu Laḥyān,[79] Najd,[80] and Khaybar.[81] He then gives more detail, in the form of long and short narrations, on the conquest of Makkah,[82] the campaign of Taif, and the battle of Mu'tah. In the Makkan period of the Prophet's biography, there is no historical sequence, but Ibn Abi Shaybah's ordering of the material on the Madinan phase of the Prophet's career does refer to a conventional, if implicit, chronological framework.

By comparing these materials with the maghāzi section of the published *Muṣannaf,* we come to the conclusion that MS. Berlin 9409 is an identical copy of the greatest part of the maghāzi section in that text, and that the only differences are either from copying errors or due to the work of a later transmitter of the book. This is also the conclusion reached by Sprenger, who had access to extra copies of the *Muṣannaf.* This, however, contradicts the presuppositions of Brockelmann, Sezgin, Schützinger and others, who thought that the manuscript contained at least a portion of *Kitāb at-Tārīkh.* Studying the manuscript and comparing it to the maghāzi section of the *Muṣannaf* confirms that it does not include *Kitāb at-Tārīkh.*

Still, there are questions about Ibn Abi Shaybah's *Kitāb at-Tārīkh* that must be answered; these include:

- Where is it?
- Is it still available?
- Was it separate from the *Muṣannaf*?
- Does it have any relationship to the maghāzi?

According to Brockelmann and Sezgin, Ibn Abi Shaybah's *Kitāb at-Tārīkh* is retained in MS. Berlin 9409 and in another copy that was transmitted by al-Khaṭīb al-Baghdādi and now exists in al-Maktabat aẓ-Ẓāhiriyah in Damascus, under the number 18/127.[83] Sprenger had little doubt that the manuscript formed a part of the *Muṣannaf.* Sprenger means that *Kitāb at-Tārīkh* included historical materials about the Prophet's career and other events. Zaman assumes that *Kitāb al-Maghāzi* of Ibn Abi Shaybah's *Muṣannaf* is very similar in content, if not identical, to his work on tārīkh.[84]

Our supposition is that the so-called *Kitāb at-Tārīkh*, or at least part of its original form, is retained in the *Muṣannaf*, whose present shape is not the work of Ibn Abi Shaybah but rather the endeavour of one of his students or later compilers. In other words, *Kitāb at-Tārīkh* comprises a section of the published version of the *Muṣannaf*; this comes before the maghāzi section, even though the historical information in the maghāzi section is chronologically earlier. If Ibn Abi Shaybah had put the chapters in order, he would have arranged his materials chronologically by putting the book of tārīkh immediately after the section of maghāzi, since it seems to be a continuation of its events.

The original book of tārīkh might have been available to later scholars like Ibn Ḥajar al-'Asqalāni, who cited it more than once in his *Tahdhīb at-Tahdhīb*.[85] When I looked for the reports related by Ibn Ḥajar, I found them in the tārīkh section of the *Muṣannaf*. This supports the idea that the section of tārīkh in the *Muṣannaf* includes all or part of the original *Kitāb at-Tārīkh*. In addition, most of the well-known books of Ibn Abi Shaybah that were listed by Ibn an-Nadīm and others exist as sections in the *Muṣannaf*.[86] This means that the *Muṣannaf* was arranged and compiled by later students of Ibn Abi Shaybah.

The section of tārīkh in the *Muṣannaf* contains historical reports on the battle of Yamāmah, which occurred at the time of Abu Bakr aṣ-Ṣiddīq. It also includes short historical accounts of other battles such as Qadsiyah, Jalūlā', Tastur, and Yarmouk, as well as reports on the conquest of ash-Shām (the Levant). These events are elaborated in 138 reports of varying lengths, each supported with a chain of authority.

Following these, there are 96 historical reports, which seem to have been compiled with a special purpose in mind: to provide information on conventional and controversial dates related to specific narrators of hadiths, such as Companions and tābi'ūn. The dates provided in these reports help to determine specific matters in the chronological sequence of events at the time of the Prophet (ﷺ) and after his death. The reports provide information on individual narrators, indicating how long they lived and whether they accompanied the Prophet (ﷺ). They reports are short and concise, as if they might have been responses to questions addressed to Ibn Abi Shaybah in his teaching sessions, or to some of his sources; however, there is no specific indication in the text or asānīd of the reports to support this conclusion. Ibn Abi Shaybah provides lists of names and dates of birth not only for Companions of the Prophet but also for tābi'ūn. He concludes this chapter with names and surnames of Hadith compilers, some of whom are the teachers of Ibn Abi Shaybah himself. The set of informants from whom he received his materials is almost identical to that mentioned in the maghāzi section.

The contents of the book give us an idea of the kernel of the earlier books of tārīkh. Later books had a wider scope of events, as is the case with aṭ-Ṭabari, or more organization in the transmitters' names, as with the books of tārīkh written by Imam Bukhari.

2.6 The sources of Ibn Abi Shaybah as contained in MS. Berlin 9409

From even a cursory overview of the work, it is evident that almost half of its content (in terms of space) is derived from five sources, which represent 48.4% of the whole work:

- Wakī' ibn al-Jarrāḥ
- Abu Usāmah Ḥammād ibn Usāmah
- Yazīd ibn Hārūn
- 'Ubaydullāh ibn Mūsā
- 'Affān ibn Muslim

Of the 551 reports in the manuscript:

- 11.6% belong to Wakī' ibn al-Jarrāḥ,
- 9.6% were received from Abu Usāmah,
- 7.4% are from Yazīd ibn Hārūn,
- 6.3% are from 'Abdur-Raḥīm ibn Sulaymān,
- 4.9%, 4.3% and 4.1% belong to 'Abdullāh ibn Idrīs, 'Ubaydullāh ibn Mūsā and 'Affān ibn Muslim respectively.

The remaining 52.8% were received through 69 narrators, of whom all but 16 narrated only a single hadith each. If we assume for the moment that Ibn Abi Shaybah's statements of origin are correct, this would mean that the work is primarily compiled from five major sources, each of whom contributed several traditions. It is natural to suppose that they are either originally independent works or parts thereof. Alternatively, Ibn Abi Shaybah recorded, in writing, the content of the instruction by these five figures, who (in terms of age) could have been his teachers. The same supposition may be made for the whole book of *Muṣannaf*, since similar percentages apply to its claimed sources.

On the other hand, the possibility that Ibn Abi Shaybah fabricated his statements of origin in general is not to be precluded. Which of the two hypotheses is more probable? This can most readily be answered on the basis of the three most voluminous hadith collections (those reported from the three primary sources of Ibn Abi Shaybah, each of which is composed of interconnected or interwoven parts) without recourse to external sources—for instance, those of biographical or bibliographic sources. If Ibn Abi Shaybah arbitrarily attributed them to the seven people named Wakīʻ ibn al-Jarrāḥ, Abu Usāmah, Yazīd ibn Hārūn, ʻAbdur-Raḥīm ibn Sulaymān, ʻAbdullāh ibn Idrīs, ʻUbaydullāh ibn Mūsā and ʻAffān ibn Muslim, then they ought to be similar in their structure of transmission. To make a comparison possible, it will suffice to qualify the statements of origin of the first three sources and assemble them into profiles:

1. The Wakīʻ ibn al-Jarrāḥ source material is made up of: 32% from Sufyān ath-Thawri, 12% from Isrā'īl ibn Yūnus; 8% from Ismāʻīl ibn Abi Khālid, and 6% from Ḥammād ibn Salamah. The remaining 42% are distributed among 23 names. There are no personal statements in the accounts of Wākīʻ.

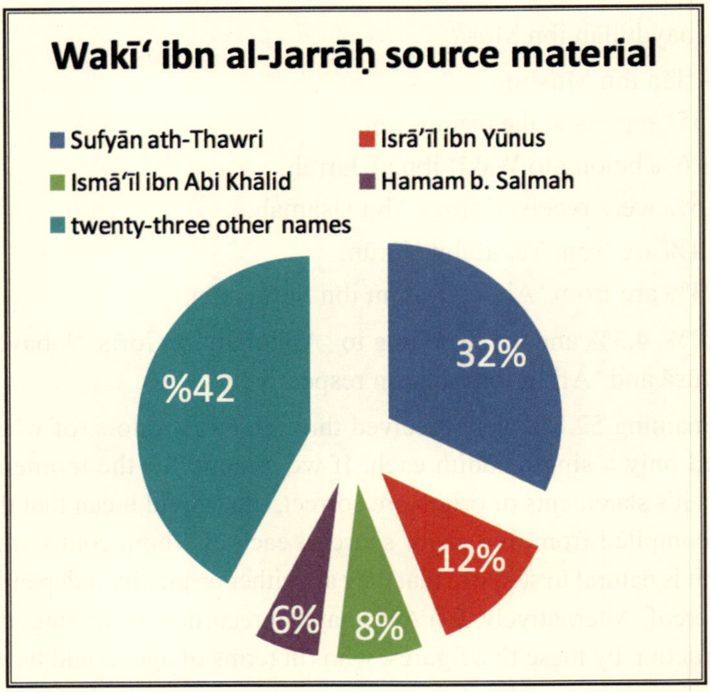

2. The Abu Usāmah source material is made up of: 19% from Hishām ibn 'Urwah, 11% from Ibn 'Awn, and 11% from Sulaymān ibn al-Mughīrah. The remaining 59% comes from 19 different narrators.

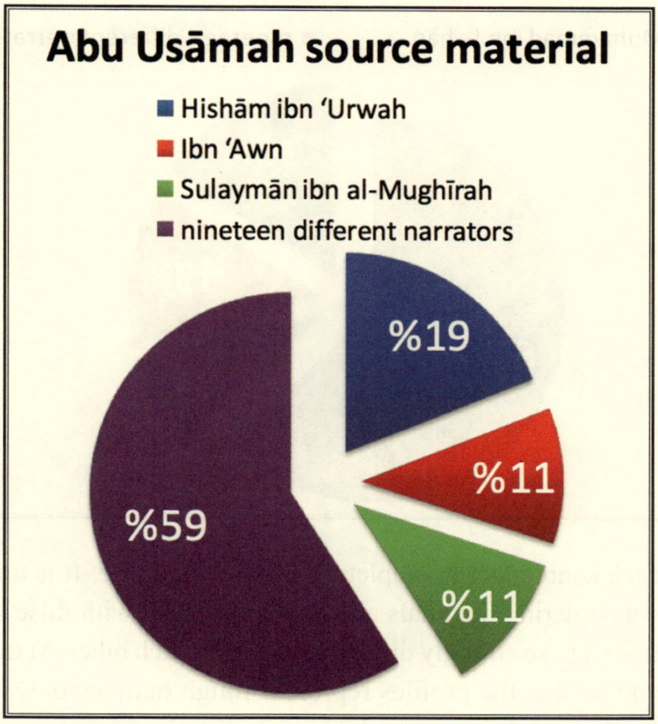

3. The Yazīd ibn Hārūn source material is made up of: 16% from Ḥammād ibn Salamah, 13% from Muhammad ibn 'Amr, and 8% from Muhammad ibn Isḥāq. The remaining 63% is distributed among 19 different names.

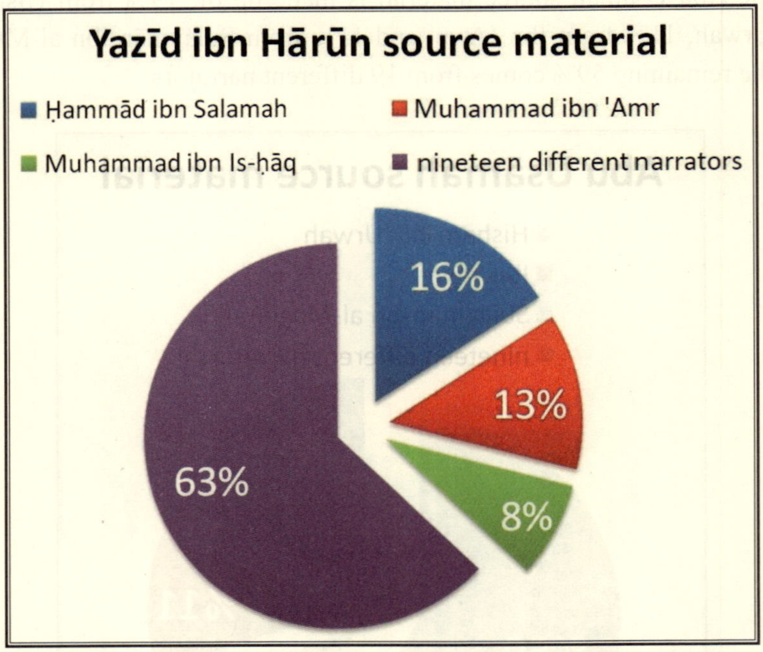

Clearly, each source has a completely individual profile. It is unlikely that a forger who was ordering materials and equipping them with false labels would create units that were so strongly differentiated from each other. At the same time, it should be noted that the profiles represent rough outlines only, and that the differences are reinforced as one goes into greater detail—for instance, by inquiring into the geographical affiliations of the sources or the formal characteristics of the texts. Greater differences will also be found in the results if we search a wider range of accounts from the whole *Muṣannaf.*

There are other formal characteristics, conspicuous in Ibn Abi Shaybah's presentation of the traditions, which point in the same direction. For example, he narrates traditions from anonymous narrators;[87] if he were fabricating his sources, he would assign the names of some of his famous authorities.

Moreover, Ibn Abi Shaybah does not claim full asānīd for all the materials he claims to have received from his sources. *Mursal* hadiths[88] and others with broken asānīd are widespread throughout the work. He does not try to attribute the sayings or actions of his sources back to the Prophet (ﷺ) or even to claim perfect chains for them. Such defects are hardly expected from a forger because they would compromise his actual objective: the feigning of a certain, unbroken transmission.

Ibn Abi Shaybah occasionally speaks of his sources receiving traditions from anonymous narrators. An example is, "Ibn Abi Shaybah from Wakī' from Nāfi' ibn 'Umar from a man who narrated from Abu Bakr…"[89] If he were a forger, why would he give only these anonymous sources when he could provide names to claim perfection in his chains of authorities?

Furthermore, Ibn Abi Shaybah provides contradictory traditions under the same topic, without necessarily providing his personal opinion. In answer to the question of how old the Prophet (ﷺ) was when he started his mission, Ibn Abi Shaybah provides nine reports that have differing views.[90] Why would he present contradictory reports in the same passage? If he wanted to enforce his point of view, he would choose only one of them and omit all those that did not support his conclusion.

The results obtained from within the work are confirmed through reports of a biographical nature contained in various later works. Separate evaluation of these sources is advisable for methodological reasons, because in Western scholarship, the authenticity of the biographical traditions is no less controversial than that of hadiths.

2.7 The author and his work in the light of the Muslim biographical sources

According to biographical sources, his full name was 'Abdullāh ibn Muhammad ibn Abi Shaybah Ibrāhīm ibn 'Uthmān ibn Khuwāstā al-'Absi, and he was commonly known as Ibn Abi Shaybah, Abu Bakr ibn Abi Shaybah, or 'Abdullāh ibn Abi Shaybah. He was born in 159 AH/ 775 CE, in Wāsiṭ in Iraq.[91]

'Ibn Abi Shaybah' was originally the surname given to his grandfather, who was the judge of Wāsiṭ[92] and a weak transmitter of hadiths. His father, a judge in Persia, was named Muhammad ibn Ibrāhīm ibn 'Uthmān ibn Khuwāstā al-'Absi (d. 182 AH/ 798 CE).

Ibn Abi Shaybah had one son, Ibrāhīm ibn Abi Shaybah (d. 265 AH/ 879 CE), and two brothers, 'Uthmān ibn Abi Shaybah (156-239 AH/ 772-853 CE) and al-Qāsim ibn Abi Shaybah (d. 241 AH/ 856 CE). According to some reports, they were also narrators of Hadith, although less reliable than Ibn Abi Shaybah.

Abu Ja'far Muhammad ibn Abi Shaybah is his nephew. Although Abu Ja'far was himself known as a weak transmitter, he wrote in the genre of *al-jarḥ wat-ta'dīl* (accreditation of Hadith narrators).

According to biographical literature, Ibn Abi Shaybah started his academic life at the age of 14 in the circles of Hadith, attending the sessions of Sharīk ibn ʻAbdullāh an-Nakhaʻi (d. 177 AH/ 793 CE).[93] This would have been between 172 AH/ 788 CE and 177 AH/ 793 CE, after Sharīk had assumed the position of judge in Kufa and towards the end of his life.

It seems that Ibn Abi Shaybah's young age was the reason why the number of materials he received directly from Sharīk was limited in comparison to the greater number of hadiths he received from Sharīk indirectly by means of Wakīʻ, Muhammad ibn al-Ḥasan, Yazīd ibn Hārūn and others. There are only three traditions from Sharīk in MS. Berlin 9409; one was received by Ibn Abi Shaybah directly, and the other two were transmitted through intermediaries.[94]

Ibn Abi Shaybah is reported to have said that he relied on his memory in retaining the traditions of Sharīk.[95] A review of the *Muṣannaf* makes it clear that almost all of the transmissions he received through Sharīk were transmitted by the method of *samāʻ* (where a teacher reads his or her materials, either from memory or from a book, and the students listen or write).

Ibn Abi Shaybah's most important teacher is Wakīʻ ibn al- Jarrāḥ (129-197 AH/ 746-812 CE), who was born in Isfahan[96] and lived and settled in Kufa. Wakīʻ was the main and the most distinguished *muḥaddith* (Hadith scholar, *pl.* muḥaddithūn) in Kufa at the time.[97] He held his teaching sessions at the main pillar in the big mosque, where the most prominent figures of Hadith in Kufa used to sit to narrate traditions. The first to sit there was ʻAbdullāh ibn Masʻūd (d. 32 AH/ 652 CE), the famous Companion of the Prophet (ﷺ); then ʻAlqamah (d. after 60 AH/ 679 CE or 70 AH/ 689 CE); followed by Ibrāhīm an-Nakhaʻi (d. 96 AH/ 543 CE); and then Manṣūr (d. 132 AH/ 749 CE). After Manṣūr came Sufyān ath-Thawri (d. 161 AH/ 777 CE), who was followed by Wakīʻ. Ibn Abi Shaybah led the session after Wakīʻ's death.[98] This indicates the close relationship between Sufyān and Wakīʻ on one side and Ibn Abi Shaybah and Wakīʻ on the other side. In 185 AH/ 801 CE, when Wakīʻ turned 56, scholars started to come to him seeking his traditions. Ibn Abi Shaybah may have studied under Wakīʻ from that time (when Ibn Abi Shaybah was 24 years of age) until Wakīʻ died in 197 AH/ 812 CE. It was probably during this period that he obtained the bulk of the materials that were transmitted from him.

As a deeply-rooted muḥaddith who was well-versed in the narration of Hadith, Wakīʻ is reported to have narrated from memory,[99] and this might have exposed him to some minor criticism from his contemporaries.[100] Nevertheless, his compilations were also written down and available if he wanted to consult them,[101] and he is reported to have checked his materials many times.[102] There are also reports confirming that he allowed the writing of traditions at his sessions.[103]

Bibliographical literature mentions books compiled by Wakī‘, including his *Sunan*[104] and his *Muṣannaf*,[105] which is similar in nature and content to the *Muṣannaf* of Ibn Abi Shaybah.[106] It is possible that Ibn Abi Shaybah received the book from Wakī‘ and then distributed parts of it throughout his *Muṣannaf*. According to bibliographical sources, Wakī‘ also had a book of history (*al-Ma‘rifah wat-Tārīkh*),[107] which may be similar to the *Tārīkh* of Ibn Abi Shaybah. Wakī‘ also compiled *Kitāb az-Zuhd*, which he was reading on his deathbed, with Yaḥyā ibn Ma‘īn.[108] The book, which contains a chapter with the same title in the *Muṣannaf*, was later found in manuscript form; it was edited in 1404 AH/ 1983 CE.[109] When we compare some of the reports of Wakī‘'s book, we find traditions with the exact same mutūn and asānīd in the *Muṣannaf*.[110] This confirms that Ibn Abi Shaybah took many reports, and even the classification of his chapters and themes, from his teacher.[111]

The same is true for another of his teachers, Abu Usāmah Ḥammād ibn Usāmah (201 AH/ 816 CE), a well-known narrator of historical reports who settled in Kufa. Abu Usāmah received over 600 accounts from Hishām ibn ‘Urwah (d. 146 AH/ 763 CE), who is therefore one of his main sources for historical accounts.[112] Abu Usāmah's reports represent 9.6% of the reports in Berlin MS. 9409, but only 3.7% of the reports in the *Muṣannaf*.

It is possible that Ibn Abi Shaybah contacted the Makkan Sufyān ibn ‘Uyaynah (107-198 AH), whose collection of Hadith still exists.[113] His book of tafsīr is quoted by ath-Tha‘labi[114] and Ibn Ḥajar, who received permission to narrate it.[115] Ibn Abi Shaybah would have had to travel to Makkah to receive Sufyān's traditions;[116] this may explain why he quotes directly from Sufyān only six times in MS. Berlin 9409, whereas he includes 35 of his traditions transmitted through intermediaries.

In addition to the people named above, other informants of Ibn Abi Shaybah are listed in the biographical works. Most of them can also be found in MS. Berlin 9409 and the *Muṣannaf*. Some of the better known ones are:

- Yazīd ibn Hārūn (d. 206 AH/ 822 CE)[117]
- ‘Abdur-Raḥīm ibn Sulaymān (d. 187 AH/ 803 CE)
- ‘Abdullāh ibn Idrīs (d.192 AH/ 808 CE)
- ‘Ubaydullāh ibn Mūsā (d. 213 AH/ 819 CE)
- ‘Affān ibn Muslim (d. 219 AH/ 834 CE)[118]

Moreover, other sources of Ibn Abi Shaybah had books with content similar to his. Al-Faḍl ibn Dukayn (d. 218-219 AH/ 833-834 CE) had a book of tārīkh that was cited in Ibn Ḥajar's *Iṣābah*, Ibn Sa'd's *aṭ-Ṭabaqāt* and Bukhari's *Tārīkh*.[119] Muhammad ibn Fuḍayl (d. 295 AH) is reported to have had a book comprising many themes (similar to a muṣannaf);[120] he has an extant collection in manuscript form at aẓ-Ẓāhiriyah[121] on the subject of supplication, and his *Kitāb az-Zuhd* is in the *Iṣābah*[122] of Ibn Ḥajar, who had a written copy of it.[123] Abu Dāwūd aṭ-Ṭayālisi (d. 204 AH/ 819 CE), a teacher of Ibn Abi Shaybah's, compiled a musnad[124] similar to Ibn Abi Shaybah's *Musnad.*

Thus, the statements in the biographical literature about Ibn Abi Shaybah's teachers correspond, to a large extent, to the information that can be gained from his work itself about his more significant sources. Because the biographical reports are not dependent on the work of Ibn Abi Shaybah, they may be regarded as independent confirmation of the conclusions drawn from the work itself.

Ibn Abi Shaybah received his materials by means of written transmissions; this was a normal method by the beginning of the second Islamic century. These written materials included a full recording of the traditions he received from his teachers, as shown by a comparison of his narrations with those of Iraqi contemporaries like Aḥmad ibn Ḥanbal and Abu Ya'lā al-Mūṣili.

The same process of circulating written records was also followed by the generation of Ibn Abi Shaybah's teachers, as proven by comparing their variations with the teachers of his contemporaries. However, in the generation before that (in the second half of the first century AH), written transmission was not used systematically. A combination of written elements and oral transmission was later transformed into fully-written texts. (This conclusion is in conformity with other conclusions on the transmission history of the Hadith in other regions of the Islamic world.)[125]

In the first quarter of the third century AH, Ibn Abi Shaybah achieved so much fame as a scholar that he attracted students from all corners of the Islamic world, among whom were:

- Ibn Ḥanbal (d. 241 AH/ 856 CE)
- Bukhari (d. 256 AH/ 870 CE)
- Muslim (d. 261 AH/ 875 CE)
- Abu Dāwūd (d. 275 AH/ 889 CE)
- Ibn Mājah (d. 273 AH/ 887 CE)
- 'Abdullāh ibn Aḥmad ibn Muhammad ibn Ḥanbal (d. 290 AH/ 903 CE)

Adh-Dhahabi also mentions other famous names in the third century AH/ ninth century CE, such as ash-Shāfi'i (d. 204 AH/ 820 CE) and Muhammad ibn Sa'd (d. 230 AH/ 845 CE), al-Wāqidi's secretary and the compiler of aṭ-Ṭabaqāt.126

Also found among the numerous students of Ibn Abi Shaybah was Baqi ibn Makhlad al-Andalusi, from whom is derived a large part of the version of the Muṣannaf that has come down to us.127

Ibn Abi Shaybah's reputation rested, above all, on his books. The earliest references to them come from his students Aḥmad ibn Ḥanbal, Bukhari, Muslim and others. We can infer only that the books came into being during the first quarter of the third century AH/ ninth century CE and that they contained hadiths, among other things, but the references provide no details about their structure. Ibn an-Nadīm (d. 385 AH/ 995 CE) mentions the following books:

- *Kitāb as-Sunan fil-Fiqh,*
- *Kitāb at-Tafsīr,*
- *Kitāb at-Tārīkh,*[128]
- *Kitāb al-Fitan,*
- *Kitāb Ṣiffīn,*
- *Kitāb al-Jamal,*
- *Kitāb al-Futūḥ* and
- *al-Musnad.*[129]

Al-Baghdādi mentions *al-Aḥkām* as one of Ibn Abi Shaybah's books.[130] The designation 'sunan' or 'aḥkām' leads one to assume that it was a work of the muṣannaf type. Further names of his books include *Kitāb al-Īmān* (which was received by Ibn Ḥajar),[131] *al-Adab*[132] and *Kitāb Thawāb al-Qur'ān.*[133] Ibn Ḥajar mentions a permission for transmitting the book of *al-Awā'il.*[134] Some of these books—including *Kitāb at-Tārīkh, Kitāb al-Fitan, Kitāb Ṣiffīn, Kitāb al-Jamal* and *Kitāb Thawāb al-Qur'ān*—were published as chapters of the *Muṣannaf.*

During the first quarter of the third century AH, the four most famous transmitters of hadiths in Iraq were:

- 'Ali ibn al-Madīni,
- Yaḥyā ibn Ma'īn,
- Aḥmad ibn Ḥanbal, and
- Ibn Abi Shaybah.[135]

They were known for detecting the defects in traditions, clarifying the errors of muḥaddithīn, working out the legal issues of hadiths, and classifying traditions according to themes.

Ibn Abi Shaybah became the main muḥaddith of Kufa. Other scholars who accompanied him during his sessions included his brother 'Uthmān, Mushkanah, and 'Abdullāh ibn al-Barā'. According to 'Abdān al-Ahwazi, no one dared to narrate traditions in the presence of Ibn Abi Shaybah.[136]

According to biographical sources, Ibn Abi Shaybah was highly respected in terms of authenticity, accuracy and memory retention; he is said to have possessed the most retentive memory of his time.[137] According to Ibn Ḥanbal[138] and Yaḥyā ibn Ma'īn,[139] he was truthful. Ibn Abi Shaybah used to criticize Yaḥyā ibn Ma'īn in narrating traditions from Ḥafṣ ibn Ghayyāth, due to his possession of the latter's books.[140] Al-'Ajli, Abu Ḥātim ar-Rāzi and Ibn Kharāsh said, "He is trustworthy."[141]

He moved to Baghdad the same year he passed away (234 AH/ 849 CE). Ibrāhīm ibn Nafṭawayh related that one year before his death, the caliph al-Mutawakkil invited muḥaddithīn—including Muṣ'ab az-Zubayri, Is-ḥāq ibn Isrā'īl and Ibrāhīm ibn 'Abdullāh al-Harawi, in addition to Abu Bakr and 'Uthmān ibn Shaybah—to meet for the purpose of narrating traditions opposing the heretical Mutazilites and their subgroup, the Jahmites.[142]

In *Tārīkh Baghdād*, it is narrated that when Ibn Abi Shaybah reached Baghdad, a pulpit was erected for him in ar-Raṣafah mosque, where 30,000 people assembled to receive his hadiths.[143] At first, he narrated a tradition from his memory, but due to the critical attitude of his audience, he started reading from his books.[144]

Therefore, we know that Ibn Abi Shaybah had his traditions written and compiled in book form at least by this time (not long before his death). For the most part, they were in the possession of his son Ibrāhīm,[145] and it is probable that Ibrāhīm assisted him in classifying the material and categorizing it into books and chapters. This conclusion is supported by the way he classified his materials in the *Muṣannaf.*

Abu 'Ubaydah al-Qāsim ibn Salām (d. 224 AH/ 839 CE) remarked that Ibn Abi Shaybah was distinguished by his classifying and ordering his materials.[146] Ar-Rāmahurmuzi (d. 360 AH/ 970 CE)[147] also regarded him as unique in the thematic organization of his materials and compilations. This means that Ibn Abi Shaybah had a prominent role in arranging his materials, at least in the years immediately before his death. His powerful memory helped him to retain the materials and to retrieve them during his sessions.[148]

The *Muṣannaf* edition that contains the maghāzi section found in MS. Berlin 9409 is based mainly on the materials transmitted by Baqi ibn Makhlad (201-276 AH/ 816-889 CE). Baqi travelled to Kufa and received the *Muṣannaf* from Ibn Abi Shaybah himself, seemingly at the end of the latter's life. He uses the form '*ḥaddathanā Abu Bakr ibn Abi Shaybah* (Abu Bakr ibn Abi Shaybah informed us)' throughout the *Muṣannaf*. Baqi's riwāyah is usually introduced at the beginning of each book (rarely at the beginning of a chapter) with the phrase '*ḥaddathanā* (he informed us)', and then mostly confines itself to giving only the name Abu Bakr at the head of the isnād.

Biographical sources mention that Baqi returned to Andalusia two years before his death and started narrating the book for the first time in that land, but a controversy erupted over its differing and contradictory reports and verdicts. This controversy was settled when Muhammad ibn 'Abdur-Raḥmān ibn al-Ḥakam ibn Hishām, the emir of Andalusia from 275-300 AH/ 888-912 CE, perused the book and then asked to have it copied for him.[149] The *Muṣannaf* proliferated in Andalusia and was circulated only there until the sixth century AH/ twelfth century CE.[150] The only surviving copy was narrated by 'Abdullāh ibn Yūnus ibn 'Abdullāh al-Murādi al-Qabri, who transmitted both the *Muṣannaf* of Ibn Abi Shaybah and the *Musnad* of Baqi ibn Makhlad.

Ibn Khayr al-Ishbīli had different permissions for transmitting the book.[151] In Egypt, this book was received by Ibn Ḥajar in the eighth century AH/ fourteenth century CE, in the narration of 'Abdullāh ibn Yūnus from Baqi ibn Makhlad.[152]

2.8 Conclusion

In this chapter, we tried to answer three preliminary questions.

1) Does MS. Berlin 9409 contain the work of Abu Bakr 'Abdullāh ibn Muhammad ibn Abi Shaybah?

After reviewing the names of Ibn Abi Shaybah's teachers as mentioned in his own published books, and then comparing them to other relevant books of Hadith, we came to the conclusion that MS. Berlin 9409 is indeed the work of Ibn Abi Shaybah—with the exception of the first 17 traditions. These 17 do not include the names of Ibn Abi Shaybah's teachers, nor are they from sources he used anywhere else. They are most probably the work of Maslamah ibn al-Qāsim, the compiler of Ibn Abi Shaybah's *Kitāb al-Awā'il*.

2) Does the manuscript contain the well-known book *at-Tārīkh*, as claimed by some Western scholars?

After comparing the published book of the *Muṣannaf* with the manuscript at hand, we came to the conclusion that the manuscript is an identical copy of the chapter of maghāzi and that it does not contain the book *at-Tārīkh*, as was commonly argued in previous studies of the manuscript. The book is, however, wholly or partially included in the *Muṣannaf* under the same title, a point which is proven by later citations of *at-Tārīkh* and by Ibn Abi Shaybah's method of classifying his chapters.

3) If the manuscript does represent part of Ibn Abi Shaybah's work, are the sources maintained in the manuscript proven to actually be his sources, or are they mere forgeries that he arbitrarily ascribed to imaginary persons?

We employed two independent methods for answering this question about the authenticity of Ibn Abi Shaybah's sources.

By means of source criticism of the manuscript's chains of authority, we concluded that his sources formed independent individual profiles of their respective materials, thus precluding the possibility of an organized attribution of materials by Ibn Abi Shaybah. His use of anonymous sources, broken asānīd and contradictory texts supports this conclusion.

We also reviewed the life and works of the author in Muslim biographical sources, and this confirmed—through a separate evaluation of these sources—the results obtained from the work itself.

Therefore, we conclude that Ibn Abi Shaybah's sources are real; he must have received the materials from similar compilations received from his teachers.

Chapter Three

The development of early biographical sources about the life of Prophet Muhammad (ﷺ): The Kufan sources in the first two Islamic centuries

3.1 Introduction

In the second chapter, we answered the question of authorship; it was proven that MS. Berlin 9409 must be regarded as the work of Ibn Abi Shaybah. We provided preliminary answers to further questions regarding his sources—for instance, stating that he must have received his material from the teachers he named in MS. Berlin 9409. This investigation was conducted by means of source criticism based on the analysis of asānīd.

Although the question of authorship was convincingly answered, there are still questions about the development of Ibn Abi Shaybah's materials. The transmission history of these materials during the first two Islamic centuries and the reliability of his teachers' reports are still in question. To tackle these two questions, I will choose a group of traditions from MS. Berlin 9409 and compare them to variants in the Iraqi and Ḥijāzi sources by means of isnād-cum-matn analysis, which is regarded as one of the more effective tools of source criticism.

3.2 Method of investigation

In this chapter, I will make use of isnād-cum-matn analysis to check Ibn Abi Shaybah's sources against the sources of his Iraqi and Ḥijāzi contemporaries. The aim of this process, as defined by Motzki, is to trace the transmission history of a hadith by comparing its variants found in the different compilations of traditions that are available;[1] therefore, the tradition under investigation should have variants. This method uses both isnād analysis and the scrutiny of mutūn. The isnād analysis follows the methodological principles that were introduced by J. Schacht[2] and further refined by G. H. A. Juynboll, but the premises—and therefore the conclusions—are different. The study of mutūn is based on principles worked out in the historical disciplines to determine the origin of written transmissions such as manuscripts. It examines their development and their dependence on, or relationship to, each other.

This method proceeds from several premises, which were described by Motzki as follows:

1. Variants of a tradition are (at least partially) the result of a process of transmission.
2. The asānīd of the variants reflect (at least partially) the actual paths of transmission.
3. Cases in which the content of the text (mutūn) is correlated with the common links in the asānīd are most likely instances of real transmission.[3]

The method of isnād-cum-matn analysis used in this investigation consisted of several steps:

1. A tradition (or group of traditions) was chosen from MS. Berlin 9409.
2. As many variants as possible, equipped with asānīd (or fragments of them), were collected from all available legal, biographical and historical compilations of hadiths.
3. The lines of transmission were compiled in order to detect common links in the different generations of transmitters. A diagram of the isnād bundles was drawn for each tradition alone, in the form of Juynboll's method of isnād analysis of single traditions. This diagram shows the common links, partial common links, printed compilations and asānīd provided without the mutūn.
4. The variant texts were compared in order to identify relationships and differences among them in terms of their structure and wording. This also allowed us to formulate statements about their transmission history.
5. The mutūn were compared in order to identify their correlations and differences.
6. The results of isnād and matn analyses were compared. At this point, we were able to draw conclusions about the transmission history of the tradition and to provide an approximate date for when it was introduced.

The isnād-cum-matn analysis has proved to be a powerful tool for investigating historical traditions.[4] It was tested by Schoeler,[5] Motzki, A. Görke,[6] and others, and these studies showed that it is possible to reconstruct historical traditions concerning the biography of the Prophet (ﷺ). There is conformity and consistency between the asānīd and the mutūn, and accurate dating of traditions going back to the first century AH becomes tenable. Although some scholars consider the detailed analysis of asānīd to be tedious, it is an indispensable method for dating traditions and transmitted books.

It should also be mentioned that there is an alternative methodological framework that is widely adopted in Western studies of the process of transmitting hadiths in early Islam. This methodology relies intensively on the framework of 'oral history'. I chose not to adopt this methodological framework because recent research by Motzki and others (such as Schoeler and Sebastian Günther) has shown that although the transmission of traditions in early Islam was essentially oral, it left the phase of informal, purely oral transmission relatively early (by the second half of the first Islamic century). It was cultivated by organized teaching, in which the written preservation of orally transmitted knowledge was common.[7]

Although we must bear in mind that Muslims have various opinions concerning the use of writing and the written word, we know that even the earliest authorities were already practising writing and that written materials were used for a variety of purposes.[8] According to Motzki, Schoeler and Günther, this was the case as early as the first century of Islam.

The forms of this written preservation varied. They could be fixed as notes during or after lectures, scrupulously written down from dictation, or copied from a manuscript and read again to the teacher.[9] In the first Islamic century, the method by which transmission was recorded depended on the subject, time, place, teacher and student, and different methods could be in vogue at the same centre of learning at the same time.[10]

3.3 The story of the *mi'rāj* (ascension of the Prophet [ﷺ] to the heavens)

For the experimental material of this chapter, I will provide a historical study of the transmission of three hadiths recorded by Ibn Abi Shaybah on the subject of the mi'rāj. We will compare these traditions to those in other available Hadith compilations, at the level of the asānīd and the mutūn.[11]

One advantage of choosing the story of the mi'rāj is that it was mentioned in various versions within the work of Ibn Abi Shaybah. Since most of these versions have parallels in other Iraqi and Ḥijāzi sources, we will be able to compare these versions and examine their development.

Another advantage is that there are varying accounts of this story preserved in different sources, and this is a prerequisite for the application of sanad-cum-matn analysis.

Ibn Abi Shaybah provides nine reports on the story of the mi'rāj, all of which have uninterrupted chains of authorities going back to the Prophet (ﷺ). In Hadith compilations, the complete story mainly goes back to the Companion Anas ibn Mālik (d. 92-93 AH/ 711-712 CE), so we will start with this tradition.

3.4 The tradition of Anas narrated directly from the Prophet (ﷺ)

Ibn Abi Shaybah provides two versions of Anas ibn Mālik's tradition on the story of the mi'rāj. The first is narrated directly from the Prophet (ﷺ), and the second—provided with its isnād only[12]—is narrated from Mālik ibn Ṣa'ṣa'ah, who belongs to the tribe of Anas ibn Mālik. (There is a third version that names Abu Dharr as the informant of Anas ibn Mālik, but this version is not included in the work of Ibn Abi Shaybah.)

Ibn Abi Shaybah received the first tradition of Anas from al-Ḥasan ibn Mūsā al-Ashyab (d. 209-210 AH/ 824-825 CE), who received it from Ḥammād ibn Salamah al-Baṣri (d. 167 AH/ 783 CE). The latter received it from Thābit al-Bunāni (d. 123-127 AH/ 741-745 CE), the student of Anas ibn Mālik. Diagrams 1 to 6 in Appendix 1 show that the common link seems to be Anas ibn Mālik.[13] He passed the hadith to six students, most of whom should be regarded as what G.H.A. Juynboll terms 'partial common links'.[14] Let us analyze them in turn:

1) THĀBIT AL-BUNĀNI (shown on Diagram 1):

Thābit al-Bunāni is well-known for his expertise in Anas' traditions. He, along with his students, came from Basra. He passed the tradition to Ḥammād ibn Salamah (d. 167 AH/ 783 CE) and Sulaymān ibn al-Mughīrah (d. 165 AH/ 782 CE), both of whom are similarly regarded as partial common links.

Ḥammād ibn Salamah is a partial common link by virtue of six transmitters:

a. al-Ḥasan ibn Mūsā (d. 209-210 AH/ 824-825 CE), whose version is included in Ibn Abi Shaybah's *Muṣannaf*[15] and Aḥmad's *Musnad*;[16]

b. al-Ḥajjāj ibn Minhāl, whose version is found in Ibn Mandah's *Kitāb al-Īmān*;[17]

c. Aḥmad ibn Is-ḥāq, found in Abu 'Awānah's *Musnad*;[18]

d. Hudbah ibn Khālid (d. 233-239 AH/ 848-853 CE), whose version is found in Abu Ya'lā's *Musnad*[19] and Abu Nu'aym's *Mustakhraj*;[20]

e. Shaybān ibn Farrūkh (d. 235-236 AH/ 849-850 CE), whose version is found in Muslim's *Ṣaḥīḥ*[21] and Ibn Mandah's *Kitāb al-Īmān*;[22] and

f. al-Faḍl ibn 'Anbasah (d. 200 AH/ 816 CE), whose transmission is found in aṭ-Ṭabari's *Tafsīr*.[23]

The second narrator from Thābit, Sulaymān ibn al-Mughīrah, is a partial common link by virtue of four transmitters:

a. Yūnus ibn Ismā'īl,

b. Bahz ibn Ḥakīm,

c. Muhammad ibn Is-ḥāq and

d. Hāshim ibn al-Qāsim.

2) SHARĪK IBN 'ABDULLĀH IBN ABI NAMIR (shown on Diagram 2):

Sharīk ibn 'Abdullāh ibn Abi Namir (d. 140-144 AH/ 757-761 CE)[24] also claimed to have received the story from Anas. His version is included in Abu Nu'aym's *Mustakhraj*.[25] Almost all transmitters after Sharīk are from Madinah, so the isnād would be Ḥijāzi; Sharīk, therefore, represents the Ḥijāzi line in this tradition.

He passed the tradition to just one transmitter: Sulaymān ibn Bilāl at-Taymi al-Madani (d. 177 AH/ 793 CE), who is regarded as a partial common link by virtue of four transmitters:

a. 'Abdullāh ibn Wahb ibn Muslim,[26]

b. 'Abdul-'Azīz ibn 'Abdullāh ibn 'Abdullāh ibn 'Umar ibn al-Khaṭṭāb al-Madani,[27]

c. 'Abdul-Ḥamīd ibn 'Abdullāh ibn 'Abdullāh ibn Uways (d. 202 AH/ 817 CE)[28] and

d. ‘Abdul-‘Azīz al-Uways.

3) YAZĪD IBN ABI MĀLIK (shown on Diagram 3):

Yazīd ibn ‘Abdur-Raḥmān ibn Abi Mālik ad-Dimashqi (d. 130 AH/ 748 CE) allegedly received the story from Anas ibn Mālik. Yazīd had two students who transmitted the report:

a. Sa‘īd ibn ‘Abdul-‘Azīz (a partial common link), whose version is contained in an-Nasā’i’s *Sunan*,[29] Ibn ‘Asākir’s *Tārīkh*[30] and aṭ-Ṭabarāni’s *Musnad as-Shāmiyyīn*;[31]

b. Yazīd’s son, Khālid ibn Yazīd, whose version is included in a later compilation: Ibn Kathīr’s *Tafsīr*.[32] This version is commonly criticized by Muslim muḥaddithūn for containing inauthentic additions.[33]

4) ‘ABDUR-RAḤMĀN IBN HĀSHIM (shown on Diagram 4):

‘Abdur-Raḥmān ibn Hāshim has a version of the hadith that is included in aṭ-Ṭabari’s *Tafsīr*,[34] aṭ-Ṭabarāni’s *Tahdhīb*[35] and al-Bayhaqi’s *Dalā’il*.[36] There are two partial common links included in this transmission: Ibn Wahb and Yūnus ibn ‘Abdul-A‘lā.

5) ḤAMĪD AṬ-ṬAWĪL (shown on Diagram 5):

Ḥamīd aṭ-Ṭawīl’s version is included in aṭ-Ṭabari’s *Tafsīr*,[37] Aḥmad’s *Musnad*[38] and Ibn Abi Shaybah’s *Muṣannaf*.[39] Ḥamīd transmits an abridged version of the tradition of Anas and is regarded as a partial common link. He is known as one who disguises narrators within traditions, especially the traditions of Anas ibn Malik.[40]

6) QATĀDAH IBN DI‘ĀMAH (shown on Diagram 6):

The version of Qatādah ibn Di‘āmah is received by Sa‘īd ibn Abi ‘Arūbah[41] and Ma‘mar ibn Rāshid, whose narration is included in ‘Abdur-Razzāq’s *Muṣannaf*.[42] ‘Abdur-Razzāq is a partial common link who allegedly gave the tradition to aṭ-Ṭabari,[43] ‘Abd ibn Ḥumayd,[44] Aḥmad,[45] Ibn Ḥibbān,[46] al-Bayhaqi,[47] Ibn al-‘Arābi,[48] and al-Khaṭīb al-Baghdādi (in his *Tārīkh*).[49] Qatādah’s version is similarly short, but its text is different from that of Ḥamīd; this affirms the probability that Qatādah or a later transmitter is responsible for this version.

If we accept that Anas ibn Mālik is the common link in the isnād bundle, we can provisionally conclude that the tradition about the ascension of the Prophet (ﷺ) to the heavens, connected with the name of the Companion Anas ibn Mālik as its original transmitter, was spread by him in Basra in the first quarter of the second century AH. By identifying the common link and partial common links, we have taken the first step towards dating the transmission groups; still, certainty about their origin and development cannot be gained from transmission lines alone. The dating can be made more accurate by thoroughly analyzing the texts and then combining the results with those obtained through the scrutiny of the asānīd.

As far as I know, the oldest collection containing reports about the story of the Prophet's ascension to the heavens, as transmitted on the authority of the Companion Anas ibn Mālik, is the *Muṣannaf* of Ibn Abi Shaybah. The version that he presents is the most suitable as a starting point for textual analysis because it has variants in other sources. The tradition (whose transmission is shown on Diagram 1) reads:

Al-Ḥasan ibn Mūsā al-Ashyab—Ḥammād ibn Salamah—Thābit al-Bunāni—Anas ibn Mālik—the Messenger of Allah (ﷺ) said:

«(1)[50] I was brought a *burāq*, and it is a white animal, above the donkey and below the mule (in size), whose every stride carried it as far as its eyes could reach.

(2) I mounted it until it came to Jerusalem's temple.

(3) Then I tethered the beast to the ring where the prophets used to tie (it before).

(4) I entered al-Masjid al-Aqṣâ (the 'Farthest Mosque') and performed two units of prayer in it, and then came out,

(5) and Gabriel brought me a vessel of wine and a vessel of milk. I chose the milk, and Gabriel said: You have chosen the fiṭrah (the true, primeval religion).

(6) Hence, he took me to the earthly heaven. Gabriel asked for admittance, and it was said: Who is it?

He replied: Gabriel.

It was said: Who is with you?

He answered: Muhammad.

It was asked: Has it been revealed to him (to ascend to the heavens)?

He answered: Yes, indeed it has been revealed to him.

Then we were admitted (to enter), where I saw Adam, who welcomed (us) and called down God's blessings on me.

(7) Then we were brought to the second heaven, where Gabriel asked for admittance, and it was said: Who is it?

He said: Gabriel.

It was said: And who is with you?

He answered: Muhammad.

It was asked: Has it been revealed to him (to ascend to the heavens)?

He answered: Indeed, it has been revealed to him.

Then we were admitted (to the second heaven), where I saw the two maternal cousins John and Jesus, who welcomed (me) and called down God's blessings on me.

(8) Then we were brought to the third heaven, where Gabriel asked for admittance.

It was said: Who is it?

He answered: Gabriel.

It was asked: And who is with you?

He answered: Muhammad.

They said: Has it been revealed to him (to ascend to the heavens)?

He replied: Indeed, it has been revealed to him to ascend to the heavens.

Then we were admitted to where I saw Joseph, who was given half of the (earthly) beauty. He welcomed (me) and called down God's blessings on me.

(9) Then we were raised to the fourth heaven, where Gabriel asked for admittance.

It was asked: And who is it?

He answered: It is Gabriel.

It was asked: And who is with you?

He answered: Muhammad.

It was asked: Has it been revealed to him (to ascend to the heavens)?

He answered: Indeed it has been revealed to him to ascend.

Then we were admitted to where I saw Enoch, who welcomed (me) and called down God's blessings on me.

Then he (the Messenger of Allah) said: Allah says:

﴿ورفعنه مكانا عليا ﴿٥٧﴾﴾ (سورة مريم: ٥٧)

﴿And we raised him to a high station.﴾ *(Qur'an 19: 57)*

(10) Then we were brought to the fifth heaven, where Gabriel asked for admittance, and it was asked: Who is it? And who is with you?

He answered: Muhammad.

It was said: Has it been revealed to him (to ascend to the heavens)?

He answered: Indeed, it has been revealed to him to ascend to the heavens.

Then we were admitted to where I saw Aaron, who welcomed me and called God's blessings on me.

(11) Then we were brought to the sixth heaven, where Gabriel asked for admittance, and it was asked: Who is it?

He answered: It is Gabriel.

It was further asked: And who is with you?

He answered: Muhammad.

It was said: Has it been revealed to him (to ascend to the heavens)?

He answered: Indeed, it has been revealed to him to ascend to the heavens.

Then we were admitted to where I saw Moses, who welcomed me and called down God's blessings on me.

(12) Then we were raised to the seventh heaven, where Gabriel asked for admittance. It was asked: And who is it?

He answered: It is Gabriel.

It was asked: And who is with you?

He answered: Muhammad.

It was asked: Has it been revealed to him (to ascend to the heavens)?

He answered: Indeed, it has been revealed to him.

Then we were admitted to where I saw Abraham.

(13) He was reclining against *al-Bayt al-Ma'mūr*,[51] where 70,000 angels enter every day, never to visit (this place) again.

(14) Then I was taken to the *sidrat al-muntahā*,[52] whose leaves were like elephants' ears and its fruit like big earthenware vessels. When it was covered by the command of Allah, it underwent such a change that none amongst the creation has the power to praise its beauty.

(15) Then Allah revealed to me a revelation, and He made obligatory for me 50 prayers every day and night.

(16) When I went down to Moses, he asked: What has your Lord enjoined upon your community?

I replied: Fifty prayers.

He instructed: Return to your Lord and beg for a reduction (in the number of prayers), for your community shall not be able to bear this burden, as I have put to test the children of Israel and tried them (and found them too weak to bear such a heavy burden).

He (the Messenger of Allah [ﷺ]) said: I went back to my Lord and said: My Lord, make things lighter for my Ummah.

(My Lord) reduced five prayers for me. I went down to Moses and said: (My Lord) reduced five (prayers) for me.

He said: Verily, your people shall not be able to bear this burden; return to your Lord and ask Him to make things lighter. I then kept going back and forth between my Lord, Blessed and Exalted be He, and Moses, until He said: There are five prayers every day and night, O Muhammad, each being credited as 10, so that they make 50 prayers.

(18) He who intends to do a good deed and does not do it will have a good deed recorded for him, and if he does it, will have it recorded for him as 10; whereas he who intends to do an evil deed and does not do it will not have it recorded for him; if he does it, only one evil deed will be recorded.

I then came down, and when I came to Moses and informed him, he said: Go back to your Lord and ask Him to make things lighter.

Upon this, the Messenger of Allah (ﷺ) remarked: I returned to my Lord until I felt ashamed before Him.» (A sound hadith recorded by Ibn Abi Shaybah and Aḥmad)

Al-Ḥasan ibn Mūsā al-Ashyab's version is not extant in Ibn Abi Shaybah's *Muṣannaf* alone; it is also contained in the *Musnad* of Aḥmad. By comparing both texts, we reach the conclusion that the differences are typical transcription errors, and this confirms that both texts must be derived from a common source through a written transmission. Aḥmad and Ibn Abi Shaybah were contemporaries who could both have received the text from al-Ḥasan at the same or very nearly the same time. Both Aḥmad and Ibn Abi Shaybah could have received the text in written records and could have also read it back to al-Ḥasan. This would explain the rare differences between the two variants, which could be mere scribal errors. There would have been no need for Aḥmad to copy the text from Ibn Abi Shaybah, or vice versa, since al-Ḥasan was available for both of them in Iraq.

In order to answer the question of whether al-Ḥasan received the tradition from his alleged informant (Ḥammād ibn Salamah), we need to compare his version with those of other Iraqis around that time. Five students, all Iraqis, were claimed to be recipients of the same text from Ḥammād ibn Salamah:

- al-Ḥajjāj ibn Minhāl,
- Aḥmad ibn Is-ḥāq,
- Hudbah ibn Khālid,

- Shaybān ibn Farrūkh, and
- al-Faḍl ibn 'Anbasah.

All of them are Iraqis. A comparison among the five variants of Ḥammād shows that the basic outline and structure are the same, which confirms that all the texts emanate from a common source through a written transmission. There are, however, a number of differences in terms of additions and omissions. Since these go beyond normal copyist errors, this excludes the possibility that the compilers of the written sources (or any of their informants) copied from each other and provided texts with fabricated asānīd. Among the most significant differences are the following:

a. In al-Ḥasan's and Shaybān's versions, *ṭawīl* (lofty) is added to the description of the animal the Prophet (ﷺ) rode, whereas it is missing in the other versions.

b. The noun *ad-dābbah* (beast) is added in al-Ḥajjāj's and Hudbah's versions, but in the other versions, the burāq was referred to by a pronoun.

c. The adjective *ad-dunyā* (earthly) is added in all the versions except that of Shaybān.

d. The versions of al-Ḥajjāj and Shaybān have the addition *dhahrahu* (his back) in reference to Abraham resting his back against al-Bayt al-Ma'mūr.

e. Al-Ḥajjāj has an addition that is not found in other versions: *faraja'tu ḥattā antahaytu ilā Mūsā* (then I went down to Moses). The same addition is found in Aḥmad ibn Is-ḥāq's version, except that the word *faraja'tu* (then I returned) is replaced by *fanazaltu* (I descended).

f. Grammatical variants—such as *ataynā* (we came) instead of *ataytu* (I came), and *ḥattā intahaytu* (until I reached) instead of *fantahaytu* (then I reached)—are found in all versions.

g. There are variant synonyms such as *fa'tāni* (then came to me) instead of *jā'ni* (went to me), *ursila* (sent) instead of *bu'itha* (raised as a messenger), and *yan'itihā* (naming it) instead of *yaṣifuhā* (describing it).

h. Different sequences are noticeable throughout the five variants. For instance, Jesus (عليه السلام) is mentioned first in Shaybān's version, but John (عليه السلام) comes first in all the other versions.

i. Similarly, the vessel of wine is mentioned first in most of the versions, but it is mentioned second (after the vessel of milk) in the version of al-Ḥajjāj.

j. Al-Ḥajjāj's version also has a missing sentence: *Wa man hamma bi ḥasanatin fa lam ya'malahā kutibat ḥasanatan wāḥidah fa in 'amilahā kutibat 'asharah.* (He who intends to do a good deed and does not do it will have a good deed recorded for him, and if he does it, will have it recorded for him as 10.) This was deemed to be a later copyist error.

To summarize, there are meaningful differences in wording but not in the basic structure and outline of the narration. The peculiarities of these five texts show that they are independent transmissions going back to a common source. This common source, according to the isnād, is the text transmitted by Ḥammād ibn Salamah.

This conclusion may be bolstered by an analysis of the two short versions received through Ḥammād ibn Salamah. One is received through Hudbah and is included in Abu Ya'lā's *Musnad,* while the other is received through al-Faḍl ibn 'Anbasah and is included in aṭ-Ṭabari's *Tafsīr*. The version of Abu Ya'lā reads as follows:

Shaybān—Ḥammād—Thābit—Anas—the Prophet (ﷺ):

«When I ascended to the seventh heaven, I was taken to the sidrat al-muntahā, where (I found out that) its leaves are like the ears of elephants and its fruits are like jars. When it was covered by the command of Allah, it underwent such a change that no one amongst people can describe its beauty.»

The shorter version of Abu Ya'lā is similar in wording and style to the detailed versions of Muslim and Abu Nu'aym. There is one minor difference: The use of *mā ghashiyahā* (whatever covers it) instead of *mā ghasha* (what covers) in the short one and the choice of a different word: *an-nās* (people) instead of *khalqullāh* (the creation of Allah).

These minor differences affirm that the short version is neither dependent on their detailed versions nor an imitation of a portion thereof. If we compare Abu Ya'lā's short version with his detailed version, the differences are greater, meaning that his short version is not based on his own longer narration. Thus, this short version should go back to the same common source from whom Muslim took his detailed version; according to the isnād, this is Shaybān ibn Farrūkh.

There is another short version found in aṭ-Ṭabari through al-Faḍl ibn 'Anbasah. Al-Faḍl is one of the students of Ḥammād, and his version should be compared to those of his contemporaries who claimed to have received material from Ḥammād. When this version is compared to the other detailed variants of the students of Ḥammād, minor differences in wording become apparent. It is not obvious that it is based on any of the five variants; therefore, it should not be regarded as dependent on any of them. Nevertheless, it matches them in terms of its main structure and should therefore be traced to the same common source: Ḥammād ibn Salamah.

A comparison of the short version of Shaybān (included in Abu Ya'lā) with that of al-Faḍl ibn 'Anbasah (included in aṭ-Ṭabari) shows that both versions have variations in wording, not only when compared to each other but also when compared to other detailed versions. This finding rules out the explanation that one of those short versions is an imitation of the other or of any of the detailed versions. The conformity of structure among these short and long versions, moreover, affirms that they must have come from one common source, who, according to the isnād, is Ḥammād ibn Salamah. Therefore, we can provisionally conclude that those short and detailed versions were introduced by Ḥammād ibn Salamah in written transmission in Iraq before his death in 167 AH/ 783 CE.

According to isnād and matn, there is another version of Thābit's transmission that was received by Sulaymān ibn al-Mughīrah. This variant is included in Ibn Mandah's *Kitāb al-Īmān,* Ibn 'Asākir's *Tārīkh* and aṭ-Ṭabari's *Tafsīr.* A mere glance at this version confirms that it differs much more from Ḥammād's matn. The version of Sulaymān ibn al-Mughīrah includes additional details that are not contained in Ḥammād's text.

a. It states that the journey started in the Prophet's house and that the Prophet's breast was opened, washed with *Zamzam*[53] water and then filled with faith and wisdom by means of a golden utensil sent down from the heavens. This segment is contained in the version of Mālik ibn Ṣa'ṣa'ah, which will be discussed later. Sulaymān's variant similarly affirms that Anas saw marks on the Prophet (ﷺ) indicating where his chest had been split open.

b. When the Prophet (ﷺ) met Adam (عليه السلام) in the first earthly heaven, Adam welcomed the Prophet (ﷺ) by saying, "Welcome (O Muhammad) my son and Messenger." The rest of the messengers welcomed the Prophet (ﷺ) by calling him their brother and the Messenger of God. Ḥammād's version states only that the Prophet (ﷺ) was welcomed; it does not mention the exact words.

c. In Ḥammād's version, the description of al-Bayt al-Ma'mūr is introduced immediately upon narrating the Prophet's meeting with Abraham. In Sulaymān's version, it is introduced upon the Prophet's question to the angel. This might be the addition of a transmitter, especially if the tradition is not narrated verbatim.

d. In Ḥammād's version, Abraham (ﷺ) was described as resting his back against al-Bayt al-Ma'mūr, but this is not mentioned in Sulaymān's version.

e. God's multiplication of good deeds is missing in Sulaymān's version.

In addition to these major differences between the versions of Ḥammād and Sulaymān, there are several variations in wording. The differences, however, cannot hide the fact that the structure of the narration and a substantial portion of the text are identical. We can conclude from this that the two versions are not copied from each other but must be independently derived from a common source. According to the isnād, this is Thābit al-Bunāni, who narrated both abridged and detailed versions of the tradition of Anas ibn Mālik concerning the Prophet's ascension to the heavens. The short version originated before 123 AH/ 741 CE.

Sulaymān ibn al-Mughīrah has another abridged version, which is included in Muslim's *Ṣaḥīḥ* and Abu Nu'aym's *Mustakhraj*.[54] The former is received through Bahz, from Sulaymān from Thābit al-Bunāni, while the latter is received through Hāshim ibn al-Qāsim from Sulaymān. There is no relationship between this abridged version and the one discussed earlier. Let us introduce the translation of this version as contained in Muslim's *Ṣaḥīḥ*:

'Abdullāh ibn Hāshim—Bahz ibn Ḥakīm—Sulaymān ibn al-Mughīrah—Thābit—Anas—the Prophet (ﷺ):

«I was visited (by a group of angels) who took me to Zamzam, where my breast was opened and washed out with Zamzam water. Then I was released.»

By comparing the short variant of Sulaymān with his detailed text, we can safely reach the conclusion that they are not dependent on each other, simply because of one difference that is not the result of scribal error: the use of the word *fanṭalaqtu* (then I was released), which uses the first singular pronoun, as opposed to *fanṭalaqu* (they departed), with the first plural pronoun. The rest of the content and wording are identical; therefore, they must go to Sulaymān ibn al-Mughīrah as the common source.

There remains a question about this version: does it go back to Thābit, or does it stop at Sulaymān? There is a similar version that goes through 'Abd Rabbuh ibn Sa'īd from Thābit al-Bunāni and is contained in an-Nasā'i's *Sunan*. When we compare the short version of Sulaymān's to that of 'Abd Rabbuh, it appears that differences among the two versions exceed the scope of variant wording. There are additional details that appear in this version:

- Prayer has been made obligatory toward Makkah,
- Two angels took the Prophet (ﷺ) to the well of Zamzam; two angels opened the Prophet's breast, took out its contents and put it on a golden tray. After washing him, they filled his breast with wisdom and faith.

In addition to those extra details, there are other structural and wording differences. This version may be an elaboration of the variant of Muslim. Despite all these additions and differences, the main outline is the same; that is, the Prophet (ﷺ) was taken to the well of Zamzam, where his breast was opened and then washed. Therefore, those two variants could come from one source, which, according to the isnād, is Thābit al-Bunāni.

If I am correct in concluding that the versions of Ḥammād and Sulaymān must go back, independently of each other, to a common source, then the difference between the two versions must be explained by supposing that Thābit al-Bunāni related the story in at least two different ways, one as abridged and the other detailed. The detailed version was the original one that he related to his students, and it was the one received by Ḥammād ibn Salamah and Sulaymān ibn al-Mughīrah.

Ḥammād has more expertise in Thābit's traditions than does Sulaymān, but he suffered from confusion towards the end of his life; many biographers accused him of *wahm* (illusion), especially in his final days. Imam Bukhari did not include any of his traditions in his *Ṣaḥīḥ,* but Muslim included the traditions he transmitted before reaching old age, especially those he received from Thābit.[55]

Therefore, the version of Sulaymān may be regarded as the original; it must have been received in Iraq during the first half of the second century. Thābit was also asked about the story of opening the Prophet's breast and whether it happened once, during the Prophet's youth, or if it occurred again immediately before the Prophet's ascension to the heavens. He answered by relating the abridged story of the opening of his breast, which happened while the Prophet (ﷺ) was in Makkah. Sulaymān ibn al-Mughīrah transmitted both versions, while Ḥammād transmitted only the detailed one. My conclusion—that Sulaymān's more detailed version should be taken as the most accurate transmission—is supported by comparing his version of this tradition to others.

The closest version to that of Thābit al-Bunāni is the version of Yazīd ibn Abi Mālik. Yazīd's version is related by aṭ-Ṭabarāni, Ibn 'Asākir and an-Nasā'i through Sa'īd ibn 'Abdul-'Azīz, who is regarded as a partial common link. (See Diagram 3 of Appendix 1.) This is affirmed by comparing his texts as included in the foregoing compilations. The variants go back to Sa'īd, who must be regarded as the common source to transmit his text through the written media. There is another version included in Ibn Kathīr's *Tafsīr*; this is claimed to have been received from Yazīd through his son Khālid. By comparing the two versions of Yazīd ibn Abi Mālik, it becomes evident that Khālid's variant includes many additional details that are missing in the variant of Sa'īd. Khālid is known as a weak transmitter; he probably added these details to the version he received from his father.

Let us now compare the version of Yazīd ibn Abi Mālik with that of Thābit al-Bunāni. In my comparison, I will rely on the variant of Sa'īd ibn 'Abdul-'Azīz as related by an-Nasā'i.

In Yazīd's version, the Prophet (ﷺ) was taken by Gabriel to offer prayer in Ṭībah (Madinah), and he was told that this would be his place of migration. He offered a second prayer at aṭ-Ṭūr, where God had spoken to Moses, and then a third prayer at Bethlehem, where Jesus is said to have been born. Prophets were then gathered for him in Jerusalem, where he led them in prayer. (There is no mention of the two vessels of wine and milk in this version.) He ascended to the seven heavens, where he saw the other prophets. When he reached the sidrat al-muntahā, a fog shaded him, and he prostrated. Thereafter, prayers were prescribed as 50 in number. The Prophet (ﷺ) returned to God after Moses advised him to ask his Lord to reduce the number of prayers.

The differences between Thābit's and Yazīd's versions are such that any dependence of one on the other is not probable. What they have in common must go back to a common source, which may be ascertained by examining the version of Sharīk ibn 'Abdullāh. (See Diagram 2 of Appendix 1.)

Sharīk's is the third version that allegedly goes back to Anas, and it has greater differences than that of Thābit. The following is a translation of Sharīk's version from Bukhari's *Ṣaḥīḥ al-Bukhāri*:[56]

«(1) The night Allah's Messenger (ﷺ) was taken for a journey from the Sacred Mosque (of Makkah), the Kaaba: Three persons came to him in a dream while he was sleeping in the Sacred Mosque before the divine inspiration was revealed to Him.

One of them said: Which of them is he?

The middle (second) angel said: He is the best of them.

The last (third) angel said: Take the best of them.

(2) Only that much happened on that night, and he did not see them until they came on another night (after the divine inspiration was revealed to him), and he saw them; his eyes were asleep but his heart was not, and so is the case with the prophets: their eyes sleep while their hearts do not sleep. Those angels did not talk to him until they carried him and placed him beside the well of Zamzam. From among them, Gabriel took charge of him. Gabriel cut open (the part of his body) between his throat and the middle of his chest (heart) and took all the material out of his chest and abdomen and then washed it with Zamzam water with his own hands until he had cleansed the inside of his body. Then a gold tray, containing a gold bowl full of belief and wisdom, was brought, and Gabriel filled his chest and throat with it before sealing it up.

(3) He then ascended with him to the nearest heaven and knocked on one of its doors. The dwellers of the heaven asked: Who is it?

He said: Gabriel.

They asked: Who is accompanying you?

He replied: Muhammad.

They inquired: Has he been called?

He affirmed: Yes.

They said: He is welcomed.

The dwellers of the heaven became pleased with his arrival, and they did not know what Allah would do to the Prophet (ﷺ) on the earth unless Allah informed them. The Prophet (ﷺ) met Adam over the nearest heaven.

Gabriel said to the Prophet (ﷺ): He is your father; greet him.

The Prophet (ﷺ) greeted him, and Adam returned his greeting and said: Welcome, my son! Oh, what a good son you are!

(4) Behold, he saw two flowing rivers while he was in the nearest heaven. He asked: What are these two rivers, Gabriel?

Gabriel said: These are the sources of the Nile and the Euphrates.

(5) Then Gabriel took him around that heaven and behold, he saw another river, at the bank of which there was a palace built of pearls and emeralds. He put his hand into the river and found its mud-like, pungent musk. He asked: What is this, Gabriel?

Gabriel said: This is al-Kawthar (the name of a river in paradise, the banks of which are made of pearls), which your Lord has kept for you.

(6) Then Gabriel ascended (with him) to the second heaven, and the angels asked the same questions as those on the first heaven: Who is it?

Gabriel replied: Gabriel.

They asked: Who is accompanying you?
He responded: Muhammad.

They inquired: Has he been sent for?

He affirmed: Yes.

Then they said: He is welcomed.

(7) Then he (Gabriel) ascended with the Prophet (ﷺ) to the third heaven, and the angels said the same as the angels of the first and the second heavens had said.

(8) Then he ascended with him to the fourth heaven, and they said the same.

(9) Then he ascended with him to the fifth heaven, and they said the same.

(10) Then he ascended with him to the sixth heaven, and they said the same.

(11) Then he ascended with him to the seventh heaven, and they said the same. In each heaven, there were prophets whose names he had mentioned, of whom I remember Enoch in the second heaven; Aaron in the fourth heaven; and another prophet, whose name I do not remember, in the fifth heaven. Abraham was in the sixth heaven, and Moses in the seventh heaven because of his privilege of talking to Allah directly.

(12) Moses said (to Allah): O Lord! I thought that none would be raised above me. But Gabriel ascended with him (the Prophet [ﷺ]) for a distance above that, the distance of which only Allah knows, until he reached the sidrat al-muntahā (beyond which none may pass).

(13) Then he approached the Irresistible, the Lord of Majesty, and drew closer until he was two bow lengths or even nearer.

(14) Among the things that Allah revealed to him then was the enjoinment of 50 prayers upon his followers in a day and a night.

(15) Then the Prophet (ﷺ) descended until he met Moses. Moses stopped him and asked: O Muhammad! What did your Lord enjoin upon you?

The Prophet (ﷺ) replied: He enjoined upon me to perform 50 prayers in a day and a night.

Moses said: Your followers cannot do that. Go back so that your Lord may reduce it for you and for them.

The Prophet (ﷺ) turned to Gabriel as if he wanted to consult him about that issue. Gabriel expressed his opinion, saying: Yes, if you wish.

Gabriel ascended with him to the Irresistible, and he said while he was in his place: O Lord, please lighten our burden, for my followers cannot do that.

Thus, Allah deducted for him 10 prayers, whereupon he returned to Moses, who stopped him again and kept on sending him back to his Lord until the number of enjoined prayers was reduced to only five. Then Moses stopped him when the prayers had been reduced to five and said: O Muhammad! By Allah, I tried to persuade my nation, the children of Israel, to do less than this, but they could not do it and gave it up. However, your followers are weaker in body, heart, sight and hearing, so return to your Lord so that He may lighten your burden.

The Prophet (ﷺ) turned towards Gabriel for advice, and Gabriel did not disapprove of that. So he ascended with him for the fifth time. The Prophet (ﷺ) said: O Lord, my followers are weak in their bodies, hearts, hearing and constitution, so lighten our burden.

On that, the Irresistible said: O Muhammad!

The Prophet (ﷺ) replied: Here I am at Your service.

Allah said: The Word that comes from Me does not change, so it will be as I enjoined on you in the Mother of the Book.

Allah added: Every good deed will be rewarded 10 times, so it is 50 (prayers) in the Mother of the Book (in reward), but you are to perform only five (in practice).

The Prophet (ﷺ) returned to Moses, who asked: What have you done?

He said: He has lightened our burden; He has given us for every good deed a tenfold reward.

Moses said: By Allah! I tried to make Bani Israel observe less than that, but they gave it up. So go back to your Lord that He may lighten your burden further.

Allah's Messenger (ﷺ) said: O Moses! By Allah, I feel shy about returning too many times to my Lord.

(16) On that, Gabriel said: Descend in Allah's name.

The Prophet (ﷺ) then awoke within the Sacred Mosque (at Makkah).» (Bukhari)

This version seems to be an elaboration of Thābit's version.

a. It introduces the whole story as a dream.

b. The incident of opening the Prophet's heart, according to this variant, occurs twice: once before the Prophet's mission and the other at the time of his ascension.

c. The description of opening the breast is more elaborate.

d. The prophets who meet the Messenger (ﷺ) in the heavens are not named.

e. The Prophet (ﷺ) sees two rivers in the first heaven.

f. Moses speaks to his Lord about the elevated status of Muhammad (ﷺ).

g. At the end of the narration, the Prophet (ﷺ) wakes up at the Kaaba.

The differences between the two versions are so many, and sometimes so substantial, that it is not conceivable that Bukhari's text is based on Ibn Abi Shaybah's version or vice versa. Sharīk's version seems to be another independent transmission from Anas ibn Mālik. Those additional details will be discussed later.

There are three versions left in this isnād bundle, and they are all short. The first of them (the fourth in the isnād bundle) is that of 'Abdur-Raḥmān ibn Hāshim ibn 'Utbah ibn Abi Waqqāṣ. (See Diagram 4 of Appendix 1.) It departs from the preceding versions by adding a conversation between Gabriel and the burāq, the Prophet's meeting with an elderly woman on his way to Jerusalem, a man who calls out to him, and a group of creatures who greet him by the road. Gabriel is then recorded as explaining that the woman represents the remaining lifetime of the world and the man represents Satan. The only correspondence with the previous versions is that the Prophet (ﷺ) is offered a vessel of milk and one of wine.

Given the insufficient bibliographical information on 'Abdur-Raḥmān ibn Hāshim in the sources, and the fact that no other narrator transmits the same text, we cannot determine whether or not he actually received this text from Anas. Muslim muḥaddithūn judged this version as including additions not substantiated by other reliable transmitters. There is, however, a great deal of similarity between this version and the tradition of Abu Sa'īd al-Khudri as contained in aṭ-Ṭabari's *Tahdhīb al-Āthār*.[57] Most probably, 'Abdur-Raḥmān ibn Hāshim received the text from Abu Sa'īd al-Khudri and attributed it to Anas ibn Mālik. This supposition is supported by the conclusion that most of the content of this hadith is not included in any of the transmissions of Anas. The only aspect included in Anas' tradition is the part about vessels of wine and milk. Moreover, if we compare this version to that of Abu Sa'īd al-Khudri, we find that they have substantial differences in wording but they have similar outlines. Such a similarity suggests an oral transmission in the generation after the common link, that is, at the time of 'Abdur-Raḥmān ibn Hāshim, who is an unknown transmitter of hadiths.

The fifth version that it is claimed to have been received from Anas is that of Ḥamīd aṭ-Ṭawīl. (See Diagram 5 in Appendix 1.) It is included in Ibn Abi Shaybah's *Muṣannaf,* Aḥmad's *Musnad* and aṭ-Ṭabari's *Tafsīr.* The following text is a translation of Ibn Abi Shaybah's version.

Abu Khālid al-Aḥmar—Ḥamīd aṭ-Ṭawīl—Anas ibn Mālik—the Prophet (ﷺ): «When I reached the sidrat al-muntahā, its leaves were like the ears of elephants, and its jujube (fruits) were like jars. When it was covered by the command of Allah, it changed (into something) reminding me of jacinth and emerald.» (A sound hadith recorded by Ibn Abi Shaybah and others)

Let us compare these three variants first. While Aḥmad's variant is identical to aṭ-Ṭabari's in wording and structure, it is different from Ibn Abi Shaybah's in wording.

a. The full name of the tree is mentioned in Ibn Abi Shaybah's, whereas it is referred to as *as-sidrah* in Aḥmad's version.

b. In both, the leaves of the tree are compared to jars, but Ibn Abi Shaybah's version uses the word *qilāl*, whereas Aḥmad's version uses the word *jirār*. This is due to the narrators' variant choice of synonyms.

c. In Ibn Abi Shaybah's version, the leaves of the lote tree are described first, but in Aḥmad's version, they are mentioned after the fruit.

d. The mention of jacinth and emerald are additions that are not provided in the other versions.

The fact that Ibn Abi Shaybah's variant is different from—and thus independent of—those of Aḥmad and aṭ-Ṭabari is explained by the difference in their respective informants. Ibn Abi Shaybah's informant is Abu Khālid al-Aḥmar, whereas Muhammad ibn Ibrāhīm ibn Abi 'Adiyy is the transmitter from whom Aḥmad and aṭ-Ṭabari received their variants. Therefore, the three versions should belong to one source, who, according to the isnād, is Ḥamīd. Ibn Abi Shaybah and Aḥmad received their materials through written transmission, while their teachers received them aurally.[58]

Thus, the three versions should at least belong to Ḥamīd aṭ-Ṭawīl, who might have fabricated the tradition or might have really received it from Anas, as he claimed. This last question may be tested if we compare the short version transmitted by Ḥamīd with the relevant short version of Thābit al-Bunāni. I will compare Thābit's version as recorded in Abu Ya'lā's *Musnad* with Ḥamīd's version as included in Ibn Abi Shaybah. There are differences in the wording:

- *dhahaba bi* (went with me) is used instead of *intahaytu* (I reached),
- *ka'ādhān al-fiyalah* (like elephants' ears) instead of *amthāl al-fiyalah* (like elephants),
- *thamaruhā* (its fruits) instead of *nabquhā* (its lotus fruits),
- *taghayyarat* (changed) instead of *taḥawwālat* (transformed).

There are some additions in Thābit's version:

- *famā aḥadun yastaṭī'u an yan'itahā min ḥusnihā* (no one can describe it because of its beauty) and
- *fa'awḥā Allāhu ilayyā mā awḥā* (Allah revealed to me what he revealed).

There is one addition in Ḥamīd's version: the mention of jacinth and emerald. This addition, which is missing in all other detailed and short versions of the story, is most likely the work of Ḥamīd aṭ-Ṭawīl.

The three variants evoke doubt about the exact words, and the differences blur the possibility that any of these short versions is dependent on another. In spite of these differences in wording, though, the outline is the same. This similarity strongly suggests that there is only one source from whom this version was received, so we should accept what the isnād indicates until the contrary is proven. According to the isnād, this source is Anas ibn Mālik.

The possibility that Ibn Abi Shaybah fabricated this version is untenable since it is not an imitation of his detailed version, which he received from al-Ḥasan ibn Mūsā al-Ashyab. If he had intended to fabricate such a hadith, it would have been much easier to use the name of al-Ḥasan ibn Mūsā, whose detailed version is included in his book. In addition, comparing his variant to the one included in Aḥmad and aṭ-Ṭabari proves that the tradition was circulated in Iraq not only in the generation of Ibn Abi Shaybah and that of his informant, but also in the previous generation. This leads us to the conclusion that the sources of Ibn Abi Shaybah, when compared to the other Iraqi sources, are real sources.

The conclusion reached by analyzing the isnād bundle—that there is a common link for the tradition of Anas concerning the Prophet's ascension—is corroborated by the matn analysis. Additionally, the isnād analysis shows that this common link is Anas ibn Mālik, and that it was not artificially created by the so-called 'spread of asānīd'. There are contrasts among the variants deriving from the second generation (Thābit, Sharīk and Yazīd), in which the differences among the texts are much more substantial. The reason seems to be that in the generation of Thābit al-Bunāni's pupils, who received their texts from him in the first quarter of the second Islamic century, the methods of preserving them were not yet as sophisticated as they would become a generation later.

According to Anas ibn Mālik, to whom the different versions of the story go back, he received the hadith from the Prophet (ﷺ), who died when Anas was 20 years old.[59] Anas is well-known for his close contact with the Prophet (ﷺ) throughout the entire Madinan phase of the Prophet's mission. He was one of the most prolific narrators of hadiths and the longest living of the Companions, living until the year 92 or 93 AH/ 711 or 712 CE. He had moved to Basra, where he transmitted this tradition (of the Prophet's ascension) between 23 AH/ 644 CE and 92 AH/ 711 CE.

Anas was not with the Prophet (ﷺ) when the incident occurred, but he is said to have heard a report of it from another Companion. The veracity of this ascription cannot be ascertained on the basis of this tradition alone. The only thing that we can say at this stage of our analysis is that if it is true, there are long periods between the times when Anas heard the story (before the year 10 AH/ 631 CE), when Thābit al-Bunāni might have received it (between 50 AH/ 670 CE and 91 AH/ 710 CE), and when it was transmitted to Thābit's students (between 91 AH/ 710 CE and 123 AH/ 741 CE). During these periods, the story was probably only preserved by memory, with its form changed—even if only slightly—every time it was retold, as the two different versions of Thābit illustrate. Therefore, we can conclude that the two paths of transmission that are included in Ibn Abi Shaybah are based on real sources. Ibn Abi Shaybah's informants did not fabricate their asānīd, nor did their respective teachers.

3.5 The tradition of Anas received from Mālik ibn Ṣa'ṣa'ah

Ibn Abi Shaybah provided the tradition of Mālik ibn Ṣa'ṣa'ah in the isnād without text. We need to verify whether this isnād was fabricated or whether it had a text that was circulated at the time of Ibn Abi Shaybah's informants. Variants of this tradition equipped with isnād can be found in 17 sources. The oldest compilation is Ibn Abi Shaybah's; its isnād starts with Ḥammād ibn Usāmah, who received the tradition from Sa'īd ibn Abi 'Arūbah. Sa'īd identifies Qatādah as his informant, and Qatādah allegedly transmits the story from Anas ibn Mālik, whom Mālik ibn Ṣa'ṣa'ah cites as his ultimate authority. The common link in this isnād bundle is Qatādah. (See Diagram 8 of Appendix 1.)

Sa'īd ibn Abi 'Arūbah, one of the six transmitters who allegedly received the story from Qatādah, is what G. H. A. Juynboll terms the 'partial common link'. He is from Basra and is known for his expertise in the traditions of Qatādah. Eleven transmission lines are attributed to him. Three of them are provided only with asānīd: that of Ḥammād ibn Usāmah (d. 201 AH/ 816 CE)[60] contained in Ibn Abi Shaybah's *Muṣannaf*,[61] that of Muhammad ibn Bakr ibn 'Uthmān al-Barsāni (d. 204 AH/ 819 CE)[62] contained in Aḥmad's *Musnad*,[63] and that of Khālid ibn al-Ḥārith ibn 'Ubayd ibn Sulaymān al-Hujaymi al-Baṣri (120-186 AH/ 738-802 CE) contained in aṭ-Ṭabari's *Tafsīr*.[64]

There are two variant short versions: that of Muhammad ibn Ibrāhīm ibn Abi 'Adiyy al-Baṣri (d. 194 AH/ 810 CE), included in aṭ-Ṭabari's *Tafsīr*,[65] and that of 'Abdah ibn Sulaymān in Muhammad ibn Naṣr al-Marwazi's *Ṣalāt al-Witr*.[66] The rest are detailed versions given with asānīd and mutūn. They include the version of Yazīd ibn Zuray' al-'Ayshiy al-Baṣri (d. 182 AH/ 798 CE), who may also be regarded as a partial common link. His version is contained in Bukhari's *Jāmi'*,[67] Abu 'Awānah's *Musnad*,[68] an-Nasā'i's *as-Sunan al-Kubrā*[69] and Ibn 'Asākir's *Tārikh*.[70] Among the detailed versions are those of the following:

a. 'Abdul-Wahhāb ibn 'Aṭā' al-Khaffāf al-Baṣri[71] (d. 204-206 AH/ 819 CE) within Ibn Mandah's *Kitāb al-Īmān*,[72] al-Bayhaqi's *Dalā'il*[73] and Abu 'Awānah's *Mustakhraj*;[74]

b. Muhammad ibn Ja'far al-Baṣri (d. 139 AH/ 756 CE) recorded by Aḥmad in his *Musnad*;[75] and

c. Muhammad ibn Sulaymān, included in Ibn Mandah's *Kitāb at-Tawḥīd*.[76]

The second partial common link who received the tradition from Qatādah is Hishām ibn Abi 'Abdullāh ad-Dastwā'i (d. 154 AH/ 771 CE), who is also from Basra. (See Diagram 9 of Appendix 1.) Eight transmission lines go through Hishām. Three of them are provided with asānīd only:

a. That of his son Mu'ādh ibn Hishām (d. 200 AH/ 816 CE), which is contained in Ibn 'Asākir's *Tārīkh*,[77] aṭ-Ṭabari's *Tafsīr*[78] and Ibn Mandah's *Kitāb al-Īmān*;[79]

b. That of Yaḥyā ibn Sa'īd al-Qaṭṭān (d. 198 AH/ 814 CE), which is included in Ibn 'Asākir's *Tārīkh*;[80] and

c. That of Yazīd ibn Zuray' (d. 182 AH/ 798 CE), which is contained in Ibn Mandah's *Kitāb al-Īmān*.[81]

From Hishām also comes a short version that is received by Mu'ādh ibn Hishām and contained in Muslim's *Ṣaḥīḥ*.[82] There are three other versions of Hishām:

1. One is received by Yazīd ibn Zuray'; it is contained in Bukhari,[83] an-Nasā'i's *Sunan*[84] and Abu 'Awānah's *Mustakhraj*.[85]
2. The second is received by 'Abduṣ-Ṣamad ibn 'Abdul-Wārith (d. 207 AH/ 822 CE); it is included in Ibn Mandah's *Kitāb al-Īmān*.[86]
3. The third is found in Abu 'Awānah[87] and aṭ-Ṭabarī,[88] through Abu Dāwūd aṭ-Ṭayālisi.

The third student who is reported to have received the tradition from Qatādah is Hammām ibn Yaḥyā ibn Dinār al-Baṣri (d. 156-64 AH/ 781-783 CE), whose version is included in Ibn Mandah's *Kitāb al-Īmān*,[89] Ibn Ḥibbān,[90] Bukhari,[91] Aḥmad[92] and Ibn 'Asākir.[93] (See Diagram 7 in Appendix 1.)

There are, however, two additional single transmitters who claim to have received the story from Qatādah:

1. Shaybān ibn Farrūkh (d. 235-236 AH/ 849-850 CE), whose version is included in Abu Nu'aym's *Ma'rifat aṣ-Ṣaḥābah*,[94] and
2. Abu 'Awānah al-Waḍḍāḥ ibn 'Abdullāh al-Yashkuri (d. 175 AH/ 791 CE), whose version is extant in aṭ-Ṭabarāni's *al-Mu'jām al-Kabīr*[95] and Abu 'Awānah's *Mustakhraj*.[96]

Given the fact that Qatādah is the common link in the isnād bundle, we can provisionally conclude that the tradition about the ascension of the Prophet (ﷺ) connected with the name of the Companion Mālik ibn Ṣa'ṣa'ah as its original transmitter was spread in Basra in the first quarter of the second century by Qatādah ibn Di'āmah (d. 117-118 AH/ 735-736 CE). This conclusion about the common link will be revised later, but for now it is accepted provisionally based on the analysis of the isnād alone.

Furthermore, classifying the asānīd of all the variants of Mālik ibn Ṣa'ṣa'ah's traditions has given us a clue about how to classify the different versions. By identifying the common link and partial common links, we have taken the first step towards dating the transmission groups, but we cannot be certain of their origin and development based on the transmission lines alone. The dating can be made more accurate by thoroughly analyzing the texts and then combining the results of that analysis with the results obtained through a scrutiny of the asānīd.

As mentioned previously, Ibn Abi Shaybah's variant is only provided with its isnād. In analyzing the matn of this tradition, I will proceed from the variant of Hammām ibn Yaḥyā, which, it is claimed, was received from Qatādah. (See Diagram 7 of Appendix 1.) It reads as follows:

Hudbah ibn Khālid—Hammām ibn Yaḥyā—Qatādah—Anas ibn Mālik—Mālik ibn Ṣa'ṣa'ah—the Prophet (ﷺ):

«Allah's Messenger (ﷺ) described to them his Night Journey, saying:

(1) While I was lying in *al-ḥaṭīm*—or it is said: *al-ḥijr* (both of which are names for a place close to the Kaaba)—suddenly someone came to me and cut my body open from here to here.

I (Qatādah) asked al-Jārūd, who was by my side: What does he mean by it?

He replied: It means from his throat to his pubic area. And he said: From the top of the chest.

The Prophet (ﷺ) said: He then took out my heart. Thereupon, a gold tray of faith was brought to me, and my heart was washed and was filled (with faith) and then returned to its original place.

(2) Then a white animal, which was smaller than a mule and bigger than a donkey, was brought to me.

At this, al-Jārūd asked: Was it the burāq, Abu Ḥamzah?

I (Anas) replied in the affirmative.

The Prophet (ﷺ) said: The animal's stride reached the farthest point of its sight.

(3) I was carried on it, and Gabriel set out with me until we reached the nearest heaven. When he asked for the gate to be opened, it was asked: Who is it?

Gabriel answered: Gabriel.

It was asked: Who is accompanying you?

Gabriel replied: Muhammad.

It was asked: Has Muhammad been called?

Gabriel replied in the affirmative.

Then it was said: He is welcomed. What an excellent visit his is!

The gate was opened, and when I went into the first heaven, I saw Adam there. Gabriel said (to me): This is your father, Adam; pay him your greetings.

I greeted him, and he returned the greeting to me and said: You are welcomed, O pious son and pious prophet.

(4) Then Gabriel ascended with me until we reached the second heaven. Gabriel asked for the gate to be opened.

It was asked: Who is it?

Gabriel answered: Gabriel.

It was asked: Who is accompanying you?

Gabriel replied: Muhammad.

It was asked: Has he been called?

Gabriel answered in the affirmative.

Then it was said: He is welcomed. What an excellent visit his is!

The gate was opened. When I went into the second heaven, I saw John and Jesus, who were cousins. Gabriel said (to me): Here are John and Jesus; pay them your greetings.

I greeted them, and both of them returned my greetings to me and said: You are welcomed, O pious brother and pious prophet.

(5) Then Gabriel ascended with me to the third heaven and asked for its gate to be opened.

It was asked: Who is it?

Gabriel replied: Gabriel.

It was asked: Who is accompanying you?

Gabriel replied: Muhammad.

It was asked: Has he been called?

Gabriel replied in the affirmative.

Then it was said: He is welcomed. What an excellent visit his is!

The gate was opened, and I went to where I saw Joseph.

Gabriel said (to me): This is Joseph; pay him your greetings.

I greeted him, and he returned the greeting to me and said: You are welcomed, O pious brother and pious prophet.

(6) Then Gabriel ascended with me to the fourth heaven and asked for its gate to be opened.

It was asked: Who is it?

Gabriel replied: Gabriel.

It was asked: Who is accompanying you?

Gabriel replied: Muhammad.

It was asked: Has he been called?

Gabriel replied in the affirmative.

Then it was said: He is welcomed. What an excellent visit his is!

The gate was opened, and when I went into the fourth heaven, there I saw Enoch. Gabriel said (to me): This is Enoch; pay him your greetings.

I greeted him, and he returned the greeting to me and said: You are welcomed, O pious brother and pious prophet.

(7) Then Gabriel ascended with me to the fifth heaven and asked for its gate to be opened.

It was asked: Who is it?

Gabriel replied: Gabriel.

It was asked: Who is accompanying you?

Gabriel replied: Muhammad.

It was asked: Has he been called?

Gabriel replied in the affirmative.

Then it was said: He is welcomed. What an excellent visit his is!

When I went over the fifth heaven, there I saw Aaron.

Gabriel said: This is Aaron; pay him your greetings.

I greeted him, and he returned the greeting to me and said: You are welcomed, O pious brother and pious prophet.

(8) Then Gabriel ascended with me to the sixth heaven and asked for its gate to be opened.

It was asked: Who is it?

Gabriel replied: Gabriel.

It was asked: Who is accompanying you?

Gabriel replied: Muhammad.

It was asked: Has he been called?

Gabriel replied in the affirmative.

It was said: He is welcomed. What an excellent visit his is!

When I went (into the sixth heaven), there I saw Moses.

Gabriel said: This is Moses; pay him your greeting.

I greeted him, and he returned the greetings to me and said: You are welcomed, O pious brother and pious prophet.

(9) When I left him (Moses), he wept.

Someone asked him: What makes you weep?

Moses said: I weep because after me there has been sent (as a prophet) a young man whose followers will enter paradise in greater numbers than my followers.

(10) Then Gabriel ascended with me to the seventh heaven and asked for its gate to be opened.

It was asked: Who is it?

Gabriel replied: Gabriel.

It was asked: Who is accompanying you?

Gabriel replied: Muhammad.

It was asked: Has he been called?

Gabriel replied in the affirmative.

Then it was said: He is welcomed. What an excellent visit his is!

(11) So when I went (into the seventh heaven), there I saw Abraham.

Gabriel said (to me): This is your father; pay your greetings to him.

I greeted him, and he returned the greetings to me and said: You are welcomed, O pious son and pious prophet.

(12) Then I was made to ascend to the sidrat al-muntahā. Behold! Its fruits were like the jars of Ḥijr (a place near Madinah), and its leaves were as big as the ears of elephants.

Gabriel said: This is the sidrat al-muntahā.

(13) Behold! There ran four rivers; two were hidden and two were visible. I asked: What are these two kinds of rivers, Gabriel?

He replied: As for the hidden rivers, they are two rivers in paradise, and the visible rivers are the Nile and the Euphrates.

(14) Then al-Bayt al-Ma‘mūr was shown to me, and a container full of wine, another full of milk, and a third full of honey were brought to me. I took the milk. Gabriel remarked: This is the pure state, which you and your nation are upon.

(15) Then the prayers were enjoined on me, 50 prayers a day. When I returned, I passed by Moses, who asked (me): What have you been ordered to do?

I replied: I have been ordered to offer 50 prayers a day.

Moses said: Your followers cannot bear 50 prayers a day, and by Allah, I have tested people before you, and I have tried my level best with the children of Israel (in vain). Go back to your Lord and ask for a reduction to lessen your followers' burden.

I went back, and Allah reduced 10 prayers for me. Then again I came to Moses, but he repeated what he had said before. Thus, I again went back to Allah, and He reduced 10 more prayers. When I came back to Moses, he said the same. I went back to Allah, and He ordered me to observe 10 prayers a day. When I came back to Moses, he repeated the same advice. Hence, I went back to Allah and was ordered to observe five prayers a day.

When I came back to Moses, he asked: What have you been ordered?

I replied: I have been ordered to observe five prayers a day.

He said: Your followers cannot bear five prayers a day, and no doubt, I have experience with the people before you, and I have tried my level best with the children of Israel. Go back to your Lord and ask for a reduction to lessen your followers' burden.

I said: I have requested so much of my Lord that I feel ashamed, but I am satisfied now and surrender to Allah's order.

When I left, I heard a voice saying: I have passed My order and have lessened the burden of My worshippers.»

This text resembles the structure and wording of the version of 'Affān ibn Muslim that is contained in Aḥmad's *Musnad*. The differences extant in the two other variants that go back to Hammām—a partial common link in the isnād bundle[97]—are mostly due either to copyist errors or to some slight editing by the transmitters, but a comparison of Hammām's version with that of Sa'īd ibn 'Arūbah[98] or Hishām ad-Dastwā'i[99] brings to light further differences. This is similar to the previous tradition of Anas ibn Mālik, in that the differing versions of the hadith transmitted by each of these three narrators from Qatādah vary more than the set of variants originating from their transmission to their students. Therefore, we can say that each of the three possesses a characteristic form of the hadith.

A comparison between Hishām's and Hammām's versions reveals that Hishām's is somewhat shorter and more concise, and it does not contain a repetition of narrative elements such as *marḥaban bi al-ibn aṣ-Ṣāliḥ wa an-Nabiy aṣ-Ṣāliḥ, fafatḥa falammā khalaṣtu, thumma ṣa'ada bi ḥattā atā'*. (You are welcomed, O pious brother and pious prophet. Then he opened [the gate]. When I had finished [there], I ascended until I reached…)

In Hammām's version, Qatādah is reported as being unsure of the exact word for the place from which the Prophet (ﷺ) started the journey (whether it is al-ḥaṭīm or al-ḥijr, although both of them are variant names for the same place).[100] In Hishām's version, the place is somewhere closer to the (Sacred) House (*al-bayt*).

Hammām's narration describes the burāq as a white animal smaller than a mule and bigger than a donkey, but its colour is missing in Hishām's version. Similarly, Moses is described as weeping after the Prophet (ﷺ) left him, a detail included only in Hammām's version. In Hishām's version, al-Bayt al-Ma'mūr is described in more detail and before the Lote Tree, but in Hammām's version, it is mentioned briefly and only after the four rivers. The detailed description of al-Bayt al-Ma'mūr is an insertion by Qatādah, as explained in Hammām's version included in Aḥmad's *Musnad*. Qatādah took it from Abu Hurayrah's transmission of the story. Moreover, the vessels of wine and other liquids that Gabriel introduced to the Prophet (ﷺ) are mentioned only in Hammām's version. At the end of Hishām's version, there is a short sentence describing Allah's multiplication of one good deed into 10 good deeds; this final phrase is missing in Hammām's version.

There is one more noticeable difference between the two texts. Hammām has the following matn:

«[1] While I was lying in al-ḥaṭīm—or it is said: al-ḥijr (both of which are names for a place close to the Kaaba)—suddenly someone came to me and cut my body open from here to here.

I (one of the narrators) asked al-Jārūd, who was by my side: What does he mean by it?

He said: It means from his throat to his pubic area. And he said: From the top of the chest.»

In Hishām's version, as preserved in al-Bayhaqi's *Dalā'il,*[101] there is no mention of this question. There is another similar addition, which is related to al-Jārūd and is only contained in Hammām's version. He is reported as asking Anas ibn Mālik a question about the burāq, but there is no mention of this question in Hishām's version.

The version of Sa'īd ibn Abi 'Arūbah, the third version to be transmitted from Qatādah, is found in Ibn Abi Shaybah's *Muṣannaf,* aṭ-Ṭabari's *Tafsīr,* Muslim's

Ṣaḥīḥ, an-Nasā'i's *Sunan,* Bukhari's *Ṣaḥīḥ al-Bukhāri,* Aḥmad's *Musnad* and other compilations. This version is distinct from those of both Hammām and Hishām, but it is closer to Hammām's version in its basic structure. The differences appearing in Sa'īd's version can be summarized as follows:

1. The Prophet (ﷺ) starts the journey from a place close to the Kaaba.
2. The angels talk to each other while searching for the Prophet (ﷺ), who is lying down between two men.
3. A golden bowl is full of Zamzam water before the opening of the chest.
4. The animal is white, and its strides carry it as far as it can see.
5. The Prophet (ﷺ) is carried with Gabriel, who never leaves him (until the point of the sidrat al-muntahā).
6. There is doubt over whether he describes Jesus and John as maternal cousins.
7. Qatādah recites the Qur'ānic verse:

﴿وَرَفَعۡنَٰهُ مَكَانًا عَلِيًّا ۝٥٧﴾ (سورة مريم: ٥٧)

﴾And we raised him to a high station.﴿ *(Qur'an 19: 57)*

8. Al-Bayt al-Ma'mūr is mentioned immediately after the Prophet's meeting with Abraham.
9. The Prophet (ﷺ) is offered only two vessels, one of milk and one of wine. (A vessel of honey is added in Hammām's version.)
10. It is stated that prayers are reduced by 10.
11. It is mentioned that deeds are multiplied tenfold.

From a study of all the variations among Hammām's, Hishām's and Sa'īd's texts, we can conclude that none of them was copied from one of the others. All are identical in structure and, for the most part, in wording as well; thus, they must be derived from a common source. According to their asānīd, Qatādah's narration is the common link among the three transmissions, and it is very unlikely that his status as a common link in the isnād is the result of a 'spread of asānīd.' This conclusion is substantiated by adding the versions of Abu 'Awānah and Shaybān to the previously analyzed variants.

Aṭ-Ṭabari's *Tafsīr* contains only the following short version of this tradition. (See Diagram 8 of Appendix 1.)

Muhammad ibn al-Muthannā—Muhammad ibn Ibrāhīm ibn Abi 'Adiyy—Sa'īd—Qatādah—Anas ibn Mālik—Mālik ibn Ṣa'ṣa'ah—the Prophet (ﷺ):

«When I arrived at the seventh heaven, I came to Abraham and said: Gabriel, who is this?

Gabriel answered: He is your father Abraham.

I greeted him, and he said: Welcome, righteous son and righteous Prophet.

Then I was raised to the sidrat al-muntahā.

The Prophet (ﷺ) then related that its fruits were like the jars of Ḥijr (a place near Madinah) and its leaves were like the ears of elephants.»

This short version does not have any further parallels other than that of Muhammad ibn al-Muthannā, the informant of aṭ-Ṭabari who narrated a detailed version of the same hadith. A comparison of these two shows that neither of them is copied from the other. An example of the divergence between them is that Ibn al-Muthannā's version did not mention the sidrat al-muntahā.

Similarly, the short version above is not identical to any of the other detailed variants of Qatādah through Sa'īd ibn Abi 'Arūbah. Sa'īd's variants associate Prophet Abraham with al-Bayt al-Ma'mūr, but the short version associates him with the sidrat al-muntahā. This short version is, however, similar (although not identical) to the detailed version of Qatādah through Hammām. Therefore, it could be supposed that it would go back to Qatādah, a conclusion that is corroborated by isnād analysis. Thus, the conclusion drawn about the origin of the detailed version may also be applicable to the short one. I assume that Qatādah related the story at different times with a slightly varying isnād and matn. Additionally, he used one element within it as a legal argument, and this was transmitted later on his authority as a separate hadith.

A very important question is: is Qatādah merely a common link in the transmission of the hadith of the Prophet's ascension, or should he be credited as its ultimate source? To answer this question, it is useful to make a detailed comparison between the tradition of Mālik ibn Ṣa'ṣa'ah and the tradition of Anas (narrated by Thābit al-Bunāni). For the latter tradition, we shall use the version of Sulaymān ibn al-Mughīrah, which we concluded is the original of the two variants of Thābit al-Bunāni and which is found within Ibn Mandah's *Kitāb al-Īmān*,[102] aṭ-Ṭabari's *Tafsīr*[103] and Ibn 'Asākir's *Tārīkh.* We will compare this hadith with one of the variants of Qatādah as contained in Bukhari's *Jāmi'*.[104] Table 1 summarizes the points of concordance between the two traditions (with the differences underlined):

The tradition of Anas ibn Mālik	**The tradition of Mālik ibn Ṣa'ṣa'ah**
[1] While I was with my family, I was taken to the well of Zamzam where my chest was cut open. Thābit said: Anas ibn Mālik said that he (the Prophet [ﷺ]) showed us the trace of this (opening). Then his chest was washed by Zamzam water. Then a gold tray full of faith and wisdom descended, and my heart was filled with it.	[1] While I was lying in al-ḥaṭīm—or it is said: al-ḥijr (both of which are names for a place close to the Kaaba)—suddenly someone came to me and cut my body open from here to here. I (Qatādah) asked al-Jārūd, who was by my side: What does he mean by it? He said: It means from his throat to his pubic area. And he said: From the top of the chest. The Prophet (ﷺ) said: He then took out my heart. Thereupon, a gold tray of faith was brought to me, and my heart was washed and was filled (with faith) and then returned to its original place.
[2] Then I was made to ascend to the earthly heaven where admittance was sought. It was asked: Who is it? Gabriel answered: Gabriel. It was asked: Who is accompanying you? Gabriel replied: Muhammad. It was asked: Has Muhammad been called? Gabriel replied in the affirmative. The gate was opened, and I saw Adam there. He said: You are welcomed, O son and prophet.	[2] Then a white animal, which was smaller than a mule and bigger than a donkey, was brought to me. At this, al-Jārūd asked: Was it the burāq, Abu Ḥamzah? I (Anas) replied in the affirmative. The Prophet (ﷺ) said: The animal's stride reached the farthest point of its sight.
[3] Then I was made to ascend the second heaven. It was asked: Who is it? Gabriel answered: Gabriel. It was asked: Who is accompanying you? Gabriel replied: Muhammad. It was asked: Has he been called? Gabriel answered in the affirmative. The gate was opened. When I went into the second heaven, there I saw Jesus and John, who said: You are welcomed, O brother and prophet.	[3] I was carried on it, and Gabriel set out with me until we reached the nearest heaven. When he asked for the gate to be opened, it was asked: Who is it? Gabriel answered: Gabriel. It was asked: Who is accompanying you? Gabriel replied: Muhammad. It was asked: Has Muhammad been called? Gabriel replied in the affirmative. Then it was said: He is welcomed. What an excellent visit his is! The gate was opened, and when I went into the first heaven, I saw Adam there. Gabriel said (to me): This is your father,

	Adam; pay him your greetings. I greeted him, and he returned the greeting to me and said: You are welcomed, O pious son and pious prophet.
[4] Then we ascended to the third heaven and asked for its gate to be opened. It was asked: Who is it? Gabriel replied: Gabriel. It was asked: Who is accompanying you? Gabriel replied: Muhammad. It was asked: Has he been called? Gabriel replied in the affirmative. The gate was opened, and then I went over the third heaven where I saw Joseph. He said: You are welcomed, O brother and prophet.	[4] Then Gabriel ascended with me until we reached the second heaven. Gabriel asked for the gate to be opened. It was asked: Who is it? Gabriel answered: Gabriel. It was asked: Who is accompanying you? Gabriel replied: Muhammad. It was asked: Has he been called? Gabriel answered in the affirmative. Then it was said: He is welcomed. What an excellent visit his is! The gate was opened. When I went into the second heaven, I saw John and Jesus, who were cousins. Gabriel said (to me): Here are John and Jesus; pay them your greetings. I greeted them, and both of them returned my greetings to me and said: You are welcomed, O pious brother and pious prophet.
[5] Then we ascended to the fourth heaven and asked for its gate to be opened. It was asked: Who is it? Gabriel replied: Gabriel. It was asked: Who is accompanying you? Gabriel replied: Muhammad. It was asked: Has he been called? Gabriel replied in the affirmative. Then it was said: He is welcomed, what an excellent visit his is! The gate was opened, and I met Enoch. He said: You are welcomed, O brother and prophet.	[5] Then Gabriel ascended with me to the third heaven and asked for its gate to be opened. It was asked: Who is it? Gabriel replied: Gabriel. It was asked: Who is accompanying you? Gabriel replied: Muhammad. It was asked: Has he been called? Gabriel replied in the affirmative. Then it was said: He is welcomed. What an excellent visit his is! The gate was opened, and I went to where I saw Joseph. Gabriel said (to me): This is Joseph; pay him your greetings. I greeted him, and he returned the greeting to me and said: You are welcomed, O pious brother and pious prophet.

[6] Then we ascended to the fifth heaven and asked for its gate to be opened. It was asked: Who is it? Gabriel replied: Gabriel. It was asked: Who is accompanying you? Gabriel replied: Muhammad. It was asked: Has he been called? Gabriel replied in the affirmative. It was opened and I saw Aaron. He said: You are welcomed, O brother and prophet.	[6] Then Gabriel ascended with me to the fourth heaven and asked for its gate to be opened. It was asked: Who is it? Gabriel replied: Gabriel. It was asked: Who is accompanying you? Gabriel replied: Muhammad. It was asked: Has he been called? Gabriel replied in the affirmative. Then it was said: He is welcomed. What an excellent visit his is! The gate was opened, and when I went into the fourth heaven, there I saw Enoch. Gabriel said (to me): This is Enoch; pay him your greetings. I greeted him and he returned the greeting to me and said: You are welcomed, O pious brother and pious prophet.
[7] Then we ascended to the sixth heaven and asked for its gate to be opened. It was asked: Who is it? Gabriel replied: Gabriel. It was asked: Who is accompanying you? Gabriel replied: Muhammad. It was asked: Has he been called? Gabriel replied in the affirmative. It was opened and there I saw Moses. He said: You are welcomed, O brother and prophet.	[7] Then Gabriel ascended with me to the fifth heaven and asked for its gate to be opened. It was asked: Who is it? Gabriel replied: Gabriel. It was asked: Who is accompanying you? Gabriel replied: Muhammad. It was asked: Has he been called? Gabriel replied in the affirmative. Then it was said: He is welcomed. What an excellent visit his is! So when I went over the fifth heaven, there I saw Aaron. Gabriel said: This is Aaron; pay him your greetings. I greeted him, and he returned the greeting to me and said: You are welcomed, O pious brother and pious prophet.
[8] Then I was made to ascend to the seventh heaven where admittance was sought. It was asked: Who is it? Gabriel replied: Gabriel. It was asked: Who is accompanying you? Gabriel replied, Muhammad. It was asked: Has he been called? Gabriel replied in the affirmative. It was opened and there I saw Abraham who said: You are welcomed O son and prophet.	[8] Then Gabriel ascended with me to the sixth heaven and asked for its gate to be opened. It was asked: Who is it? Gabriel replied: Gabriel. It was asked: Who is accompanying you? Gabriel replied: Muhammad. It was asked: Has he been called? Gabriel replied in the affirmative. It was said: He is welcomed. What an excellent visit his is!

	When I went (into the sixth heaven), there I saw Moses. Gabriel said: This is Moses; pay him your greeting. I greeted him, and he returned the greetings to me and said: You are welcomed, O pious brother and pious prophet.
[9] Then I reached a building. I said to the angel: What is that (building)? He said: It is a building which Allah constructed for the angels. Seventy thousand angels enter every day to sanctify and glorify Allah. They never return to it (but always a fresh batch comes into it daily).	[9] When I left him (Moses), he wept. Someone asked him: What makes you weep? Moses said: I weep because after me there has been sent (as a prophet) a young man whose followers will enter paradise in greater numbers than my followers.
[10] Then I reached the sidrat al-muntahā. I knew that it was a lote tree by its leaves and fruits. When it was covered by Allah's command it was changed so that nobody can describe it.	[10] Then Gabriel ascended with me to the seventh heaven and asked for its gate to be opened. It was asked: Who is it? Gabriel replied: Gabriel. It was asked: Who is accompanying you? Gabriel replied: Muhammad. It was asked: Has he been called? Gabriel replied in the affirmative. Then it was said: He is welcomed. What an excellent visit his is!
[11] Then the prayers were enjoined on me, fifty prayers a day. When I returned, I passed by Moses who asked (me): What have you been ordered to do? I replied: I have been ordered to offer fifty prayers a day. He said: Your people will not bear that, so return to your Lord and ask him to reduce the number. I returned back to my Lord who reduced ten. I kept going between my Lord and Moses until Allah made them five. I returned to Moses who asked me to go back to my Lord to ask Him for reduction. I said: I submit. I was then called (by my Lord): I have made my decree and have reduced the burden on My slaves, and I shall reward each prayer as if it were ten prayers.	[11] So when I went (into the seventh heaven), there I saw Abraham. Gabriel said (to me): This is your father; pay your greetings to him. I greeted him, and he returned the greetings to me and said: You are welcomed, O pious son and pious prophet.

	[12] Then I was made to ascend to the sidrat al-muntahā. Behold! Its fruits were like the jars of Ḥijr (a place near Madinah) and its leaves were as big as the ears of elephants. Gabriel said: This is the sidrat al-muntahā.
	[13] Behold! There ran four rivers: two were hidden and two were visible. I asked: What are these two kinds of rivers, O Gabriel? He replied: As for the hidden rivers, they are two rivers in paradise, and the visible rivers are the Nile and the Euphrates.
	[14] Then al-Bayt al-Maʿmūr was shown to me, and a container full of wine, another full of milk, and a third full of honey were brought to me. I took the milk. Gabriel remarked: This is the pure state, which you and your nation are upon.
	[15] Then the prayers were enjoined on me, fifty prayers a day. When I returned, I passed by Moses, who asked (me): What have you been ordered to do? I replied: I have been ordered to offer fifty prayers a day. Moses said: Your followers cannot bear fifty prayers a day, and by Allah, I have tested people before you, and I have tried my level best with the children of Israel (in vain). Go back to your Lord and ask for a reduction to lessen your followers' burden. He said: Your followers cannot bear five prayers a day, and no doubt, I have experience with the people before you, and I have tried my level best with the children of Israel. Go back to your Lord and ask for a reduction to lessen your followers' burden. I said: I have requested so much of my Lord that I feel ashamed, but I am satisfied now and surrender to Allah's order. When I left, I heard a voice saying: I have passed My order and have lessened the burden of My worshippers.

	I went back, and Allah reduced ten prayers for me. Then again I came to Moses, but he repeated what he had said before. Thus, I again went back to Allah, and He reduced ten more prayers. When I came back to Moses, he said the same. I went back to Allah, and He ordered me to observe ten prayers a day. When I came back to Moses, he repeated the same advice. I went back to Allah and was ordered to observe five prayers a day.
	When I came back to Moses, he said: What have you been ordered?
	I replied: I have been ordered to observe five prayers a day.
	He said: Your followers cannot bear five prayers a day, and no doubt, I have experience with the people before you, and I have tried my level best with the children of Israel. Go back to your Lord and ask for a reduction to lessen your followers' burden.
	I said: I have requested so much of my Lord that I feel ashamed, but I am satisfied now and surrender to Allah's order.
	When I left, I heard a voice saying: I have passed My order and have lessened the burden of My worshippers.

Table 1

The comparison of the content of Anas' tradition with that going back to Mālik ibn Ṣa'ṣa'ah shows that they correspond to a great extent. There is an obvious structural similarity between the two texts, which is further affirmed by the fact that the sequence of the units is nearly the same. In addition, there are a number of cases of equivalency in content and in specific wording.

Such similarities could give credence to the idea that one may be based on the other, but the structural and textual differences and additions noticed in both the texts rule this out.

For instance, there is no reason to suppose that Thābit abridged the text of Qatādah (Mālik's tradition) by deleting some segments. In fact, such an inference is ruled out by the fact that other variants of Thābit, specifically those transmitted through Ḥammād ibn Salamah, include some of the missing segments. Therefore, the structural similarities and the textual correspondence of the mutūn quoted above cannot be the result of one's dependence on the other; they must both be derived from one or more common sources.

Such a conclusion is in accordance with the evidence from the relevant asānīd. Both versions purport to go back to Anas ibn Mālik, so the common source for the tradition of Mālik ibn Ṣa'ṣa'ah is Anas—not Qatādah, who should instead be regarded as one of the partial common links who received the tradition from Anas. The only difference is that he names Mālik as the original transmitter of the tradition.

Most probably, Anas ibn Mālik himself is responsible for this problem. Sometimes he narrates the tradition by providing the name of the Prophet (ﷺ) immediately, but at other times, he provides the tradition quoting Mālik. Anas and Mālik belong to the same tribe and are contemporaries, so the tradition of Mālik should be dated at approximately the same time as the tradition of Anas, or even earlier.

We can conclude by mentioning the significance of these results in confirming the historical authenticity of this tradition within the *Muṣannaf* of Ibn Abi Shaybah. We have demonstrated that the tradition of Mālik was circulated and transmitted in Iraq at the time of Sa'īd ibn Abi 'Arūbah (before his death in 156 AH/ 782 CE). When we compared Qatādah's version with the previous versions of Anas ibn Mālik, it became evident that the tradition was already well-known in Iraq—especially in Basra—before 100 AH/ 718 CE.[105] Therefore, it is certain that the isnād provided by Ibn Abi Shaybah without a matn is a genuine chain for a tradition that he possessed. It is not fabricated by Ibn Abi Shaybah or by any of his informants at any stage of transmission. It is difficult to provide the exact matn for this isnād since it is missing in the manuscript of the *Muṣannaf,* but it should be presumed that it would match other versions transmitted by Sa'īd ibn Abi 'Arūbah, and that it would share many characteristics with the tradition of Thābit al-Bunāni, which was textually transmitted by Ibn Abi Shaybah, as previously discussed.

3.6 The tradition of Abu Dharr

Variants that report the story of the Prophet's ascension to the heavens on the authority of Abu Dharr, and that are provided with asānīd, are found in a number of sources: Aḥmad's *Musnad,* Bukhari's *Jāmi',* Muslim's *Ṣaḥīḥ,* an-Nasā'i's *Sunan,* al-Bayhaqi's *Dalā'il,* Ibn 'Asākir's *Tārīkh,* Abu Nu'aym's *Mustakhraj,* Ibn Ḥibbān's

Ṣaḥīḥ, Abu 'Awānah's *Musnad,* Ibn Mandah's *Kitāb al-Īmān,* al-Ājjuri's *ash-Sharī'ah,* al-Bazzār's *Musnad,* al-Firyābi's *Qadar* and al-Fākihi's *Akhbar Makkah.* (See Diagram 10 of Appendix 1.)

As with Anas' tradition, there are versions with both short and long mutūn. The short version is recorded by the well-known Madinan scholar Ibn Shihāb az-Zuhri, who provides an isnād that ends with Anas ibn Mālik directly quoting the Prophet (ﷺ). This short version is sometimes inserted into the detailed one. Thus, it may be dated at least to 124 AH/ 742 CE, the year az-Zuhri died. When an isnād bundle is compiled from all variants, az-Zuhri appears as a common link above the alleged transmitter, Anas ibn Mālik.

Two transmitters claim to have received the story from him: Yūnus ibn Yazīd and 'Aqīl ibn Khālid.[106] The former is termed a partial common link, whereas the latter is a so-called 'dive'.[107] Yūnus is a partial common link by virtue of five transmitters:

1. al-Layth ibn Sa'd,[108]
2. 'Abdullāh ibn Wahb,[109]
3. 'Abdullāh ibn al-Mubārak,[110]
4. 'Anbasah ibn Khālid ibn Yazīd[111] and
5. Anas ibn 'Iyāḍ.[112]

The asānīd in the lower part—Anas and 'Anbasah—are Madinan; in the upper part, 'Abdullah ibn Wahb and al-Layth are Egyptians. 'Abdullāh ibn al-Mubārak is Marwazī.

It should be pointed out that there is a difference with regard to who originally transmitted the hadith to Anas ibn Mālik. According to one of the transmissions, the name of his informant is Abu Dharr, but Ubayy ibn Ka'b's name is given in another transmission.

This problem can be easily solved based on an analysis of the asānīd. In Aḥmad's *Musnad*, the two variant chains are given. It seems that Anas ibn 'Iyāḍ is the one who is responsible for changing the name of Abu Dharr into Ubayy. It is a transcription error; the word Dharr was omitted from the hadith and was later read by copyists as Ubayy instead of Abu Dharr.[113]

In analyzing the matn, we will proceed from the version contained in Muslim's *Ṣaḥīḥ*:

Ḥarmalah ibn Yaḥyā—'Abdullāh ibn Wahb—Yūnus ibn Yazīd—az-Zuhri—Anas ibn Mālik—Abu Dharr—the Prophet (ﷺ):

«[1]The roof of my house was cleft when I was in Makkah. Gabriel descended, opened my heart and washed it with the water of Zamzam. He then brought a gold basin full of wisdom and faith, and after emptying it into my breast, he closed it up.

[2] Then, taking me by my hand, he ascended with me to the heaven. When we came to the lowest heaven, Gabriel asked the guardian of the lowest heaven to open (its gate).

The guardian asked: Who is there?

Gabriel replied: It is Gabriel.

He again asked: Is there someone with you?

Gabriel answered: Yes, Muhammad is with me.

He asked: Has he been called?

Gabriel replied: Yes.

Then he opened (the gate). When we ascended the lowest heaven, I saw a man seated with parties on his right side and parties on his left side. When he looked up to his right, he laughed and when he looked to his left, he wept. He said: Welcome, O pious prophet and pious son.

I asked Gabriel who he was. He replied: It is Adam, and these parties on his right and on his left are the souls of his descendants. Those on his right are the inmates of paradise and the parties which are on his left side are the inmates of hell; when he looked towards his right side, he laughed, and when he looked towards his left side, he wept.

[3] Then Gabriel ascended with me to the second heaven. He asked its guardian to open (its gate), and its guardian replied in the same way as the guardian of the lowest heaven and opened it.

Anas ibn Mālik said: He (the Prophet [ﷺ]) mentioned that he found in the heavens Adam, Enoch, Jesus, Moses and Abraham, but he did not ascertain the nature of their abodes except that he had found Adam in the lowest heaven and Abraham in the sixth heaven.

[4] When Gabriel and the Messenger of Allah (ﷺ) passed by Enoch (عليه السلام), he said: Welcome, O pious prophet and pious brother.

He (the narrator) said: He (the Prophet [ﷺ]) then proceeded and asked: Who is he? Gabriel replied: It is Enoch.

[5] Then I passed by Moses (عليه السلام), who said: Welcome, O pious prophet and pious brother.

I asked (Gabriel): Who is he?

He replied: It is Moses.

[6] Then I passed by Jesus, who said: Welcome, O pious messenger and pious brother.

I asked (Gabriel): Who is he?

He replied: It is Jesus, son of Mary.

[7] Then I went to Abraham (ﷺ), who said: Welcome, O pious prophet and pious brother.

I asked: Who is that?

He (Gabriel) replied: It is Abraham.»

A comparison of the two versions received from az-Zuhri, one by Yūnus ibn Yazīd and the other by 'Aqīl ibn Khālid, makes it evident that both of them were received through written transmission, since their differences are only scribal. Analysis of the two texts proves that az-Zuhri is the common source from whom both variants were received through written transmission. Despite the comparison of both versions that allegedly go back to az-Zuhri, and the establishment of the content of the common sources from which both must be derived, the issue of the common source is still not fully explored. The reader of the texts of the tradition of Abu Dharr will have realized that it displays some correlation with the traditions of Qatādah and Anas ibn Mālik discussed earlier. Therefore, the relationships among the three traditions should be studied before a definitive answer to the issue of the source (or sources) of the versions can be given.

The appropriate units of text of the three traditions have been put alongside one another in Table 2. Mālik's tradition has been taken as the reference for the other three (Anas' tradition through Ḥammād ibn Salamah, Anas' tradition through Sulaymān ibn al-Mughīrah, and Abu Dharr's tradition). In Anas' tradition, we chose two variants of Thābit al-Bunāni, the first received through Ḥammād and the other through Sulaymān. There are some segments that are mentioned in the first but that do not appear in the second. For Mālik's tradition, we chose the version of Hammām as contained in Bukhari. For Abu Dharr's tradition, we used the variant of Yūnus ibn Yazīd as contained in Muslim's *Ṣaḥīḥ*.

Mālik	Anas, through Ḥammād ibn Salamah	Anas, through Sulaymān ibn al-Mughīrah	Abu Dharr
1	-	1	(1)
2	1	-	-
3	6	2	(2)
4	7	3	(3), (4)
5	8	4	-
6	9	5	(4)
7	10	6	-
8	11	7	(3), (5)
9	-	-	-
10	12	8	(7)
11	14	10	-
12	-	-	-
13	(13)	9	-
14	(5)	-	-
15	15	11	-

Table 2

The units of the contents of Malik's text are listed in the first column; the equivalent units of the others are shown in the second, third and fourth columns respectively. Plain numbers mean that the units correspond in content; numbers in parentheses mean that the content is similar only. A dash means that there is neither exact correspondence nor similarity. The results of the comparison are as follows:

Regarding the first variant of Mālik ibn Anas, namely Anas' tradition through Ḥammād ibn Salamah:

- Ten of Mālik's units (2-8, 10-11 and 15) display clear correspondence.
- Two of Mālik's units (13 and 14) show similarities.
- Three of Mālik's units (1, 9 and 12) have no equivalents.

For the second variant, Anas' tradition through Sulaymān ibn al-Mughīrah:

- Eleven of Mālik's units display clear correspondence.
- There are no units that are merely similar in content.
- Four of Mālik's units have no equivalents.

The tradition of Abu Dharr shows the greatest contrast with the other traditions.

- No units display a clear correspondence to the texts of Mālik's (or Anas') traditions.
- Only six of Mālik's units (1, 3, 4, 6, 8 and 10) have some similarity in content, and even those appear in a different sequence.
- Nine of Mālik's units have no equivalents.

We can conclude from this comparison that the source of the traditions of Anas and Mālik is different from that of Abu Dharr, a conclusion which is confirmed by the isnād. The obvious correspondence between the traditions of Anas and of Mālik ibn Ṣa'ṣa'ah strongly supports the conclusion that both traditions were originally received from Mālik. The problem of identifying the original transmitter of the tradition can be solved easily by the supposition that Anas ibn Mālik narrated the tradition on more than one occasion. Sometimes he quoted the Prophet (ﷺ) directly; at other times, he quoted Mālik ibn Ṣa'ṣa'ah. Mālik is thus the original narrator of this strand of the biographical tradition in question.

Although the text of Abu Dharr's hadith is different from the other two, this does not mean that the similarities between the two strands should be attributed to chance. Rather they must derive from the fact that they refer to an original event that is prior to them. If we remove the points in which they vary, we are left with an outline of this original event that is agreed upon by all narrators. This can be summarized as follows:

The Prophet (ﷺ) was in Makkah when the incident happened. An angel opened his heart and washed it with the water of Zamzam. He then brought a gold basin full of wisdom and faith, emptied it into his breast, and closed it up. The angel made the Prophet (ﷺ) ascend to heaven. When they came to the lowest heaven, Gabriel asked for admittance and it was granted to them. They met Adam in the first heaven. Then Gabriel ascended with the Prophet to the other heavens where they met Enoch, Jesus, Moses and Abraham.

This presents the absolute core of the ascension narrative transmitted by the Companion Anas ibn Mālik, who is the only early figure common to all the asānīd that we have analyzed; in other words, he is the earliest common link. Given the differences between the two main strands we have identified, it seems that Anas received the ascension story from two sources: Mālik ibn Ṣa‘ṣa‘ah and Abu Dharr. Abu Dharr's version is shorter than Mālik's, but neither is dependent upon the other, and both men presumably heard it directly from the Prophet (ﷺ). Anas transmitted each of them with its own particular details; sometimes he told the narrative without attributing it to another Companion, in which case his version was closer to that of Mālik.

3.7 Conclusion

In this chapter, we tried to check the reliability of the sources of Ibn Abi Shaybah and his informants, as contained in MS. 9409. By using isnād-cum-matn analysis, we investigated the transmission history of specific traditions, mostly with Iraqi asānīd, of the ascension of the Prophet (ﷺ) to the heavens. On the basis of isnād comparison, we have singled out three different complexes of traditions, each going back to a Companion of the Prophet (ﷺ): Anas ibn Mālik, Mālik ibn Ṣa‘ṣa‘ah and Abu Dharr. The analysis of the groups of asānīd compiled from the variants of the three tradition complexes has produced the following results:

1. The isnād bundles of the two most common traditions (that of Anas ibn Mālik and that of Mālik ibn Ṣa‘ṣa‘ah) show common links who died around 93 AH/ 712 CE and 113 AH/ 731 CE (in the case of Anas ibn Mālik and Qatādah ibn Di‘āmah respectively).
2. The third tradition, of Abu Dharr, shows a common link who died in 125 AH (az-Zuhri).

On the basis of the isnād analysis, the hypothesis was made that traditions about the Prophet's ascension to the heavens must have originated earlier than the time of the sources in which they first appear. They must go back at least to Anas ibn Mālik, Qatādah and az-Zuhri.

This hypothesis was checked by a matn analysis of the variants of the different traditions. For traditions ascribed to Anas ibn Mālik, the results showed that the texts of the variants of each tradition complex seem to be independent of each other; thus they must go back to a common source. The text analysis showed that Thābit al-Bunāni, Sharīk, and ‘Abdur-Raḥmān ibn Hāshim all had differences in the wording. We can conclude that the common source of the differing mutūn in the later collections must be the common link of all the various asānīd.

The matn analysis of the versions ascribed to Anas ibn Mālik and Mālik ibn Ṣa‘ṣa‘ah has revealed many essential structural elements in common, but in the tradition of Abu Dharr, there is less direct correspondence (although there are some similarities). We concluded that Anas ibn Mālik should be regarded as the earliest common link for the three traditions, which are divergent narratives of an original prior event. They should, in fact, be reduced into two major strands of tradition: one ascribed to Mālik and the other to Abu Dharr. Anas received the two traditions from those two Companions and transmitted them separately. This all confirms the hypothesis that the common link in these biographical traditions was not artificially created by the so-called 'spread of asānīd'.

The idea that Ibn Abi Shaybah's informants fabricated their materials is untenable. This conclusion is attested by comparing his variants to those transmitted by his Iraqi contemporaries, such as Aḥmad and Abu Ya'lā, as well as by contemporaries of his informants. It has been proven that at least three traditions recorded by Ibn Abi Shaybah in MS. Berlin 9409 were circulated in Iraq, not only in his generation and that of his informants but also in the generation prior to that. This, along with the other evidence cited in this study, leads us to the conclusion that the sources claimed by Ibn Abi Shaybah are genuine and that the chains of transmission are to be taken seriously by historical scholarship.

This chapter also tackled the thorny question of which of the two versions of the ascension narrative is earlier: the longer or shorter one. In analyzing the isnād and matn of Anas' tradition, we reached the conclusion that there are two different abridged texts; one of them goes back at least to az-Zuhri, who died in 124 AH/ 742 CE, while the other goes back at least to Qatādah, who died in 93 AH/ 712 CE. We provided a detailed argument to show that the manner of variation recorded in the detailed versions of this hadith show that they must be dated prior to Qatādah, back to Anas ibn Mālik himself. This conclusion contradicts the conclusion of Joseph Schacht, who claimed that shorter traditions are the older ones. Our study shows there is no plausible reason why such a generalization should be accepted.

Chapter Four

Origin of early biographical sources about the life of Prophet Muhammad (ﷺ)

4.1 Introduction

This chapter will introduce a more comprehensive answer to the question of the original standard material of the Prophet's biography. This problem has been controversial in Western scholarship since Joseph Schacht contradicted Muslim, and some Western, scholars by claiming that the origin of the Sunnah is in Iraq and that Ḥijāzi tradition always lags behind Iraqi tradition. Schacht's conclusion is based on the supposition that, "Sources show that the term '*sunna* of the Prophet' is early Iraqian and not Medinese."[1]

Schacht thus argues that the idea of Madinah as the homeland of the Prophet's example was invented in the early third century AH and unknown previously. As for how this concept came into being, Schacht assumes that differences noticed among ancient Iraqi, Madinese or Syrian sources prior to ash-Shāfi'i's *Kitāb al-Umm* are due to the fact that these ancient schools did not uphold the concept of the overriding authority of the Prophet's Sunnah:

> Only Shāfi'i, obviously under the influence of the pressure group of traditionists, upholds consistently the doctrine that when there exists a tradition from the Prophet, no other argument is valid. Shāfi'i's work is full of monotonous repetitions of this essential doctrine of his, and it is clear that this doctrine was a startling innovation in his time.[2]

According to Schacht, "The great mass of legal traditions which invoke the authority of the Prophet, originated in the time of ash-Shāfi'i and later."[3] Afterwards, he says, the concept moved to Madinah under "the activity of a pressure group of traditionists, whose aims were the same as those of a corresponding group in Iraq."[4] Schacht argues that these traditions started to appear in the second quarter of the second century and represent a counter-movement to the original flourishing of juristic activity:

> This explains why the doctrine of Madinah as established by Mālik in his Muwaṭṭā' disagrees often with traditions from the Prophet with Madinan asānīd, related by Mālik himself.[5]

In his attempt to prove these claims, Schacht relied on a comparison of Mālik's *Muwaṭṭā'* and ash-Shāfi'i's *Kitāb al-Umm*. Schacht was particularly interested in the theory that the emergence of the Prophet's authority in the legal sphere caused the phenomenon of the backwards growth of the asānīd of traditions. He used the example of ash-Shāfi'i extensively, saying about him:

> In the course of his polemics against the ancient schools of law… continuously reproaches them for relying on traditions from persons other than the Prophet himself.[6]

Schacht compared Yaḥyā ibn Yaḥyā al-Laythi's transmission of Mālik's *Muwaṭṭā'* with ash-Shaybāni's transmission; in the later transmission, he noticed an increase in the percentage of accounts that claimed to go back to the Prophet (ﷺ). He made the same claim when he compared the *Āthār* of Abu Yūsuf with that of ash-Shaybāni. Schacht explains some key elements of his analysis:

> It cannot be doubted that the stage of referring to the teaching and the example of the Prophet was preceded by, and grew out of, an earlier stage in which reference was made to Companions (and Successors) only.… The several schools adopted rather one or the other Companion as their eponym, putting their doctrine as a whole under his aegis and referring to him as their authority in general terms. In the case of the Kufians, for whom Ibn Mas'ud fills this role, we can still see clearly that the general reference to Ibn Mas'ud himself grew out of a similar reference to the Companions of Ibn Mas'ud as the alleged founders of the Kufian doctrine, and most of the members of this group who are mentioned by name, turn out to be relatives of the Kufian successor, Ibrāhim an-Nakhā'i…[7]

Schacht returns to the starting point that he inherited from Goldziher:

> Isnāds have a tendency to grow backwards; that after going back to, say, a Successor to begin with, they are subsequently often carried back to a Companion and finally to the Prophet himself.[8]

Schacht says that this is true not only for legal traditions but also for the historical hadiths, especially the sīrah traditions. In his view, historical traditions served to provide precedents for those who held opposing points of view. He calls this phenomenon a 'transformation of legal propositions into pseudo-historical information,'[9] which essentially means that, "Historical information on the Prophet is only the background for legal doctrines and therefore devoid of independent value."[10] Accordingly, Madinan biographical sources are of late origin, and:

> A considerable part of the standard biography of the Prophet at Medina, as it appeared in the second half of the second century A.H. was of very recent origin and is therefore without independent historical value.[11]

By studying a fragment of the lost book *Kitāb al-Maghāzi* by Mūsā ibn 'Uqbah, Schacht tried to prove that his theory of legal traditions could also be applicable to biographical accounts.[12] Accepting his theory about the value of Islamic historical traditions deeply blurs the possibility of reconstructing Muslim sources about the biography of the Prophet (ﷺ) and puts scholars at an impasse.

However, there are recent advances in the field of sources and research methodologies that were not available to Schacht and that make his theory open to reconsideration. With regard to sources, a considerable number of early biographical and Hadith compilations have been discovered and edited in the last few decades; these were not available for Schacht to study. They include the two *Muṣannaf* works of 'Abdur-Razzāq and Ibn Abi Shaybah, *Tārīkh al-Madīnah* by 'Umar ibn Shabbah, *Akhbār Makkah* by al-Fākihi, the *Tafsīr* of 'Abdur-Razzāq aṣ-Ṣan'āni, and many others.

Moreover, during the last few years, there have been influential advancements in the field of methodology, and these have brought about fruitful results in providing a clearer vision of the early history of Islam. These methodologies are principally the sanad analysis of single traditions and the isnād-cum-matn analysis of multiple hadiths. The latter method has achieved considerable progress by combining the investigation of asānīd with literary analysis and by using an exhaustive corpus of sources.[13]

In addition, there have been many refutations of Schacht's theory of the development of legal traditions. Recent critical work by Schoeler, Motzki, and others demonstrates the value of testing his theories about biographical traditions. The remainder of this chapter will be devoted to my use of the techniques of isnād-cum-matn analysis to challenge Schacht's views on the origin of early biographical sources about the life of Prophet Muhammad (ﷺ).

4.2 Investigation materials

The materials used in this investigation are the hadiths recorded by Ibn Abi Shaybah about the bounty hunter Surāqah's pursuit of the Prophet (ﷺ) and Abu Bakr during their Hijrah (migration) from Makkah to Madinah.[14] There are two main groups of transmissions that deal with this story, namely that of al-Barā' ibn 'Āzib and that of Surāqah ibn Mālik ibn Ju'shum. Both versions are included in MS. Berlin 9409.

There are two reasons for choosing this tradition:

1. It has different versions preserved in different sources; this is a prerequisite for the application of isnād-cum-matn analysis.
2. Surāqah's tradition was reported through parallel Iraqi and Ḥijāzi lines of transmission. This will enable us to make comparisons about these two centres of Islamic knowledge, which, it should be remembered, were of particular interest to Schacht.

Some of the reports in Muslim sources about Surāqah's pursuit of the Prophet (ﷺ) have been discussed in two articles. In 1935, Schacht studied the version of Surāqah that was contained in the fragment of the lost maghāzi text of Mūsā ibn 'Uqbah.[15] He claims in his analysis that this tradition, which is transmitted by Mūsā ibn 'Uqbah from az-Zuhri, is fictitious. Schacht considers Mūsā's sources, which always originate from az-Zuhri, to be invented.[16] This is argued in pursuit of his general theory, which contends that traditions grow in a backward direction; therefore, the traditions of az-Zuhri should be attributed to later authorities. In other words, he claims that Mūsā ibn 'Uqbah or one of his transmitters invented the traditions and then ascribed them to az-Zuhri as a source of authority. Schacht was content with analyzing the sanad of the version in his possession, without comparing it to alternate versions.

In 2000, Gregor Schoeler published an article reconsidering some of Schacht's conclusions.[17] After using isnād-cum-matn analysis and comparing versions of the tradition as transmitted in other Hadith compilations that were not available to Schacht, Schoeler concluded:

> Because of the different characteristics of the two transmissions reported by az-Zuhri—the distinctive quality that az-Zuhri's text has in both strands of tradition—it is improbable that 'Abdur-Razzāq or Ma'mar have imitated Musa's text (or vice versa). On the contrary, 'Abdur-Razzāq—Ma'mar and Musa's versions of the text must go back to a common source: az-Zuhri.[18]

Schoeler further authenticated az-Zuhri's sources by studying a different tradition of the fragment of Mūsā ibn 'Uqbah, but he did not compare the Madani version of az-Zuhri with Iraqi versions. He went no further than to make the point that this tradition must be attributed to az-Zuhri.

4.3 The tradition of Surāqah ibn Mālik ibn Ju'shum

Variants of this version equipped with an isnād are found in 13 different sources. (See Diagram 11 of Appendix 1.) Principal among them are: Muhammad Ibn Is-ḥāq's *Sīrah,* 'Abdur-Razzāq's *Muṣannaf,* Ibn Abi Shaybah's *Muṣannaf,* Aḥmad's *Musnad,* Ibn Abi 'Āṣim's *al-Āḥād wal-Mathāni,* al-Ḥārith's *Bughyah,* Ibn Ḥibbān's *Ṣaḥīḥ,* Ibn al-Mundhir's *al-Awsaṭ,* aṭ-Ṭabarāni's *al-Mu'jam al-Kabīr* and Abu Nu'aym's *Dalā'il.* Ibn 'Asākir's variant is short, but the rest provide detailed variants.

According to the method of G.H.A. Juynboll, the common link in this bundle is the Madinan scholar Ibn Shihāb az-Zuhri. He is a common link by virtue of four transmitters:

1. 'Aqīl, whose variant is included in al-Ḥakim's *Mustadrak.*[19]
2. Ma'mar ibn Rāshid, whose variant found its way into different compilations, such as al-Ḥākim's *Mustadrak*[20] and 'Abdur-Razzāq's *Muṣannaf.*[21] ('Abdur-Razzāq may himself be a partial common link by virtue of three transmitters: Aḥmad ibn Ḥanbal,[22] Ibn Abi as-Sirri[23] and Is-ḥāq ibn Ibrāhīm.)[24]
3. Mūsā ibn 'Uqbah, whose variant is transmitted by Muhammad ibn Fulayḥ[25] and Ismā'īl ibn Ibrāhīm ibn 'Uqbah.[26]
4. Muhammad ibn Is-ḥāq.[27]

Az-Zuhri received the tradition from 'Abdur-Raḥmān ibn Mālik ibn Mālik ibn Ju'shum, who received it from his father Mālik, the brother of the original narrator Surāqah, who is claimed to have played a major role in the story.

According to the isnād bundle, Mālik ibn Mālik ibn Ju'shum is not the only one who is claimed to have received the tradition from Surāqah. Al-Ḥasan al-Baṣri is also claimed to have received it. Al-Ḥasan transmitted the tradition to 'Ali ibn Zayd, who conveyed it to Bishr ibn 'Umar, whose variant is found in al-Ḥārith's *Bughyah,*[28] and to Aswad ibn 'Āmir, whose variant is found in Ibn Abi Shaybah's *Muṣannaf.*[29]

According to the method of Hadith criticism developed by G. H. A. Juynboll, al-Ḥasan is a so-called 'dive', whose reliability is hardly tenable. Juynboll claims that the deeper a single chain dives under a common link, the more recent the date of origin of that particular strand. Thus, this strand, which dives under the common link and ends up with a Companion, should be considered more recent than those ending with the common link, but older than those ending up with the Prophet (ﷺ).[30]

The different transmission lines also display family connections. ‘Abdur-Raḥmān ibn Mālik transmits from his father Mālik ibn Mālik ibn Ju‘shum, who transmits from his brother Surāqah ibn Mālik ibn Ju‘shum. Since Ibn Shihāb az-Zuhri (d. 124 AH/ 742 CE) is the common link in the isnād bundle, we can provisionally assume that the tradition about Surāqah's pursuit of the Prophet (ﷺ) during his Hijrah was shared widely in Madinah in the first quarter of the second century AH.

In analyzing the text of this tradition, I will start with the version of Mūsā ibn ‘Uqbah, which is included in aṭ-Ṭabarāni's *al-Mu'jam al-Kabīr,* Ibn Abi ‘Āṣim's *al-Āḥād wal-Mathāni* and al-Bayhaqi's *Dalā'il.* This tradition is also included in a fragment of the lost book of *Maghāzi* by Mūsā ibn ‘Uqbah,[31] which was received by Mūsā's nephew Ismā‘īl ibn Ibrāhīm ibn ‘Uqbah. The tradition goes as follows:

Mūsā—az-Zuhri—‘Abdur-Raḥmān ibn Mālik ibn Mālik ibn Ju‘shum—Mālik ibn Mālik ibn Ju‘shum (‘Abdur-Raḥmān's father)—Surāqah ibn Mālik ibn Ju‘shum (Mālik's brother):

«While I was sitting in my people's assembly, one of our men came up, stopped and said: By God, I have just seen three riders passing. I think they must be Muhammad and his Companions.

I gave him a wink, enjoining silence, and said: They are the so-and-so looking for a lost camel.

He said: Perhaps so. Then he remained silent.

I remained there for a short while; then I mentioned my house, got up and ordered my horse to be readied.»

By comparing this version to Mūsā's version in al-Bayhaqi's *Dalā'il,* I found out that the version contained in the fragment is abridged. It seems that there was a missing text in the edition of Sachau quoted above. This conclusion is confirmed by referring to the original manuscript.[32] Therefore, the complete text of Mūsā's version, as transmitted by Ismā‘īl ibn Ibrāhim ibn ‘Uqbah, is as follows:

Az-Zuhri told me that ‘Abdur-Raḥmān ibn Mālik ibn Mālik ibn Ju‘shum told him from his father (Mālik ibn Mālik ibn Ju‘shum), from his uncle, Surāqah ibn Mālik ibn Ju‘shum:

«[1] When the Messenger (ﷺ) migrated from Makkah to Madinah, the Quraysh offered a reward of 100 camels to anyone who would bring him back.

[2] While I was sitting in my people's assembly,

[3] one of our men came up and stopped, saying: By God, I have just seen three riders passing. I think they must be Muhammad and his Companions.

[4] I gave him a wink, enjoining silence, and said: They are the so-and-so looking for a lost camel.

[5] He said: Perhaps so. Then he remained silent.

[6] I remained there for a short while;

[7] Then I mentioned my house, got up and

[8] ordered my horse to be readied, for it was tethered for me in the bottom of the valley.

[9] Then I asked for my weapons, and I went out from the back of some rooms.

[10] Then I took my divining arrows and went out, having put on my armour.

[11] Then I cast the divining arrows, and out came the arrow that I did not want: Do him no harm.

[12] I was hoping to bring him back to the Quraysh so that I might win the reward of 100 camels.

[13] I rode in pursuit of him, and when my horse was going, he stumbled and I fell. I thought this was somewhat unusual,

[14] so I resorted to the divining arrows again and out came the detestable: Do him no harm. But I refused to be put off and rode on in pursuit.

[15] Again my horse stumbled and threw me, and again I tried the arrows, with the same result.

[16] I rode on, and at last, as I saw the little band, my horse stumbled with me. Its forelegs went into the ground, and I fell.

[17] Then as it got its legs out of the ground, smoke arose like a sandstorm.

[18] When I saw that, I knew that he was protected against me and would have the upper hand.

[19] I called to them, saying who I was and asking them to wait for me, (also telling them that) they need have no concern, for no harm would come to them from me.

[20] The Messenger (ﷺ) told Abu Bakr to ask what I wanted, and I said: Write a document for me which will be a sign between you and me.

The Messenger (ﷺ) instructed Abu Bakr to do so.

[21] Then I gave no mention of what happened, until Allah opened Makkah for his Messenger (ﷺ) and he finished (conquering) Ḥunayn and Taif.

[22] Then I went out to meet him with the document, and I met him in al-Ju'rānah. I entered with a battalion of the Anṣār.[33] They started hitting me with their arrows and said: Keep away, keep away; what are you asking for?

I approached the Prophet (ﷺ) while he was on his camel. By Allah, I looked at his legs, which seemed (as white) as the core of the palm tree. I raised my hands with the document and said: O Messenger of Allah, this is your document, and I am Surāqah ibn Mālik ibn Ju'shum.

The Messenger of Allah (ﷺ) said: It is a day of fulfilment and righteousness; draw closer to me.

I approached him and accepted Islam. Then I tried to remember something to ask the Prophet (ﷺ) about. I said: If a lost camel comes to my basin to drink from the water I prepared for my own camels, should I receive a reward?

He said: In every thirsty being (whose thirst you quench) there is a reward.

I then returned to my people and proceeded (to give) my charity to the Prophet (ﷺ).»

A comparison with another version—contained in aṭ-Ṭabarāni's *al-Mu'jam al-Kabīr* and Ibn Abi 'Āṣim's *al-Āḥād wal-Mathāni* and also said to have come from Mūsā ibn 'Uqbah, but transmitted by Muhammad ibn Fulayḥ—reveals such a correlation that both texts must come from a common source by way of a written transmission. There are, however, some differences that exclude the possibility that aṭ-Ṭabarāni or his informant copied al-Bayhaqi's matn and provided it with a fabricated isnād.

There are several additions and omissions in comparison with the text of Ismā'īl ibn Ibrāhīm. Among the additions that appear in one version and are missing in the other are: *min Makkata* (from Makkah), *'alayhim* (by them), *idh jā'a rajulun minnā* (when a man of us [our tribe] came), and *wallāhi* (by Allah).

Among the differences are: *rakabatun thalāthah* (riders who were three) instead of *thalāthatu rakabah* (three riders), *wa* (and) instead of *thumma* (then), *sihāmi* (my arrows) instead of *quddaḥi* (cups). The peculiarities of each text show that they are independent transmissions going back to a common source; according to the isnād, it is the matn transmitted by Mūsā ibn 'Uqbah.

Mūsā ibn 'Uqbah is not the only one who received the tradition from az-Zuhri. In order to verify the version of az-Zuhri, we need to look at the versions of three other colleagues of Mūsā:

1. **Ma'mar ibn Rāshid.** In his version, messengers are received from the Quraysh to inform people that the blood money of the Prophet (ﷺ) and Abu Bakr will be allocated as a reward for anyone who kills or captures Muhammad (ﷺ) and his Companion. The reporter's testimony is particularly addressed to Surāqah: *Ya Surāqata, inni ra'aytu anifan* (Surāqah, I saw a little while ago…) The reporter only sees shadows of men going by the coast. Surāqah affirms that he recognized them as the Prophet (ﷺ) and his Companion: *fa-'arafu annahum hum* (I realized that they were the same). Surāqah's slave girl is called to get the horse ready: *fa-amartu jariyatan tukhrija li farasi* (I commanded a slave girl to bring me my horse). Surāqah is reported as leaving from the back of his house. Surāqah fixes the head of the arrow to the ground and drags it (as a way to evade people's attention). He is reported as divining his arrows after his horse stumbles. Surāqah hears the Prophet's recitation and notices Abu Bakr turning back and forth.

   In addition to these major differences between the versions of Mūsā and Ma'mar, there are several variations in wording. The differences, however, cannot obscure the fact that the structure of the narration and a substantial portion of the text are identical. From this, we can conclude that the two versions are not copied from one another but must be derived independently from a common source.

2. **Muhammad ibn Is-ḥāq.** In his version, the man who informs Surāqah first stops by the assembly before telling them about the riders he has seen, and Surāqah enters his house before pursuing the Prophet (ﷺ). Surāqah announces his name when he gets close to the Prophet (ﷺ), and he asks the Prophet (ﷺ) to wait to talk to him.

   In addition to these minor structural changes, there are some variant words used throughout the version: *thumma intaza'a yadahu* (then he withdrew his hand) instead of *thumma istakhraja yadahu* (then he took out his hand), and *kal-i'ṣār* (like a whirlwind) instead of *kal-'uthān* (like smoke).

Ibn Is-ḥāq's variant seems to be the closest in wording and structure to Mūsā ibn 'Uqbah's variant; perhaps it is another independent transmission from az-Zuhri.

3. **'Aqīl ibn Khālid al-Ayli (d. 144 AH/ 761 CE).** In this abridged version, the Quraysh allocate the blood money to be paid for the Prophet (ﷺ) and Abu Bakr in case they are killed, and they designate an equal amount as a reward for whoever kills or captures them. Such a structural difference affirms that this version has been independently transmitted.

Our comparison of the mutūn ascribed to different transmitters, all of whom relate on the authority of az-Zuhri, has brought to light that all of them are independent from each other and must go back to a common source. According to the isnād, this must be az-Zuhri.

It is striking that on the one hand, the versions of Mūsā and Ibn Is-ḥāq resemble each other, while on the other hand, the versions of Ma'mar and 'Aqīl resemble each other. If I am correct in concluding that the four versions go back independently of each other to a common source, then the differences between the two types of stories (or the correspondence between two of each) must be explained by supposing that az-Zuhri related the story in at least two different ways. 'Aqīl's version is an abbreviation of Ma'mar's detailed version.

According to az-Zuhri (56-124 AH/ 685-742 CE), he received the story from 'Abdur-Raḥmān ibn Mālik ibn Mālik ibn Ju'shum, who received it from his father, Mālik ibn Mālik ibn Ju'shum. According to Ibn Ḥajar, Mālik accepted Islam after the Prophet's death (11 AH/633 CE); therefore, he is regarded as a *tābi'ī.* He must have received the story from Surāqah after that date. This is confirmed by the date of Surāqah's death (24 AH/ 645 CE). Since this version includes an incident that occurred in 10 AH (631 CE), it must have been transmitted to Mālik after that. This ascription cannot be verified on the basis of this version alone; there is another line of transmission that must be studied before drawing a final conclusion. That is the version of al-Ḥasan al-Baṣri, who claimed to have received the story from Surāqah himself. It reads as follows:

Aswad ibn 'Āmir—Ḥammād ibn Salamah—'Ali ibn Zayd—al-Ḥasan al-Baṣri—Surāqah ibn Mālik ibn Ju'shum:

«[1] The Quraysh had assigned 40 ounces (of gold) for whoever could bring the Prophet (ﷺ) and Abu Bakr back.

[2] While I was sitting (with a group of people),

[3] a man came to me and said: The two men (Muhammad and Abu Bakr) for whom the Quraysh assigned (a reward) for capture are in such and such a place.

[4] So I went to my horse, which was grazing, and I took it.

[5] Then I picked up my arrow and rode,

[6] dragging it (the arrow on the ground) lest any of the people (who were pasturing) by water should share the reward with me.

[7] When I saw them, Abu Bakr said: This one who is following us is seeking (to catch us).

[8] When I turned to the Prophet (ﷺ), he said: O Allah, suffice us regarding him with (whatever protection) you will.

[9] Then my horse got scared while I was standing on a rocky land. I fell on a rock, and (the horse) stumbled.

[10] I said: Pray to the one who let my horse stumble so that it may be relieved and I will not disobey.

He prayed for him (Surāqah), and the horse stood up.

[11] The Messenger (ﷺ) asked: Are you going to give it to me as a gift?

Surāqah said: Yes, I will.

[13] Then the Messenger of Allah (ﷺ) said: So misguide the people seeking us.

[13] Then the Prophet (ﷺ) took the coastal route closest to the sea.

[14] In the early morning, I was seeking (to catch) them, and by late afternoon, I was protecting them.

[15] He told me: When we become stable in Madinah, you may come if you wish.

[16] When the Prophet (ﷺ) reached Madinah and he dominated over the people in Badr and Uḥud, and people embraced Islam, I knew that he intended to send Khālid ibn al-Walīd (to fight against) the people of Banu Madlaj. I went to him and said: I beseech you by your grace.

The people (surrounding the Prophet [ﷺ]) asked: What is the matter with him?

The Prophet (ﷺ) asked them to leave me until I said: I heard that you are going to send Khālid (to fight) against my people; I desire that you hold a treaty with them, so that they may embrace Islam, or even if they refuse, their hearts will not be hardened against each other.

The Prophet (ﷺ) grasped Khālid's hand and asked him to go and fulfil what had been proposed. He went to the people of Banu Madlaj, holding a covenant with them that they would not give assistance to anyone against the Messenger of Allah (ﷺ) and that they would embrace Islam when the Quraysh accepted it. Then Allah revealed:

﴿وَدُّوا۟ لَوْ تَكْفُرُونَ كَمَا كَفَرُوا۟ فَتَكُونُونَ سَوَآءً ۖ فَلَا تَتَّخِذُوا۟ مِنْهُمْ أَوْلِيَآءَ حَتَّىٰ يُهَاجِرُوا۟ فِى سَبِيلِ ٱللَّهِ ۚ فَإِن تَوَلَّوْا۟ فَخُذُوهُمْ وَٱقْتُلُوهُمْ حَيْثُ وَجَدتُّمُوهُمْ ۖ وَلَا تَتَّخِذُوا۟ مِنْهُمْ وَلِيًّا وَلَا نَصِيرًا ﴿٨٩﴾ إِلَّا ٱلَّذِينَ يَصِلُونَ إِلَىٰ قَوْمٍۭ بَيْنَكُمْ وَبَيْنَهُم مِّيثَٰقٌ أَوْ جَآءُوكُمْ حَصِرَتْ صُدُورُهُمْ أَن يُقَٰتِلُوكُمْ أَوْ يُقَٰتِلُوا۟ قَوْمَهُمْ ۚ وَلَوْ شَآءَ ٱللَّهُ لَسَلَّطَهُمْ عَلَيْكُمْ فَلَقَٰتَلُوكُمْ ۚ فَإِنِ ٱعْتَزَلُوكُمْ فَلَمْ يُقَٰتِلُوكُمْ وَأَلْقَوْا۟ إِلَيْكُمُ ٱلسَّلَمَ فَمَا جَعَلَ ٱللَّهُ لَكُمْ عَلَيْهِمْ سَبِيلًا ﴿٩٠﴾﴾ (سورة النساء: ٩٠)

﴿They would dearly like you to reject faith, as they themselves have done, to be like them. So do not take them as allies until they migrate [to Madinah] for God's cause. If they turn [on you],[34] then seize and kill them wherever you encounter them. Take none of them as an ally or supporter. But as for those who seek refuge with people with whom you have a treaty, or who come over to you because their hearts shrink from fighting against you or against their own people, God could have given them power over you, and they would have fought you. So if they withdraw and do not fight you, and offer you peace, then God gives you no way against them.﴾ *(Qur'an 4: 89-90)*

Al-Ḥasan said: Those who are meant by Allah's saying:

﴿...who come over to you because their hearts shrink from fighting against you...﴾

are Banu Madlaj, and anyone who reaches them will be included in their covenant.»

To facilitate a comparison between the Iraqi version (as transmitted by Ibn Abi Shaybah through al-Ḥasan al-Baṣri) and the different variants of az-Zuhri, the matn of the former has been divided into units of content as was done for the traditions about the Prophet's ascension narrative. The appropriate units of the two traditions have been put alongside one another in Table 3. Az-Zuhri's tradition has been taken as the reference point.

	az-Zuhri	
al-Ḥasan	**Ma'mar ibn Rāshid**	**Mūsā ibn 'Uqbah**
-	1	
(1)	2	1
2	3	2
(3)	4	3

-	5	4
-	6	5
-	7	6
-	8	7
4	9	8
(6)	10	-
5	11	9
-	12	10
-	13	11
-	14	12
7	-	-
8	-	-
9	15	13
10	-	-
-	16	14
-	17	15
-	18	16
-	19	17
-	20	18
11	-	-
-	21	19
-	22	20
13	-	-
-	-	21

Table 3

Comparing the contents of az-Zuhri's tradition with that of al-Ḥasan al-Baṣri's results in four correspondences, three units with similar content and 15 units with no equivalent. This shows there is some degree of structural similarity between az-Zuhri's matn and the text of al-Ḥasan al-Baṣri, and this is supported by the fact that the sequence of the shared units is nearly the same. In addition, a good number of cases of correspondence in content could be found.

The relationship between the traditions of az-Zuhri and al-Ḥasan al-Baṣri becomes evident when looking for similarities in wording. As shown in Table 4 below, az-Zuhri's shows several close textual parallels. The (m) symbolizes Ma'mar's variant of az-Zuhri's tradition, the (i) Ibn Is-ḥāq's variant, and the (q) that of Mūsā ibn 'Uqbah.

Ḥasan al-Baṣri	az-Zuhri
Qurayshan ja'alat fī rasūlallāhi wa Abi Bakrin arba'īnā ūqiyyah (Quraysh assigned for [those who can capture] the Messenger of Allah and Abu Bakr forty ounces [of gold]).	*Ja'alat qurayshun liman raddahu mi'at nāqatin* (Quraysh assigned for whoever can return him one hundred camels). **(q)**
Fabaynamā anā jālisun idh jā'ani rajulun faqāla innar-rajulayni al-ladhīna ja'alat Qurayshu fīhimā mā ja'alat minka bi makāni khadhā wa kadhā. (While I was sitting, a man came to me saying: The two men to whom the Quraysh assigned whatever it assigned are in such and such a place).	*Fabaynamā anā jālisun idh jā'a rajulun minnā faqāla laqad ra'aytu rakban thalāthatan marru 'allay ānifan inni la'arāhu Muḥammadan wa aṣḥābahu.* (While I was sitting, a man from us came and said: I have seen a riding party consisting of three. I surely see Muhammad and his Companions). **(q/i)**
Fa'ataytu farasi wa huwa fil-mar'a fanafartu bihi thumma akhadhtu rumḥi qāla farakibtuhu. (I came to my horse while it was in pasture. I hastened with it; then taking my spear, I rode it.)	*Ḥattā ataytu farasi farakabtuhā wa akhadhtu rumḥ*... (until I reached my horse, so I rode it and took my spear...) **(m)**
Faja'altu ajurrur-rumḥa. (Then I started pulling my spear).	*Fakhaṭaṭtu bihi al-arḍ fa akhfaḍtu 'āliyat ar-rumḥi.* (I drew on the ground [by the spear], then I lowered the high point of the spear). **(q/i)**
Fawajala farsi wa inni lafī jaladin min al-arḍ fawaqa'tu 'alā ḥajarin. (Then my horse became frightened when I was on a plain rocky land, so I fell upon a rock).	*'athara bi farsi fakharartu 'anhā.* (My horse made me fall, so I fell from it). **(q/i)**

Table 4

This table shows that there is considerable textual correspondence between the tradition of az-Zuhri and that of al-Ḥasan al-Baṣri in terms of wording. The structural similarities and the textual correspondence cannot, therefore, be the consequence of the dependence of one upon the other, but must be derived from one or more common sources of both. Such a conclusion is in accordance with the evidence revealed by the isnād. Thus, the common link of this tradition should be Surāqah ibn Mālik ibn Ju'shum.

We are faced with a difficulty in dating the version of al-Ḥasan al-Baṣri, who lived between 21 AH/ 642 CE and 110 AH/ 728 CE, according to biographical sources. He cannot have met Surāqah ibn Mālik ibn Ju'shum, for Surāqah died in 24 AH/ 645 CE, when al-Ḥasan was a young child. There are two possible explanations for this gap in transmission.

The first possibility is that 'Ali ibn Zayd or his informant al-Ḥasan imitated az-Zuhri's tradition, but there are indications that go against such an assumption.

1. If 'Ali ibn Zayd were going to transmit on the basis of az-Zuhri's matn, we would expect him to use one of the known versions, such as that of Ibn Is-ḥāq, Ma'mar, Mūsā ibn 'Uqbah, or even 'Aqīl. This is obviously not the case, though, because 'Ali's text resembles that of Ibn Is-ḥāq sometimes, that of Ma'mar sometimes, and that of Mūsā ibn 'Uqbah another time; it even seems to mix parts of them together. We could assume that either he used a version of az-Zuhri that did not survive or he created his own on the basis of two or three others, but neither of these assumptions is satisfactory.
2. The matn of Ali's version (al-Ḥasan's dive) displays so many substantial variations from az-Zuhri's version that we cannot consider it to be dependent on it. For example:
   - In 'Ali's version, the reward assigned by the Quraysh for the capture of the Prophet (ﷺ) and Abu Bakr is 40 ounces of gold. The variants of az-Zuhri, Mūsā ibn 'Uqbah and Ibn Is-ḥāq specify 100 camels, whereas Ma'mar says that it is equal to the amount of each one's blood money.
   - In 'Ali's version, Surāqah hides the shining head of the arrow so that no one will see him and share the reward with him.
   - According to al-Ḥasan's version, the Prophet (ﷺ) asks Surāqah for his horse.
   - In az-Zuhri's version, the Prophet (ﷺ) and Abu Bakr refuse his offer to give them his money or provisions.

These differences mean that it is very unlikely that 'Ali ibn Zayd fabricated the tradition. However, the question of inconsistency in the ages of al-Ḥasan and Surāqah remains.

The second, and more probable, explanation for this gap is that al-Ḥasan received the tradition from 'Abdur-Raḥmān ibn Mālik ibn Mālik ibn Ju'shum, the nephew of Surāqah, but deleted both his name and the name of his informant, Mālik ibn Mālik ibn Ju'shum. This was a common practice of al-Ḥasan, who is known for ascribing traditions to the higher authority without mentioning his direct informant.[35] Ibn Ḥajar confirmed that al-Ḥasan's transmission from Surāqah has at least two transmitters missing between him and Surāqah.

The independence of each text from the other and the similarities in the texts support the conclusion that both Iraqi and Ḥijāzi lines of transmission emanate from the same source through oral transmission. Moreover, the peculiarities of each text are not enough to exclude the possibility that such a common source is the one from whom az-Zuhri received his tradition. Al-Ḥasan must have received the tradition from 'Abdur-Raḥmān ibn Mālik ibn Mālik ibn Ju'shum and then omitted the names of his informants.

Therefore, the actual latest common link in this tradition must be 'Abdur-Raḥmān ibn Mālik ibn Mālik ibn Ju'shum, who transmitted the tradition on two different occasions, once to al-Ḥasan al-Baṣri and another time to az-Zuhri—with the latter Madinan transmission being the closest to the original version. 'Abdur-Raḥmān ibn Mālik ibn Mālik ibn Ju'shum, according to Ibn Ḥajar, probably saw the Prophet (ﷺ) but is not regarded as one of his Companions.[36] Ibn Ḥibbān held that he died in 92 AH/ 711 CE,[37] so he could have received the tradition from his father Mālik between 24 AH/ 645 CE and 92 AH/ 711 CE. Mālik did not participate in the incident; he claimed to have received the narration from his brother Surāqah ibn Mālik ibn Ju'shum, who is the original narrator and protagonist. Surāqah transmitted it before his death in 24 AH/ 645 CE; therefore, the tradition about Surāqah's pursuit of the Prophet (ﷺ) and Abu Bakr during their migration from Makkah to Madinah spread in Madinah between 24 AH/ 645 CE and 92 AH/ 711 CE. However, the veracity of this ascription cannot be substantiated on the basis of this tradition alone.

4.4 The tradition of al-Barā' ibn 'Āzib

Variants of this tradition (reporting the pursuit of the Prophet [ﷺ] and Abu Bakr during their migration to Madinah) are found in a number of sources with an isnād through the Companion al-Barā' ibn 'Āzib. These are: Ibn Abi Shaybah's *Muṣannaf,* Abu Nu'aym's *Dalā'il,* Bukhari's *Ṣaḥīḥ al-Bukhāri,* Muslim's *Jāmi',* Aḥmad's *Musnad,* al-Fākihi's *Akhbār Makkah,*[38] Ibn Abi Ḥātim's *Tafsīr,* al-Bayhaqi's *Dalā'il an-Nubuwwah,* Abu Ya'lā's *Musnad,* Ibn Ḥibbān's *Ṣaḥīḥ, Musnad al-Bazzār,* al-Lūwayn's *Juz',* al-Marwazi's *Musnad Abi Bakr* and ar-Rūyāni's *Musnad.* (See Diagram 12 of Appendix 1.)

There are some versions with a short matn and others with a detailed one. Bukhari provides four variants: two detailed and two short. The longer traditions go back to two different transmitters, Zuhayr ibn Mu'āwiyah and Isrā'īl ibn Yūnus, both of whom have Abu Is-ḥāq as-Sabī'i as their informant. Abu Is-ḥāq, who allegedly transmits the story from al-Barā' ibn 'Āzib, is the common link in this isnād bundle.[39] Isrā'īl, Zuhayr ibn Mu'āwiyah and Shu'bah, three of the four transmitters from Abu Is-ḥāq, are what G. H. A. Juynboll terms 'partial common links'. Isrā'īl is a grandson of Abu Is-ḥāq and is known for his expertise concerning the traditions of his grandfather. Four transmission lines go via Isrā'īl:

(1) That of 'Abdullāh ibn Rajā', which is contained in Bukhari's *Ṣaḥīḥ al-Bukhāri*,[40] Ibn Abi Ḥātim's *Tafsīr*,[41] Ibn Ḥibbān's *Ṣaḥīḥ*,[42] Abu Nu'aym's *Dalā'il*[43] and al-Bayhaqi's *Dala'il*;[44]

(2) That of 'Ubaydullāh ibn Mūsā, which is contained in al-Bayhaqi's *Dalā'il*[45] and Ibn Abi Shaybah's *Muṣannaf*;[46]

(3) That of 'Uthmān ibn 'Umar, which is contained in Abu Ya'lā's *Musnad*;[47] and

(4) That of 'Amr ibn Muhammad, which is contained in al-Bazzār and Aḥmad's *Musnad*.[48]

Zuhayr ibn Mu'āwiyah is the second student of Abu Is-ḥāq. Two transmission lines go via him: that of Abul-Ḥasan al-Ḥarrāni, which is found in Bukhari's *Ṣaḥīḥ al-Bukhāri*,[49] and that of al-Ḥasan ibn 'Ayn, which is found in al-Bayhaqi's *Dalā'il*[50] and Muslim's *Ṣaḥīḥ*.[51]

The short versions display a peculiarity in that they have a partial common link in Shu'bah ibn al-Ḥajjāj (d. 160 AH/ 777 CE). This suggests that Shu'bah is the one who is to be held responsible for the shortened version of al-Barā's tradition. Shu'bah provided both short and detailed versions of the tradition. The short version is found in Bukhari's *Ṣaḥīḥ al-Bukhāri*,[52] ar-Rūyāni's *Musnad*,[53] Muslim's *Jāmi'*,[54] Abu Ya'lā's *Musnad*,[55] al-Marwazi's *Musnad*[56] and Aḥmad's *Musnad*.[57] The detailed version is found in ar-Rūyāni's *Musnad*[58] and al-Marwazi's *Musnad*.[59]

There is also a single line of transmission that goes from Abu Is-ḥāq to Ḥudayj ibn Mu'āwiyah and is found in al-Lūwayn's *Juz'*.[60]

Knowing that Abu Is-ḥāq is the common link in the isnād bundle, we can provisionally conclude that the tradition about the Prophet's migration to Madinah, which is connected with the name of the Companion al-Barā' as original transmitter, was spread in Kufa in the first quarter of the second century by Abu Is-ḥāq as-Sabī'i (d. 126-127 AH/ 743-745 CE). To accurately date the tradition, we need to compare its variants.

As far as I know, the oldest collection containing a report about the migration of the Prophet (ﷺ) transmitted on the authority of al-Barā' ibn 'Āzib is Ibn Abi Shaybah's *Muṣannaf*. Of the four variants going through Abu Is-ḥāq and then Isrā'īl, it utilises the narration of 'Ubaydullāh ibn Mūsā. However, for textual analysis, we shall start with the variant transmitted by 'Abdullāh ibn Rajā' and collected by Bukhari, since it has variants in other sources. The tradition reads:

'Abdullāh ibn Rajā'—Isrā'īl—Abu Is-ḥāq—al-Barā' ibn 'Āzib:

«[1] Abu Bakr bought a (camel) saddle from 'Āzib for 13 dirhams (silver coins).

[2] Abu Bakr said to 'Āzib: Tell al-Barā' to carry the saddle to my camel.

[3] 'Āzib said: No, unless you relate to me what happened to you and Allah's Messenger when you left Makkah while the pagans were in search of you.

[4] Abu Bakr said: We left Makkah, and we travelled continuously for that night and the following day until it was midday.

[5] I looked (around) searching for shade to take as shelter, and suddenly I came across a rock, and found a little shade there.

[6] So I cleaned the place and spread a bed for the Prophet (ﷺ) in the shade and said to him: Lie down, O Allah's Messenger.

The Prophet (ﷺ) lay down and I went out, looking around to see if there was any person pursuing us.

[7] Suddenly I saw a shepherd driving his sheep towards the rock, seeking what we had already sought from it.

[8] I asked him: To whom do you belong, boy?

He said: I belong to a man from the Quraysh.

He named the man, and I recognized him. I asked him: Is there any milk with your sheep?

He said: Yes.

I asked: Will you then milk (some) for me?

He replied: Yes.

[9] Then I asked him to tie the legs of one of the sheep and clean its udder, and then ordered him to clean his hands of dust. Then the shepherd cleaned his hands by striking his hands against one another. After doing so, he milked a small amount of milk.

[10] I used to keep for Allah's Messenger (ﷺ) a leather water-container, the mouth of which was covered with a piece of cloth. I poured (water) on the milk container until its lower part was cold.

[11] Then I took the milk to the Prophet (ﷺ), whom I found awake. I said to him: Drink, O Allah's Messenger.

He drank until I became pleased.

[12] Then I said: It is time for us to move, O Allah's Messenger!

He said: Yes.

We set out while the people (the Qurayshi pagans) were searching for us. However, none found us except Surāqah ibn Mālik ibn Ju'shum, who was riding his horse.

[13] I said: These are our pursuers who have found us, O Allah's Messenger!

[14] He said: Do not grieve, for Allah is with us.

[15] When he drew near to as equal as the distance of shooting one, two or three arrows, I said: O Allah's Messenger! That pursuer has reached us.

[16] I then wept.

Allah's Messenger (ﷺ) asked: Why are you weeping?

I said: By Allah, I do not weep because of myself, but I am weeping because of you.

[17] Then the Messenger of Allah (ﷺ) prayed against him (Surāqah) by saying:

[18] O Allah, suffice us with regard to him.

[19] Then his (Surāqah's) horse sank in the earth up to the belly.

[20] He jumped up and said: Muhammad, I am fully aware that it is your doing.

[21] (Surāqah said:) Supplicate to Allah that He should rescue me from this, and I will give you a solemn pledge that I shall keep this (location) a secret from all those who are coming after me.

[22] (Surāqah continued:) Take hold of an arrow out of my quiver, for you will find my camels and my slaves at such and such a place, and you can get whatever you need (on showing this arrow).

[23] The Messenger of Allah (ﷺ) said: We are not in any need of your camels.

[24] Then he prayed for him. He (Surāqah) went back to his companions, and

[25] the Prophet (ﷺ) proceeded with me until we reached Madinah.

[26] Then the Messenger of Allah (ﷺ) said: I will spend this night with Banu an-Najjār, the maternal cousins of 'Abdul-Muṭṭalib, in order to honour them.

[27] When the people went outside (waiting for the Messenger [ﷺ]) until he entered Madinah, children and slaves were standing on houses and by roads saying: Muhammad, prayers and peace be upon him, has come; the Messenger of Allah, prayers and peace be upon him, has come.

[28] In the morning, he proceeded until he dropped where Allah commanded him.

[29] The Prophet (ﷺ) prayed directing his face to Jerusalem for 16 or 17 months but wished to be directed to the Kaaba. Then Allah revealed:

﴿قَدْ نَرَىٰ تَقَلُّبَ وَجْهِكَ فِي ٱلسَّمَآءِ ۖ فَلَنُوَلِّيَنَّكَ قِبْلَةً تَرْضَىٰهَا ۚ فَوَلِّ وَجْهَكَ شَطْرَ ٱلْمَسْجِدِ ٱلْحَرَامِ ... ﴿١٤٤﴾﴾ (سورة البقرة: ١٤٤)

﴿Many a time We have seen you [Prophet (ﷺ)] turn your face towards the heavens, so We are turning you towards a prayer direction that pleases you.[61] Turn your face in the direction of the Sacred Mosque…﴾ *(Qur'an 2: 144)*

Therefore, he was told to turn to the Kaaba (in Makkah). Afterwards, the foolish amongst the people said (as mentioned by Allah):

﴿... مَا وَلَّىٰهُمْ عَن قِبْلَتِهِمُ ٱلَّتِي كَانُوا۟ عَلَيْهَا ۚ قُل لِّلَّهِ ٱلْمَشْرِقُ وَٱلْمَغْرِبُ ۚ يَهْدِي مَن يَشَآءُ إِلَىٰ صِرَٰطٍ مُّسْتَقِيمٍ ﴿١٤٢﴾﴾ (سورة البقرة: ١٤٢)

﴿…What has turned them away from the prayer direction they used to face? Say: East and West belong to God. He guides whomever He will to the right way.﴾ *(Qur'an 2: 142)*

[30] A man offered the prayer with the Messenger of Allah (ﷺ), and then he passed by a group of the Anṣār while they were bowing down in their performance of the mid-afternoon prayer, turning their faces to Jerusalem. He said: I bear witness that I prayed with the Messenger of Allah (ﷺ) when Allah commanded him to turn his face to the direction of the Kaaba.

The people consequently turned towards the Kaaba.

[31] (Al-Barā' commented): Before (the Prophet's arrival in Madinah), we received among the immigrants Muṣ'ab ibn 'Umayr, the brother of Banu 'Abd ad-Dār ibn Quṣay. We asked him: What happened to the Messenger of Allah (ﷺ)?

He said: He and his Companions are following me.

Then came 'Amr ibn Maktūm, the brother of Banu Fahr, the sightless. We asked him: What happened to those who are following you—the Messenger of Allah (ﷺ) and his Companions?

He said: He and his Companions are following me.

Then came 'Ammār ibn Yāsir, Sa'd ibn Abi Waqqāṣ, 'Abdullāh ibn Mas'ūd and Bilāl. Afterwards came 'Umar ibn al-Khaṭṭāb, following them with 20 riders.

[32] Then came the Messenger of Allah (ﷺ) and Abu Bakr. He reached Madinah after I had already recited sūrahs from al-mufaṣṣal (the last section of the Qur'an, from Sūrah 50 to Sūrah 114). We went out to receive their camels, but we found them forewarned.»

A comparison of the text of 'Ubaydullāh ibn Mūsā (as transmitted by Ibn Abi Shaybah) with that of 'Abdullāh ibn Rajā' (contained in Bukhari's *Ṣaḥīḥ al-Bukhāri,* Ibn Ḥibbān's *Ṣaḥīḥ,* Abu Nu'aym's *Dalā'il,* al-Bayhaqi's *Dalā'il* and Ibn Abi Ḥātim's *Tafsīr*) reveals a level of correlation such that both texts must be derived from a common source by way of a written transmission.

There are some differences, though, which exclude the possibility that Bukhari, or any of his informants, copied from Ibn Abi Shaybah and provided a fabricated isnād. Among the most significant additions are: *fa'aḥyaynā laylatnā wa yawmanā, thumma farashtu li rasūlallāhi farwatan, fasammāhu fa'ariftuh, fasharib rasūlallāhi ḥattā raḍītu.* (We passed our night and day awake, and then I spread for the Messenger of Allah (ﷺ) a fur. [The shepherd] named him [the owner of the sheep], whom I recognized. Then the Messenger of Allah (ﷺ) drank [of the milk] until I became satisfied.)

We also find: *raḥli* (my caravan) instead of *ahli* (my people), *ḥaythu* (where) instead of *ḥīna* (when), *anfuḍu* (I shook off [what is around him]) instead of *anẓuru* (I observe who is around him), and *annā* (how) instead of *ayna* (where). The peculiarities of both texts show that they are independent transmissions going back to a common source; according to the isnād, this source is the matn transmitted by Isrā'īl.

This conclusion is corroborated by comparison with a third variant, which is also said to be derived from the latter and is included in Abu Ya'lā's *Musnad.* It is the variant of 'Uthmān ibn 'Umar, which differs from 'Ubaydullāh's text, among others, by the additions: *min abi* (from my father) instead of 'Āzib; *ẓillin farashastuh* (shaded area so I sprinkled); *faṣababtu al-mā'a 'alā al-labani* (I poured water on the milk container); *wa ghilmāni* (my slaves) instead of *ghanami* (my sheep).

Additionally, we find variations in both of them, such as:

- *tukhbiranā* (tell us) in place of *tuḥaddithunā* (talk to us);
- *nāma* (he slept) instead of *iḍṭaji'* (he lay down);
- *inṭalaqtu* (I broke out) instead of *dhahabtu* (I went);

- *yalḥaqnā* (he catches up to us) instead of *yudriknā* (he reaches us);
- *yukhalliṣuni* (he releases me) instead of *yujannibuni* (he makes me avoid).

There are some phrases and words that are missing in 'Uthmān's variant although they appear in 'Ubaydullāh's and 'Abdullāh ibn Rajā's variants. Some of these are:

- *hal narā min ẓillin na'wi ilayhi* (do we see a shadow to seek shelter?)
- *faḍṭaja'a* (he lay down)
- *yasūqu ghanamahu ilā aṣ-ṣakhrata* (driving his sheep to the rock)
- *annā ar-raḥīlu ya rasūlallāhi* (when is the departure, O Messenger of Allah?)

In a few details, the variant of 'Uthmān ibn 'Umar corresponds with that of 'Abdullāh ibn Rajā by missing some phrases contained in 'Ubaydullāh's variant, such as:

- *fashariba rasūlallāhi ḥattā raḍītu* (the Messenger of Allah drank until I became pleased);
- *fakāna baynanā wa baynahu qadra rumh* (the distance between us and him was a spear's length);
- *Allāhuma akfinahu bimā shi'ta* (O Allah, suffice us regarding him with [whatever protection] you will).

Finally, the variant of 'Uthmān differs from the other variant by omitting the part of the story after the Prophet's arrival in Madinah.

The three texts should therefore be regarded as independent transmissions from a common source which, according to the isnād, is the transmission of Isrā'īl from Abu Is-ḥāq.

There remains one more variant of Isrā'īl, that of 'Amr ibn Muhammad, which is found in Aḥmad's and al-Bazzār's *Musnad* collections. This variant has some additions that are not mentioned in the previous ones:

- *sarjan* (saddle) instead of *raḥlan* (saddlebag)
- *manzili* (my dwelling place) instead of *raḥli* (my luggage)
- *fadlajnā* (set out to nightfall)
- *fa'ḥathathnā yawmanā* (we hastened during our day and night)
- *fa'ahwaytu ilayhā* (I aspired to it)
- *wa farashtu lahu farwatan* (I spread for him a fur)

- *kharajatu anẓuru* (I went out to look at him)
- *faṣbabtu al-mā'a 'alā al-qadaḥ* (I poured water into the pot)
- *fī arḍin ṣaldin* (at a rocky land)

It differs from the other variants by omitting the story of the changing of the direction for the prayer, an event which took place after the Prophet's migration to Madinah. 'Amr ibn 'Uthmān's version corresponds with some of the different variants in some places, while it disagrees in others. 'Amr's variant corresponds with that of 'Ubaydullāh ibn Mūsā, and they both depart from the rest of the variants, in wordings such as:

- *iḍṭaji'* (lie down)
- *min al-ghubari* (out of dust)
- *wal-qawmu yaṭlubūnanā* (people are pursuing us)
- *yudrikanā* (reach us)
- *fakāna baynanā wa baynahu qadra rumh* (the distance between us and him was a spear's length)
- *Allāhuma akfinahu bimā shi'ta* (O Allah, suffice us regarding him with [whatever protection] you will)

These differences confirm the conclusion that the four variants—'Ubaydullāh ibn Mūsā, 'Abdullāh ibn Rajā', 'Uthmān ibn 'Umar and 'Amr ibn Muhammad—are all independent and should go back to one common source, which, according to the isnād, is the text of Isrā'īl from Abu Is-ḥāq.

Our textual analysis should go further to compare the different versions of Abu Is-ḥāq's recipients: Isrā'īl, Zuhayr ibn Mu'āwiyah, Shu'bah ibn al-Ḥajjāj and Ḥudayj ibn Mu'āwiyah. A brief glance is enough to show that Zubayr's and Shu'bah's versions differ much more from each other and from Isrā'īl's matn.

In the version of Zuhayr ibn Mu'āwiyah, 'Āzib goes out of the house to get the money from Abu Bakr. The route the Prophet (ﷺ) took is described as being vacant of any passersby. The shepherd who receives them is the slave of a man from Madinah or Makkah. Abu Bakr uses a pot when he milks the sheep for the Prophet (ﷺ). Surāqah fulfils his promise to the Prophet (ﷺ), and there is no mention of his offering camels and sheep. The story stops before the Prophet's arrival into Madinah.

In addition to these major differences between the versions of Isrā'īl and Zuhayr, there are several variations in wording. The differences, however, cannot obscure the fact that the structure of the narration and a substantial portion of the text are identical. Due to those differences, we can conclude that neither of the versions is copied from the other and that they must be derived independently from a common source.

The version of Ḥudayj ibn Mu'āwiyah almost corresponds to that of Zuhayr, who is regarded as his brother. Al-Lūwayn, who received it from Ḥudayj, maintained such conformity between the two traditions. Ḥudayj is known as a weak transmitter.

Shu'bah's version is closer to Isrā'īl's but is much shorter. In it, Surāqah promises the Prophet (ﷺ) that he will not harm him, and the Prophet (ﷺ) is thirsty before meeting the shepherd. There are also small textual variations from Isrā'īl's version. Shu'bah's variant seems to be another independent transmission from Abu Is-ḥāq.

Our comparison of the mutūn ascribed to different transmitters, all of whom relate on the authority of Abu Is-ḥāq, has revealed that they are all independent of each other and must go back to a common source which, according to the isnād, is the text of Abu Is-ḥāq. The common link is not artificially created by the so-called 'spread of asānīd'. Differences among variants derived from the second generation after Abu Is-ḥāq ('Abdullāh ibn Rajā', 'Ubaydullāh ibn Mūsā, 'Uthmān ibn 'Umar, and 'Amr ibn Muhammad) seem small, whereas differences among variants derived from the first generation (Isrā'īl, Zuhayr and Shu'bah) are much more substantial. This is due to the fact, mentioned in Chapter 3, that the generation of Abu Is-ḥāq's pupils who received their texts from him in the first quarter of the second Islamic century used methods of preservation that were not used a generation later.

According to Abu Is-ḥāq (d. 126 or 127 AH/ 743-745 CE), to whom the different versions of the story go back, he received the story from the Companion al-Barā' ibn 'Āzib (d. 72 AH/ 691-2 CE), a Madinan from the tribe of Aws, on whose authority he transmitted many traditions. This Companion did not participate in the incident himself; according to tradition, he received the story from Abu Bakr, who died in the year 13 AH/ 634 CE. At that time, al-Barā' was approximately 25 years old. The veracity of this ascription is corroborated by the other traditions of Surāqah that were transmitted through his nephew 'Abdur-Raḥmān ibn Mālik ibn Mālik ibn Ju'shum, who narrated the story of Surāqah's pursuit of the Prophet (ﷺ) and Abu Bakr.

Therefore, it seems likely that Abu Is-ḥāq received the story from al-Barā' between 50 AH/ 670-671 CE and 72 AH/ 691-692 CE and that he transmitted it to his pupils in approximately 125 AH/ 742 CE.

After dating each tradition separately, our preliminary conclusion is that the Ḥijāzi tradition that is narrated on the authority of the Companion Surāqah ibn Mālik ibn Ju'shum started spreading earlier than the Iraqi tradition that is transmitted on the authority of the Companion al-Barā' ibn 'Āzib. To substantiate this conclusion, we need to compare the two traditions in order to discern any traces of imitation or any effect of one tradition on the other. This will help us decide whether the Ḥijāzi or the Iraqi line of transmission was the original.

To facilitate a comparison of the two texts that are said to derive from Surāqah ibn Mālik ibn Ju'shum (az-Zuhri's tradition) and that of al-Barā' ibn 'Āzib (Abu Is-ḥāq's tradition), both texts were divided into units of content, with the appropriate units of the two traditions put alongside one another in Table 5. First, Surāqah's tradition is taken as the reference for that of al-Barā':

Surāqah ibn Mālik ibn Ju'shum (az-Zuhri's tradition)	**al-Barā' ibn 'Āzib (Abu Is-ḥāq's tradition)**
1	-
2	-
3	-
4	-
5	-
6	-
7	-
8	-
9	-
10	-
11	-
12	-
13	(13)
14	-
15	19
16	-
17	-
18	20
19	-
20	-
21	-
22	-

Table 5

The same two traditions are then compared again, this time with the tradition of al-Barā' taken as the reference for that of Surāqah:

al-Barā' ibn 'Āzib (Abu Is-ḥāq's tradition)	**Surāqah ibn Mālik ibn Ju'shum (az-Zuhri's tradition)**
1	-
2	-
3	-
4	-
5	-
6	-
7	-
8	-
9	-
10	-
11	-
12	-
13	(13)
14	-
15	-
16	-
17	-
18	-
19	(15)
20	(18)
21	(19)
22	-
23	-
24	-
25	-
26	-
27	-
28	-
29	-
30	-
31	-
32	-

Table 6

Tables 5 and 6 show that there are not many textual correspondences between the tradition of Surāqah and that of al-Barā' ibn 'Āzib: only four units of meaning are similar. Clearly, each tradition originated independently; there is no influence whatsoever of an Iraqi version on a Ḥijāzi version or vice versa.

In addition to the results of this comparison, we showed before that the tradition of Surāqah spread in Madinah a considerable time before that of al-Barā'. This conclusion goes against Schacht's generalized claim that Iraq is the origin of the Hadith and that any Ḥijāzi tradition is later than an Iraqi tradition.

4.5 Conclusion

The main question addressed in this chapter is about the original material of the Prophet's biography. According to Schacht and some other Western scholars, Iraq is the origin of the Sunnah and thus should be the origin of the standard sources of the Prophet's biography.

Their conclusion is challenged by using isnād-cum-matn analysis to study two groups of transmissions of the tradition about Surāqah ibn Mālik ibn Ju'shum's pursuit of the Prophet (ﷺ) and Abu Bakr during their Hijrah. The first is transmitted on the authority of the Companion Surāqah ibn Mālik ibn Ju'shum, and its common link is the Madinan scholar Ibn Shihāb az-Zuhri; the second is attributed to al-Barā' ibn 'Āzib, and its common link is Abu Is-ḥāq as-Sabī'i. Through a comparison of the variants of the former tradition, it became evident that 'Abdur-Raḥmān ibn Mālik ibn Mālik ibn Ju'shum should be regarded as the common source of the tradition of Surāqah, since the similarities and differences among the various versions showed that all versions are independently transmitted and originally emanate from one common source. In particular, we concluded that 'Abdur-Raḥmān ibn Mālik ibn Mālik ibn Ju'shum transmitted the tradition on two different occasions, once to al-Ḥasan al-Baṣri and once to az-Zuhri.

The tradition about Surāqah's pursuit of the Prophet (ﷺ) and Abu Bakr during their migration spread in Madinah between 24 AH/ 645 CE and 92 AH/ 711 CE. The veracity of this ascription was substantiated by studying the tradition of al-Barā' using the same method of investigation. According to Abu Is-ḥāq (d. 126 or 127 AH/ 743-745 CE), to whom different versions of the story are ascribed, he received the story from the Companion al-Barā' ibn 'Āzib (d. 72 AH/ 691-692 CE), a Madinan from the tribe of Aws, on whose authority he spread many traditions.

This Companion did not participate in the incident himself; according to tradition, he received the story from Abu Bakr, who died in the year 13 AH/ 634 CE.

A comparison of the two traditions (of Surāqah and al-Barā') makes it evident that, in general, there are more differences than similarities. For this reason, it is improbable that either tradition relied on the other. By dating the two traditions, we see that the Ḥijāzi version is a few years older than the Iraqi one. If one tradition did rely on the other, then the Iraqi one would have to be secondary, since it is of a later origin. Since such reliance is improbable and the Iraqi tradition is later, we can conclude that Schacht's hypothesis about the origin of early biographical sources for the life of Prophet Muhammad (ﷺ) is a generalization that fails when these sources are tested. Therefore, his hypothesis is to be completely rejected.

Conclusion

Interest in Muslim sources for the biography of the Prophet (ﷺ) was intensified by the development of Christian theology, the appearance of historical-critical studies on the life of Jesus (ﷺ), and the rise of a source-critical approach to Biblical studies. The period from Weil (1843) to Muir (1856) is mainly distinguished by recourse to Arabic original sources, accompanied by a growing interest in unearthing original sources. During this period, the general assumption was that if a certain amount of careful sifting were done, then a considerable body of reliable tradition—on which we could rely for biographical purposes—could be found.

With the publication of Goldziher's *Muhammedanische Studien* in 1890, and the impact it made on the study of the Hadith in the West, the reliability of Muslim sources became controversial. This stance was further intensified by Schacht's publication of *The Origins of Muhammadan Jurisprudence,* in which he claimed that none of the Hadith literature was authentic. Although his verdict (like that of Goldziher) resulted from a study of hadiths related to legal matters, Schacht claimed that his thesis was applicable to early Muslim traditions in general, and he tried to prove this through analysis of some maghāzi material. Needless to say, Schacht's thesis had a great impact on Western research from the second half of the nineteenth century until today.

Current Western research is characterized by two groups of researchers who stand directly opposed to one another. The pessimistic group holds that it is impossible to reconstruct the life of the Prophet (ﷺ) from existing Muslim sources; in contrast, the other group maintains a more optimistic view of the possibilities available through the use of source-critical methods.

The optimistic attitude faces certain challenges, such as the fact that systematic source-critical studies of the biographical traditions are somewhat lacking in both Muslim and Western scholarship. Another challenge is the limited number of biographical sources employed in the process of writing modern biographies of the Prophet (ﷺ). Moreover, the texts contained in earlier and later Islamic sources have not yet been studied systematically and compared to one another.

In this study, we utilized the methodology of Harald Motzki in testing the basis for a more convincing optimistic approach. We tried to tackle some of these problems by presenting a critical study of MS. Berlin 9409 (the so-called *Tārīkh Ibn Abi Shaybah*) and thereby challenging some of the problems raised by the pessimistic group.

By looking at the names of teachers that Ibn Abi Shaybah mentioned in his own published books, and comparing them to names mentioned in other relevant books of Hadith, we came to the conclusion that MS. Berlin 9409 is the work of Ibn Abi Shaybah—with the exception of the first 17 traditions, which are probably the work of Maslamah ibn al-Qāsim, the compiler of his book of *al-Awā'il*. These 17 do not include the name of Ibn Abi Shaybah's teachers, nor do they come from any of the sources he used elsewhere.

After comparing the published book of the *Muṣannaf* with MS. Berlin 9409, we came to the conclusion that the manuscript is an identical copy of the *Muṣannaf*'s chapter of maghāzi. It does not contain the book of *Tārīkh*, as was claimed in a study published in the 1970s by Schützinger. The book of *Tārīkh* is wholly or partially included in the *Muṣannaf* under the same title. Studies of later citations of the book of *Tārīkh*, and of the method used by Ibn Abi Shaybah in classifying his chapters, prove that the existing chapter of tārīkh in the *Muṣannaf* includes part or all of the well-known book.

By applying source criticism to the manuscript's chains of authorities, we discovered that the sources used by Ibn Abi Shaybah form independent individual profiles of their respective materials, which precludes the possibility that they represent an organized false attribution of materials. His use of anonymous sources, broken asānīd and contradictory texts support this conclusion.

Moreover, we reached the same conclusion by reviewing the life and works of the author in Muslim biographical sources; this confirmed, through an independent evaluation of these sources, the results obtained from the work itself. Ibn Abi Shaybah received the materials from similar compilations that he transmitted from his teachers. His sources are genuine, and they provide authentic, reliable information for writing a biography of the Prophet (ﷺ).

In order to demonstrate the reliability and development of the sources of Ibn Abi Shaybah's informants, we applied isnād-cum-matn analysis to compare his informants' material with that of contemporaneous Iraqi sources. We investigated the transmission history of specific traditions regarding two different stories: the

Prophet's ascension to the heavens and a noted incident during his Hijrah. The findings were as follows:

1. Ibn Abi Shaybah received his material from his teachers by means of written transmissions, which was the usual method at that time (around the turn of the second century AH). These written materials included a full recording of traditions he received from his teachers. This conclusion was reached by comparing the versions recorded by Ibn Abi Shaybah with those of his Iraqi contemporaries such as Aḥmad ibn Ḥanbal and Abu Ya'lā al-Mūṣili.
2. Ibn Abi Shaybah's teachers in Iraq also had written sources available to them. This can be proven by comparing the variations included in their sources with those of their contemporaries. Among the generation preceding Ibn Abi Shaybah's teachers (in the second half of the first century AH), written transmission was not used systematically in Iraq. Nonetheless, written notes, which were later turned into full transcriptions, were employed in the process of transmitting hadiths during this period. As mentioned previously, this conclusion is in agreement with other studies of transmission history in other areas of the Islamic world.
3. The proposition that Ibn Abi Shaybah's informants fabricated their materials is untenable. This conclusion is attested by comparing his variants to those transmitted by his Iraqi contemporaries, such as Aḥmad ibn Ḥanbal and Abu Ya'lā, and by his informants' contemporaries.
4. At least three of the traditions that Ibn Abi Shaybah includes in MS. Berlin 9409 were circulated in Iraq not only in his generation and that of his informants, but also in the generation before them. This leads us to the conclusion that Ibn Abi Shaybah's sources are genuine to at least two levels prior to himself.
5. Our study of the two groups of transmissions of the Hijrah tradition (relating the story of Surāqah ibn Mālik ibn Ju'shum's pursuit of the Prophet [ﷺ] and Abu Bakr during their migration) allowed us to compare Iraqi and Madinan asānīd. We found that the Ḥijāzi version should be dated a few years prior to the Iraqi one, which contradicts Schacht's thesis that Iraq was the origin of the Sunnah and hence the origin of biographical information, too.

Notes

Quotations from the Qur'an

[1] Wherever possible, Arabic terms have been translated into English. In cases where we have chosen to retain the Arabic, the transliterated word or phrase is shown in italics the first time it appears in the text; the term is also defined in the Glossary found at the end of this book. (Editor)

Arabic edition of the manuscript

[2] Ibn Abi Shaybah, *Muṣannaf*. The term 'muṣannaf' refers to a collection of hadiths arranged in chapters by subject; Sahih Bukhari and Sahih Muslim are considered to be typical examples of this genre. See Goldziher, *Muslim Studies,* 2:232-234; MacDonald, *The Development of Muslim Theology*, 79; Juynboll, "Hadith," 192; Robson, "Hadith," 24; Siddiqi, *Hadith Literature*, 16.

During my work on this dissertation, I had access to three complete editions of Ibn Abi Shaybah's work: the Bombay edition of 'Abdul-Khāliq al-Afghāni (released in parts, 1979-1983), the edition of Kamāl Yūsuf al-Ḥūt (1985), and that of Muhammad 'Abdus-Salām Shāhīn (1995). I had access to a partial edition of some parts of the work edited by 'Umar ibn Gharāmah al-'Amrawi in 1988; this does not show a publisher's name. Those editions had many typo errors, which were later verified and amended in the editions of Muḥammad 'Awwāmah (2006) and al-Luḥaydān (2004). I had access to the latter and could compare it to the manuscript. In the process of editing the draft and preparing it for publication, I used all versions to verify the Arabic texts of reports used in the work.

Introduction

[3] Weil, *Muhammad der Prophet*. Weil translated *Sīrah Ibn Hishām* into German in 1864 (as *Das Leben Mohammeds*) and was the first Western scholar to write the history of Islam from 632 to 1217 CE after studying the original sources.

[4] Motzki, *The Biography of Muhammad*, i.

[5] Vikør, "The Truth about Cats and Dogs," 1.

[6] See Schacht, "Revaluation of Islamic Traditions," 143-54; Schacht, "On Musa ibn Uqba's Kitab al-Maghazi," 288-300.

[7] Watt, *Muhammad at Mecca*; Watt, *Muhammad at Medina*. The two books were summarized in his *Muhammad: Prophet and Statesman*.

[8] Cook and Crone, *Hagarism*; Crone, *Meccan Trade and the Rise of Islam*. In *Hagarism*, Patricia Crone and Michael Cook attempted to reconstruct the history of Islam through non-Muslim sources. Although they were successful in drawing attention to problems involved in the study of Islam, they have not been able to get beyond the limitations inherent in their sources, for they are all of questionable historical authenticity.

[9] In the introduction to his *Mahomet*, Rodinson depicts the limitations he sees in Muslim sources, writing, "A biography of Muhammad limited only to absolutely unquestioned facts could amount to no more than a few dry pages." Rodinson, *Mahomet*; Rodinson, *Mohammad*, ix.

[10] This method was elaborated by Schoeler, *Charakter und Authentie der Muslimischen*. Further refinements were introduced by Motzki in his "The Murder of Ibn Abī l-Huqayq," 170-239.

[11] Pictures of the original folios of MS. Berlin 9409 can be seen in Appendix 2, and the Arabic version of hadiths quoted in the text can be found in Appendix 3.

[12] Schützinger, "Ibn Abi Šaiba und sein Tari'x," 134-46.

Chapter One

Early biographical sources of the Prophet's life used in nineteenth and twentieth century research

[1] Weil, *Muhammad der Prophet*. By scholarly, I mean a systematic study based on criticism of the sources at hand, as opposed to medieval European legends about Prophet Muhammad (ﷺ).

[2] Jeffery, "The Quest of the Historical Muhammad," 333.

[3] Recension is the practice of editing or revising a text based on critical analysis. (Editor)

[4] *Sīrah* refers to a biography, especially of Prophet Muhammad (ﷺ). Ibn Hishām's *Sīrat an-Nabi* was first edited in 1859 by Wüstenfeld in his *Das Leben Mohammeds*. It was translated into German by Gustav Weil under the title *Das Leben Mohammeds*.

[5] Weil, *Geschichte der Chalifen*.

[6] Weil, *Geschichte der Islamischen Volker*. This book of Weil's was translated into English by S. K. Bakhsh under the title *A History of the Islamic Peoples*.

[7] Weil, *The Bible, the Koran and Talmud*, vii, xvi.

[8] Weil, *Geschichte der Chalifen*, 2:290.

[9] Weil, *The Bible, the Koran and Talmud*, xvi-xvii.

[10] Jeffery, "The Quest of the Historical Muhammad," 333.

[11] Wüstenfeld, *Das Leben Mohammeds*.

[12] Jurji Zaidan remarked that Wüstenfeld edited over 200 Arabic manuscripts. See Zaidan, *Tārīkh Adab al-Lughat al-'Arabiyah*, 4:144.

[13] Hamidullah, "Muhammad Ibn Ishaq," 91.

[14] Sprenger, *The Life of Mohammed*.

[15] Sprenger, *Das Leben und die Lehre des Mohammad*.

[16] Sprenger, *Mohammed und der Koran*.

[17] Jeffery, "The Quest of the Historical Muhammad," 335.

[18] Muir, "Value of Early Mahometan Historical Sources," 103.

[19] Jeffery, "The Quest of the Historical Muhammad," 335.

[20] Muir's *The Life of Mahomet* appeared in London in four volumes between the years 1856 and 1861. It included numerous notes and references, as well as introductory chapters on the early history of Arabia, the sources for the biography of the Prophet (ﷺ), and the Qur'an and the Hadith. In the second (1876) and third (1894) editions, these introductory chapters were omitted. An abridged revision of the third edition was published with an introduction by T. H. Weir of the University of Glasgow in 1912, bearing the newly established spelling of 'Mohammad' or 'Muhammad'.

[21] This introduction is reprinted in his book *The Mohammedan Controversy*.

[22] Muir, *The Life of Mohammad*, xiv.

[23] Muir, *The Life of Mahomet*, i.

[24] Muir, *The Life of Mohammad*, xxxv.

[25] Muir, *The Life of Mohammad*, xxxv.

[26] Muir, *The Life of Mohammad*, xxxv.

[27] Muir, *The Life of Mohammad*, xxxviii.

[28] Muir, *The Life of Mohammad*, xlvi.

[29] Muir, *The Life of Mohammad*, xlii.

[30] Muir, *The Life of Mohammad*, xlii.

[31] Muir, *The Life of Mohammad*, liii.

[32] Muir, *The Life of Mohammad*, xl.

[33] Muir, *The Life of Mahomet,* vol. 1.

[34] Muir, *The Life of Mohammad*, xiv.

[35] Muir, *The Life of Mohammad*, xiv.

[36] Muir, *The Life of Mohammad*, xlix.

[37] Muir, *The Life of Mohammad*, xlix.

[38] Muir, *The Life of Mohammad*, l.

[39] Muir, *The Life of Mohammad*, l.

[40] Nöldeke, *Das Leben Muhammads*.

[41] Wellhausen, *Muhammed in Medina*.

[42] Jeffery, "The Quest of the Historical Muhammad," 341.

[43] Motzki, *The Biography of Muhammad*, xi.

[44] Goldziher, *Muhammedanische Studien*. Goldziher, *Muslim Studies*. Page numbers are based on the German edition as shown in the English translation.

[45] For a discussion of the impact made in the West by Goldziher's book, and its importance, see Juynboll, *Muslim Tradition*, 2.

[46] Goldziher, *Muslim Studies*, 81.

[47] Ansari, "The Authenticity of Traditions," 51.

[48] Goldziher, *Muslim Studies*, 71.

49 Goldziher, *Muslim Studies*, 68.

50 Goldziher, *Vorlesungen über den Islam*, 43; Goldziher, *Introduction to Islamic Theology and Law*.

51 Goldziher, *Muslim Studies*, 5.

52 Motzki, "Dating Muslim Traditions: A Survey," 206.

53 Motzki, "Dating Muslim Traditions: A Survey," 206.

54 Goldziher, *Muslim Studies*, 23-27, 138-40.

55 Goldziher, *Muslim Studies*, 25-26.

56 Goldziher, *Muslim Studies*, 29-30.

57 Goldziher, *Introduction to Islamic Theology and Law*, 5, 36.

58 Most of Goldziher's conclusions will be discussed when we elaborate on the outlines of Schacht's theory on legal and biographical traditions.

59 Motzki, *Hadith: Origin and Developments*, xxi.

60 Motzki, *Hadith: Origin and Developments,* xx.

61 Shiites have their own separate collections of hadiths; they include only narrations attributed to certain members of the Prophet's family and to certain of his close Companions. (Editor)

62 Motzki, "Dating Muslim Traditions," 207.

63 Motzki, "Dating Muslim Traditions," 207.

64 Motzki, "Dating Muslim Traditions," 207.

65 maghāzi: The plural of *ghazwah* (a battle or a raid). This normally refers to literature narrating the different excursions and skirmishes that the Prophet (ﷺ) and his Companions undertook.

66 See Nöldeke, "Zur tendenziösen Gestaltung," 16-33.

67 Becker, *Islamstudien vom Werden*, 1:521-22.

68 Caetani, *Annali dell'Islam*, 1:28-58, 121-43, 192-215 and Lammens, "Qoran et tradition," 275.

69 This theory is recently favoured by Burton, *An Introduction to the Hadith*.

70 Wensinck, *The Muslim Creed*, 52, 59. The Umayyad Caliphate ended in 750 CE/132 AH. (Editor)

71 Bell, *The Origin of Islam*.

72 Fück, "The Role of Traditionalism in Islam," 110-111.

73 Fück, "The Role of Traditionalism in Islam," 110-111.

74 Fück, "The Role of Traditionalism in Islam," 105.

75 Fück, "The Role of Traditionalism in Islam," 106.

76 Fück, "The Role of Traditionalism in Islam," 106. Mutazilites are followers of a school of speculative theology that flourished in Basra and Baghdad during the eighth to the tenth centuries. They are best known for their belief that the Qur'an was created. (Editor)

77 Fück, "The Role of Traditionalism in Islam," 108.

78 Fück, "The Role of Traditionalism in Islam," 109.

79 Fück, "The Role of Traditionalism in Islam," 110.

80 Fück, "The Role of Traditionalism in Islam," 121n47.

81 Fück, "The Role of Traditionalism in Islam," 114.

[82] Abu Sa'eed al-Khudri (﵁) narrated that the Messenger of Allah (ﷺ) said: «One should not undertake journeys except to three mosques: the Sacred Mosque (in Makkah), al-Aqṣâ Mosque (in Jerusalem), or this mosque (the Prophet's Mosque in Madinah).» (Bukhari, Muslim)

[83] Fück, "The Role of Traditionalism in Islam," 114. For an elaboration of these chronological reasons, see ar-Rahawan, "Ḥadith Textual Criticism in Muslim and Modern Western Studies."

[84] Fück, "The Role of Traditionalism in Islam," 115.

[85] Schacht, "Revaluation of Islamic Traditions," 146-47.

[86] Fück, "Review of Joseph Schacht's Origins of Muhammadan Jurisprudence," 196-9.

[87] Guillaume, "Review of Joseph Schacht's Origins of Muhammadan Jurisprudence," 175.

[88] See Sezgin, *Geschichte des Arabischen Schrifttums*, 1:53-233; Hamidullah, "History of the Early Hadith Compilation," 1-111; as-Sibā'i, *as-Sunnah wa Makanatuhā*, 1-235 (written in the 1940s); al-Khaṭīb, *as-Sunnah Qabla at-Tadwīn*; Abbott, *Studies in Arabic Literary Papyri, vol. II*, 1-83; Azami, *Studies in Early Hadith Literature*.

[89] Wansbrough, *The Sectarian Milieu*.

[90] Cook and Crone, *Hagarism*; Crone, *Slaves on Horses*.

[91] Rodinson, *Mahomet*.

[92] Watt, *Muhammad at Mecca*; Watt, *Muhammad at Medina*.

[93] Schoeler, *Charakter und Authentie*; Motzki, "The Murder of Ibn Abī l-Huqayq," 170-239.

[94] Fück, "Review of Joseph Schacht's Origins of Muhammadan Jurisprudence," 196-199.

[95] Guillaume, "Review of Joseph Schacht's Origins of Muhammadan Jurisprudence," 176.

[96] *argumentum e silentio*: Argument from silence: a conclusion derived from silence or the lack of opposing evidence. This is only considered a valid argument in certain situations.

[97] Fück, "Review of Joseph Schacht's Origins of Muhammadan Jurisprudence," 197-198.

[98] Fück, "Review of Joseph Schacht's Origins of Muhammadan Jurisprudence," 199.

[99] Watt, "The Condemnation of the Jews of Banu Qurayza," 171.

[100] Watt, *Muhammad at Mecca*, xi-xii.

[101] Watt, *Muhammad at Mecca*, xiii.

[102] Watt, *Muhammad at Mecca*, xiv.

[103] Raven, "*Sira*," 662-3.

[104] Paret, *Muhammad und der Koran*; Rodinson, *Mahomet*.

[105] Rodinson, *Mohammad,* xii.

[106] Rodinson, *Mohammad,* xii.

[107] Rodinson, *Mohammad,* xi.

[108] Blachère, *La Problème de Mahomet*.

[109] Blachère, *La Problème de Mahomet*, 18.

[110] Rippin, "Literary Analysis of Qur'an, Tafsir, and Sira," 152.

[111] Rippin, "Literary Analysis of Qur'an, Tafsir, and Sira," 154.

[112] Wansbrough, *Qur'anic Studies*, 495.
[113] Wansbrough, *Qur'anic Studies*, 495.
[114] In New Testament scholarship, the term *logia* is applied to collections of sayings credited to Jesus. (Editor)
[115] Wansbrough, *Qur'anic Studies*, 495.
[116] Wansbrough, *Qur'anic Studies*, 495.
[117] This assumption is further developed by Wildman, as will be demonstrated below.
[118] Koren and Nevo, "Methodological Approaches to Islamic Studies," 92.
[119] Koren and Nevo, "Methodological Approaches to Islamic Studies," 92.
[120] Wansbrough, *The Sectarian Milieu,* 39.
[121] Wansbrough, *Qur'anic Studies,* 117-246. These terms are drawn from the different genres of Jewish scriptural exegesis and applied to the Qur'an.
[122] Wansbrough, *The Sectarian Milieu*, 76-9.
[123] Schoeler, *Charakter und Authentie*, 142-3.
[124] Lecker, "The Death of the Prophet Muhammad's Father," 9-27.
[125] Rippin, "*The Functions of Asbab an-Nuzul in Qur'anic Exegesis*," 1-20.
[126] Rubin, *The Eye of the Beholder*.
[127] Rubin, *The Eye of the Beholder*, 3.
[128] Ibrahim, "Review of Rubin's the Eye of the Beholder."
[129] In historical studies, prosopography is an investigation of the common characteristics of a historical group, whose individual biographies may be largely untraceable, by means of a collective study of their lives. (Editor)
[130] Crone, *Slaves on Horses*, 11.
[131] Crone, *Meccan Trade and the Rise of Islam*, 223.
[132] Crone, *Meccan Trade and the Rise of Islam*, 223.
[133] Crone, *Meccan Trade and the Rise of Islam*, 224.
[134] Cook, *Early Muslim Dogma*. See especially Chapter ii.
[135] Cook, *Early Muslim Dogma*, 16.
[136] Lecker, "The Death of the Prophet Muhammad's Father," 9-27.
[137] Wildman, *Toward a Theory of Historical Narrative*, 140-1.
[138] *Tārīkh al-Bayhaqi*: Six of about 30 volumes of a history of the Ghaznavid dynasty; it was composed between 1059 and 1065 CE by Abul-Faḍl al-Bayhaqi, one of their secretarial functionaries.
[139] Motzki, *The Biography of Muhammad*, xiv. For a more detailed and thoughtful introduction to the source problems with which Western scholars are confronted when studying the Prophet's biography, see Peters, "The Quest of the Historical Muhammad," 291-315. The impossibility of a historical biography was also recently maintained by Chabbi, "Historie et Tradition Sacrée," 189-205 and Raven, "*Sira*," 660-63.
[140] Motzki, *The Biography of Muhammad*, xiv-xv.
[141] Motzki, "The Collection of the Qur'an," 16.
[142] aṣ-Ṣan'āni, *al-Muṣannaf*; Ibn Abi Shaybah, *Kitāb al-Muṣannaf*; Ibn Shabbah, *Tārīkh al-Madīnah*; see Motzki, "The Collection of the Qur'an," 16.
[143] Motzki, "The Musannaf of 'Abd al-Razzaq," 1-21.

[144] Motzki, "The Musannaf of 'Abd al-Razzaq," 1.

[145] Leites, "Sira and the Question of Tradition," 50.

[146] Motzki, "The Collection of the Qur'an," 1.

[147] H. Horst applied this method to check the authenticity of aṭ-Ṭabari's transmission. See Horst, "Zur Überlieferung in Korankommentar at-Tabari," 290-306. Similarly, G. Stauth adopted a source-critical approach based on the transmission of Mujāhid's exegesis, mostly relying on the isnād for establishing his thesis. See Stauth, "Die Überlieferung des Korankommentars Muğāhid ibn Ğabrs." See also Cook, *Early Muslim Dogma*, 204.

[148] Sezgin, *Bukharinin Kaynaklarihakkinda Arştumarlar*, 29: 406.

[149] Motzki applied this approach for checking the authenticity of 'Abdur-Razzāq aṣ-Ṣan'āni's *Muṣannaf*; see Motzki, "The Musannaf of 'Abd al-Razzaq." He further elaborated the thesis in his epoch-making titles *Die Anfänge der Islamischen Jurisprudenz* and *The Origins of Islamic Jurisprudence*.
For reviews, see:
Madelung, "Review of Motzki's Die Anfänge," 171-3;
Muranyi, "Review of Motzki's Die Anfänge," 408-10;
Hawting, "Review of Motzki's Die Anfänge," 141-3;
Juynboll, "Review of Motzki's Die Anfänge," 357-364;
Gilliot, "Review of Motzki's Die Anfänge," 75-80;
Gimaret, "Review of Motzki's Die Anfänge," 40-3;
Fierro, "Review of Motzki's Die Anfänge," 604-6;
Schneider, "Review of Motzki's Die Anfänge," 684-5;
Lekkegaard, "Review of Motzki's Die Anfänge," 552-554.

[150] Sprenger, *Das Leben und die Lehre des Mohammad*, 1:330-49.

[151] Van Ess, *Zwischen Hadith und Theologie*.

[152] Juynboll, *Muslim Tradition*, 206.

[153] Juynboll, "Some Isnad-Analytical Methods," 343-84; Juynboll, "Nafi, the Mawla of Ibn Umar," 279-300; Juynboll, "The Role of Mu'ammarun"; Juynboll, "Some Notes on Earliest Fuqaha of Islam," 287-314; Juynboll, "(Re)appraisal of Some Technical Terms," 303-349.

[154] Juynboll, *Muslim Tradition*, 9-76.

[155] Juynboll, *Muslim Tradition*, 9.

[156] Juynboll, *Muslim Tradition*, 10-23.

[157] Juynboll, *Muslim Tradition*, 71.

[158] Juynboll, *Muslim Tradition*, 71.

[159] Juynboll, *Muslim Tradition*, 206-17.

[160] Juynboll, *Muslim Tradition*, 304-6; Juynboll, "Some Isnad-Analytical Methods," 354.

[161] Juynboll, "Some Isnad-Analytical Methods," 358.

[162] For examples of dives, see Diagrams 10 and 11 in Appendix 1.

[163] Motzki, "Dating Muslim Traditions," 204-253.

[164] Motzki, "Dating Muslim Traditions," 226.

[165] Motzki, "Quo vadis, Hadit Forshung?" 43-47.

[166] Motzki, "The Collection of the Qur'an," 27.

[167] Juynboll, "Some Isnad-Analytical Methods," 352.
[168] Juynboll, "Review of Motzki's Die Anfänge," 357-364.
[169] Motzki, "Dating Muslim Traditions," 230.
[170] Schoeler, "Foundations for a New Biography of Muhammad," 21.
[171] Schoeler, "Foundations for a New Biography of Muhammad."
[172] The research presented at this colloquium was published in Motzki, *The Biography of Muhammad*.
[173] Schoeler, "Foundations for a New Biography of Muhammad," 22.
[174] Schoeler, "Foundations for a New Biography of Muhammad."
[175] A *tābi'ī* (pl. *tābi'ūn*) is one who knew or met any of the Companions and transmitted hadiths from them.
[176] Schoeler, "Foundations for a New Biography of Muhammad," 23.
[177] Motzki, *The Biography of Muhammad*, xiv.

Chapter Two:
MS. Berlin 9409 (the so-called *Kitāb at-Tārīkh* of Abu Bakr 'Abdullāh ibn Muhammad ibn Abi Shaybah [159-235 AH/ 775-849 CE]): A newly-unearthed early source for the biography of Prophet Muhammad (ﷺ)

[1] Hunwick, "Ta'rikh," 271.
[2] Hunwick, "Ta'rikh," 271.
[3] Hunwick, "Ta'rikh," 271.
[4] There are other books of maghāzi literature that are extant only as excerpts and citations of later compilations. The earliest maghāzi work existing today is that of Mūsā ibn 'Uqbah (d. 141 AH/ 758 CE). His *Kitāb al-Maghāzi* was incorporated into later works, and a few pages in extract form have survived. E. Sachau edited and translated this fragment into German in 1904, with comments on certain traditions. (Sachau, "Das Berliner Fragment des Musa ibn 'Uqba," 445-70.) A new edition of the fragment, with an Arabic preface by Mashūr Ḥusayn Salmān, has recently been edited as *Aḥādīth Muntakhabah min Maghāzi Mūsā ibn 'Uqbah*. In 1994, another Arabic recension was published by 'Abdul-Malik as *Kitāb al-Maghāzi lī Mūsā ibn 'Uqbah*.
[5] Raven, "*Sira*," 660.
[6] Hinds, "Maghāzi and Sira," 57-66; Hinds, "Maghāzi," 1161-1164.
[7] Jarrar, *Die Prophetenbiographie im Islamischen Spanien*, 1-59.
[8] Sezgin, *Geschichte der Arabischen Schrifttums*, 290.
[9] See aṣ-Ṣan'āni, *al-Muṣannaf fil-Aḥādīth*.
[10] Ibn Abi Shaybah, *Kitāb al-Muṣannaf*.
[11] Sezgin, *Geschichte der Arabischen Schrifttums*, 108.
[12] Brockelmann, *Gesschichte der Arabischen Literatur*, 1:215.

13 Unfortunately, after extensive efforts to obtain this copy, I found out that it does not exist at aẓ-Ẓāhiriyah Bibliotheca. I received a written correspondence from the director of the library affirming that there is no manuscript bearing this title, even under any well-known category or number.

14 Schützinger, "Ibn Abi Šaiba und sein Tari'x," 134-46.

15 Sprenger's view was known through his handwritten comments, which appear on MS. Berlin 9409. He has a role in classifying the manuscript, which, according to his catalogue, bears his name and the number 104.

16 Ibn an-Nadīm, *al-Fihrist*, 276.

17 His experience with the *Muṣannaf* is indicated by the corrections he made to MS. Berlin 9409 with reference to further manuscript copies of the text. Most probably, he acquired these copies from India, where he travelled and lived.

18 He alluded that it might form a part of the *Tārīkh*.

19 An edited version of MS. Berlin 9409 was rendered as a part of the dissertation on which this book is based.

20 By editing, I mean introducing the handwritten manuscript in modern publishing media after verifying the text and comparing it to other copies and Hadith compilations. Editing the work also includes verifying the names included in it, explaining difficult words, grading the traditions (according to the Muslim traditional way of classifying hadiths), and providing indexes for its content. See Appendix 3 for the Arabic versions of the hadiths from the manuscript used in this study.

21 To review the history of using source criticism in modern Western studies about Islam, refer back to Chapter One.

22 Günther, "Due Results in the Theory of Source-Criticism," 4-5.

23 Horst, "Zur Überlieferung in Korankommentar," 290-306.

24 Stauth, "Die Überlieferung des Korankommentars."

25 Sezgin, *Bukharinin Kaynaklarihakkinda Arştumarlar*.

26 Schoeler, *Charakter und Authentie*.

27 Motzki, *Die Anfänge der Islamischen Jurisprudenz*.

28 Fleischhammer, *Quellenuntersuchungen zum Kitāb al-Agānī*.

29 Günther, *Quellenuntesuchungen zu den Maqātil aṭ-Ṭālibiyyîn*.

30 The progress in this trend was not only limited to historical, exegetical and legal traditions. It was also extended to Arabic literary sources that used the isnād. Examples are the studies by Fred Donner and Sebastian Günther.

31 Abbott, *Studies in Arabic Literary Papyri, vol. 1: Historical Texts*; Abbott, *Studies in Arabic Literary Papyri, vol. 2: Qur'anic Commentary and Tradition*.

32 Motzki, *Die Anfänge der Islamischen Jurisprudenz*.

33 Possession of the manuscript was transferred to the *Königlichen Bibliothek* in Berlin in 1858.

34 Brockelmann, *Gesschichte der Arabischen Literatur*, 1:215.

35 Sezgin, *Geschichte der Arabischen Schrifttums*, 1:108.

36 Naskh: a calligraphic script used for the writing of Arabic and the basis for most modern printed texts.

[37] Ahlwardt, *A Catalogue of the Bibliotheca Orientalis Sprengeriana*, 9:29.
[38] Literally, *Kitāb al-Awā'il* means 'The Book of the Firsts'. This is a chapter in Hadith collections that specifies the individuals in early Islamic history who were the first to do certain things.
[39] Lucey, *History*, 47.
[40] MS. Berlin 9409, 209, hadith 526. Ibn Abi Shaybah's name is also mentioned in the context of two titles on pages 188 and 209.
[41] Schützinger, "Ibn Abi Šaiba und sein Tari'x," 142.
[42] al-Khaṭīb al-Baghdādi, *Tārīkh Baghdād*, 10:60; aṣ-Ṣafaḍi, *al-Wafi,* 5:46; Ibn Sa'd, *aṭ-Ṭabaqāt al-Kubrā*, 6:288; adh-Dhahabi, *Tadhkirat al-Ḥuffāẓ*, 2:28; Ibn Ḥajar al-'Asqalāni, *Tahdhīb at-Tahdhīb*, 7:149.
[43] It was edited in 1999 by Muhammad Riḍā Qahwaji, based on a rare manuscript of aẓ-Ẓāhiriyah; see Ibn Abi Shaybah, *Kitāb al-Īmān*.
[44] Ibn Abi Shaybah, *Kitāb al-Īmān*, ed. Nāsir ad-Dīn al-Albāni.
[45] For full biographical information, see adh-Dhahabi, *Sayr A'lām an-Nubalā'*, 16:110.
[46] As we shall show, the entire edited version of the *Muṣannaf* was transmitted to us through Baqi ibn Makhlad, with the exception of the book of *al-Awā'il*.
[47] See al-Khaṭīb al-Baghdādi, *Tārīkh Baghdād*, 1:287.
[48] adh-Dhahabi, *Tadhkirat al-Ḥuffāẓ*, 2:683.
[49] adh-Dhahabi, *Sayr A'lām an-Nubalā'*, 8:531.
[50] Ibn Ḥajar al-'Asqalāni, *Lisān al-Mīzān*, 6:304.
[51] This is the first tradition in MS. Berlin 9409 (*Muṣannaf*, no. 36021).
[52] This is fifth tradition in MS. Berlin 9409 (*Muṣannaf*, no. 36025).
[53] This is the sixth tradition in MS. Berlin 9409 (*Muṣannaf*, no. 36026).
[54] adh-Dhahabi, *Sayr A'lām an-Nubalā'*, 9:304; Ibn Ma'īn, *Tārīkh*, 3:349.
[55] This is the seventh report in the manuscript (*Muṣannaf*, no. 36027).
[56] This is the 11th tradition of the manuscript (*Muṣannaf*, no. 36031).
[57] MS. no. 8 and 9 (*Muṣannaf*, no. 36028 and 3629).
[58] MS. no. 10, 12, 13, 14 and 17 (*Muṣannaf*, no. 36030, 36032, 36033, 36034 and 37037).
[59] MS. no. 15 (*Muṣannaf*, no. 36035).
[60] MS. no. 16 (*Muṣannaf*, no. 36036).
[61] Shützinger concluded that the manuscript includes 531 records. He might have excluded the first 17 traditions, which do not belong to Ibn Abi Shaybah, and he did not pay attention to the last sentence, which is a part of a missing tradition on page 6 and the copyist's merging of two traditions on page 50. There is however, a third tradition, which is also missing from MS. Berlin 9409, *al-Muṣannaf*, hadith no. 36955.
[62] The original book of *Maghāzi* as published in the *Muṣannaf* also includes historical records about the third Caliph, 'Uthmān ibn 'Affān.
[63] Zaman, "Maghazi and the Muhaddithun," 2.
[64] There are three missing hadiths at the first chapter of the maghāzi section on page 6. Only the last sentence of the third hadith appears. We can find these missing hadiths in the other copies of the *Muṣannaf.*
[65] MS. Berlin 9409, 6-10.

[66] MS. Berlin 9409, 10-14.
[67] MS. Berlin 9409, 14-18.
[68] MS. Berlin 9409, 18-25.
[69] MS. Berlin 9409, 25-36.
[70] MS. Berlin 9409, 49-54.
[71] MS. Berlin 9409, 36-44.
[72] MS. Berlin 9409, 44-49.
[73] MS. Berlin 9409, 54-55.
[74] MS. Berlin 9409, 56-74.
[75] MS. Berlin 9409, 74-92.
[76] MS. Berlin 9409, 92-104.
[77] MS. Berlin 9409, 104-106.
[78] MS. Berlin 9409, 106-107.
[79] MS. Berlin 9409, 108
[80] MS. Berlin 9409, 128.
[81] MS. Berlin 9409, 130.
[82] MS. Berlin 9409, 140-167.
[83] I made extensive efforts to obtain this copy, but unfortunately I found out that it does not exist at aẓ-Ẓāhiriyah. I received formal letters from officials in the library, which is now in possession of al-Asad National Library, confirming that it is not there.
[84] Zaman, "Maghazi and the Muhaddithun," 2.
[85] See Ibn Ḥajar al-'Asqalāni, *Tahdhīb at-Tahdhīb*, 9:312; 10:312; and 9:373.
[86] Ibn an-Nadīm gives names for books claimed to be compiled by Ibn Abi Shaybah, such as *Kitāb al-Fitan, Kitāb Ṣiffīn* and *Kitāb al-Jamal.*
[87] MS. Berlin 9409*,* no. 63, where Ibn Abi Shaybah writes only, "*ḥaddathanā shaykhun lanā* (one of our teachers informed us)."
[88] A mursal hadith is a narration that a *tābi'ī* ascribes to the Prophet (ﷺ) without mentioning the Companion from whom he or she heard it.
[89] See MS. Berlin 9409, no. 69, 182, 211, 248, 273, 284 and many other traditions.
[90] MS. Berlin 9409, no. 23-31.
[91] Ibn al-Athīr, *al-Kāmil fit-Tārīkh*, 5:283.
[92] adh-Dhahabi, *Sayr A'lām an-Nubalā'*, 11:122; adh-Dhahabi, *al-'Ibar fī Khabar*, 1:79.
[93] adh-Dhahabi, *Sayr A'lām an-Nubalā'*, 11:124.
[94] MS. Berlin 9409, no. 95, 336, 461.
[95] adh-Dhahabi, *Sayr A'lām an-Nubalā'*, 11:124. Yaḥyā ibn Ma'īn did not preclude the possibility that Ibn Abi Shaybah received from Sharīk at that age.
[96] al-Mizzi, *Tahdhīb al-Kamāl*, 3:463. (Source: Wakī' ibn al-Jarrāḥ)
[97] This is confirmed by most of his contemporaries. See Ibn 'Asākir, *Tārīkh Madīnah Dimashq*, 63:61-78; ar-Rāzi, *al-Jarḥ wat-Ta'dīl*, 9:37.
[98] al-Khaṭīb al-Baghdādi, *Tārīkh Baghdād*, 10:70. It is most probably the fifth pillar in the big mosque of Kufa, as maintained by al-Ḥumawi, *Mu'jam al-Buldān*, 4:325.
[99] Ibn Ḥibbān, *ath-Thiqāt*, 562.
[100] Ibn 'Asākir, *Tārīkh Madīnah Dimashq,* 63: 68.

[101] Ibn Ḥajar al-'Asqalāni, *Tahdhīb at-Tahdhīb,* 11:109. (Source: Aḥmad ibn Ḥanbal)
[102] Ibn 'Asākir, *Tarīkh Madīnah Dimashq*, 63:67.
[103] Ibn 'Asākir, *Tārīkh Madīnah Dimashq*, 63:81. (Source: Abu 'Uthmān al-Warrāq)
[104] Ibn an-Nadīm, *al-Fihrist*, 1:283.
[105] al-Kittāni, *ar-Risālat al-Mustaṭrafah*, 1:40. Ibn Khayr al-Ishbīli claims that he received a copy of the book in Andalusia; see Ibn Khayr, *Fahrasat mā Rawāhu 'an Shuyūkhihi*, 126.
[106] Even the *Muṣannaf* of Ibn Abi Shaybah was sometimes known as *as-Sunan*; see Ibn an-Nadīm, *al-Fihrist*, 1:285.
[107] al-Bābāni, *Hadiyat al-'Ārifīn*, 2:207.
[108] Ibn 'Asākir, *Tārīkh Madīnah Dimashq*, 63:78. (Source: Yaḥyā ibn Ma'īn)
[109] Ibn al-Jarrāḥ, *Kitāb az-Zuhd*.
[110] For examples, hadiths no. 5, 6 and 15.
[111] Ibn Ḥanbal is even reported to have said, "I have never seen a man as [excellent as] Wakī' in knowledge, memory, strong chain of authorities and in classifying his themes." Quoted in an-Nawawi, *Mā Tamussu Ilayhi Ḥājat al-Qāri*.
[112] as-Suyūṭi, *Ṭabaqāt al-Ḥuffāẓ*, 1:140.
[113] Sezgin maintains that manuscripts of his Hadith collections written in the sixth/seventh centuries AH are held in libraries such as Shahīd Ali, aẓ-Ẓāhiriyah and Dār al-Kutub al-Miṣriyah; see Sezgin, *Geschichte der Arabischen Schrifttums,* 1:96. Ibn Ḥajar had a samā ', which he listed in his *al-Mu'jam al-Mufahris*, 297.
[114] See Sezgin, *Geschichte der Arabischen Schrifttums*, 1:96.
[115] Ibn Ḥajar al-'Asqalāni, *al-Mu'jam al-Mufahris*, 109.
[116] adh-Dhahabi, *Sayr A'lām an-Nubalā'*, 11:123.
[117] Ibn Ḥajar narrated a book for Yazīd, as maintained in *al-Mu'jam al-Mufahris*, 71.
[118] 'Affān has an extant collection in manuscript form in aẓ-Ẓāhiriyah and Berlin; see Sezgin, *Geschichte der Arabischen Schrifttums*, 1:102.
[119] See Sezgin, *Geschichte der Arabischen Schrifttums*, 1:101. Ibn Ḥajar al-'Asqalāni, moreover, narrated collections of Ibn Dukayn in his *al-Mu'jam al-Mufahris,* namely the book of prayer; see Ibn Ḥajar al-'Asqalāni, *al-Mu'jam al-Mufahris*, 60.
[120] Sezgin, *Geschichte des Arabischen Schrifttums*, 1:96.
[121] Sezgin, *Geschichte des Arabischen Schrifttums*, 1:96.
[122] Ibn Ḥajar al-'Asqalāni, *al-Iṣābah fī Tamyīz aṣ-Ṣaḥābah*, 3:36.
[123] Ibn Ḥajar al-'Asqalāni, *al-Mu'jam al-Mufahris*, 89.
[124] It was first published in Hyderabad in 1321 AH.
[125] These conclusions were drawn by Schoeler in his *Charakter und Authentie* and elaborated in his four articles in *Der Islam,* namely: Schoeler, "Die Frage der schriftlichen," 201-230; Schoeler, "Weiteres zur Frage der schriftlichen," 38-67; Schoeler, "Mündliche Thora und Hadit," 213-251; Schoeler, "Schreiben und Veröffentlichen," 1-43.
[126] aṣ-Ṣafadi, *al-Wāfi*, 5:462; adh-Dhahabi, *Sayr A'lām an-Nubalā'*, 11:22.
[127] Ḥabīb ar-Raḥmān al-A'ẓami maintained that Abu Bakr Aḥmad ibn 'Ali ibn Sa'īd (who received *Kitāb al-Adab* from Ibn Abi Shaybah) was the main transmitter of the *Muṣannaf* in the East, while Baqi ibn Makhlad was the main transmitter for the people of North

Africa (the current states of Morocco, Algeria, Tunisia and Libya) and Andalusia. See Muhammad Riḍā Qahwaji's introduction to the published edition of *Kitāb al-Adab*; adh-Dhahabi, *Tadhkirat al-Ḥuffāẓ*, 2:663; Ibn Ḥajar al-'Asqalāni, *Tahdhīb at-Tahdhīb*, 1:62.

[128] Ibn Ḥajar possessed a portion containing it. See Ibn Ḥajar al-'Asqalāni, *al-Mu'jam al-Mufahris*, 171.

[129] Ibn an-Nadīm, *al-Fihrist*, 1:320. This book of Ibn Abi Shaybah has been edited by 'Ādil 'Azzāzi and Aḥmad Farīd al-Muzaydi.

[130] al-Khaṭīb al-Baghdādi, *Īḍaḥ al-Maknūn*, 36; al-Khaṭīb al-Baghdādi, *Tārīkh Baghdād*, 10:66.

[131] Ibn Ḥajar al-'Asqalāni, *al-Mu'jam al-Mufahris*, 51. This book was edited by Muhammad Nāṣir ad-Dīn al-Albāni. The edition was based on a manuscript in aẓ-Ẓāhiriyah (with 279 hadiths).

[132] Sezgin, *Geschichte der Arabischen Schrifttums*, 1:108. The book was edited in 1999 by Muhammad Riḍā Qahwaji based on a rare manuscript of aẓ-Ẓāhiriyah; see Ibn Abi Shaybah, *Kitāb al-Īman*, ed. Muhammad Riḍā Qahwaji.

[133] al-Bābāni, *Hadiyat al-'Ārifīn*, 1:229. Ibn Ḥajar mentions that he received permission to transmit it. See Ibn Ḥajar al-'Asqalāni, *al-Mu'jam al-Mufahris*, 110.

[134] Ibn Ḥajar al-'Asqalāni, *al-Mu'jam al-Mufahris*, 117.

[135] al-Khaṭīb al-Baghdādi, *Tārikh Baghdād*, 10:70.

[136] adh-Dhahabi, *Sayr A'lām an-Nubalā'*, 11:124.

[137] al-Khaṭīb al-Baghdādi, *Tārīkh Baghdād*, 10:70. (Source: Ṣāliḥ ibn Muhammad)

[138] Ibn Ḥibbān, *al-'Ilal,* 1:384.

[139] al-Mizzi, *Tahdhīb al-Kamāl*, 16:40.

[140] adh-Dhahabi, *Sayr A'lām an-Nubalā'*, 11:125.

[141] al-Mizzi, *Tahdhīb al-Kamāl*, 16:39.

[142] al-Khaṭīb al-Baghdādi, *Tārīkh Baghdād*, 10:67; adh-Dhahabi, *Sayr A'lām an-Nubalā'*, 11, 122.

[143] Aḥmad ibn Ḥanbal, *al-'Ilal wa Ma'rifat ar-Rijāl*, 1:79.

[144] Ibn 'Asākir provides the first hadith that Ibn Abi Shaybah narrated when he started teaching people in Baghdad. It concerned al-'Abbās, the Prophet's uncle. See Ibn 'Asākir, *Tārīkh Madīnah Dimashq*, 10:68.

[145] Ibn 'Asākir, *Tārīkh Madīnah Dimashq*, 10:68.

[146] al-Khaṭīb al-Baghdādi, *Tārīkh Baghdād*, 51:465; Ibn 'Asākir, *Tārīkh Madīnah Dimashq*, 65:18; Ibn al-Athīr, *al-Kāmil fit-Tārīkh*, 5:283; adh-Dhahabi, *Sayr A'lām an-Nubalā'*, 10:680; Ibn Ḥajar al-'Asqalāni, *Tahdhīb at-Tahdhīb*, 6:4.

[147] ar-Rāmahurmuzi, *al-Muḥaddith al-Fāṣil*.

[148] al-Khaṭīb al-Baghdādi, *Tārīkh Baghdād*, 10:70.

[149] Ibn 'Asākir, *Tārīkh Madīnah Dimashq*, 10:356. (Source: Abu Muhammad 'Ali ibn Aḥmad ibn Sa'īd ibn Ḥazm, d. 450 AH)

[150] Ibn Khayr, *Fahrasat mā Rawāhu*, 131-133.

[151] Ibn Khayr, *Fahrasat mā Rawāhu*, 131-133.

[152] Diagram 13 in Appendix 1 shows the lines through which Ibn Khayr received the book.

Chapter Three:

The development of early biographical sources about the life of Prophet Muhammad (ﷺ): The Kufan sources in the first two Islamic centuries

[1] Motzki, "The Murder of Ibn Abī l-Huqayq," 174.

[2] Schacht, *The Origins of Muhammadan Jurisprudence*, 163-75; Johannes H. Kramers independently developed, about the same time as Schacht, similar but on the whole superior methods for the investigation of hadiths, but his contribution remained nearly unnoticed. See Kramers, "Une tradition á tendance manichéenne," 10-22.

[3] Motzki, "The Murder of Ibn Abī l-Huqayq," 174.

[4] The method in principle was already used by Johannes H. Kramers in his "A Tradition of Manichaen Tendency," 245-57 and Van Ess, *Zwischen Hadith und Theologie*.

[5] See Schoeler, *Charakter und Authentie* and Schoeler, "Musa ibn Uqba's Maghazi," 67-97.

[6] Görke, "The Historical Tradition about al-Hudaybiya," 240-275.

[7] Mozki, *Die Anfänge der Islamischen Jurisprudenz*, 87-95; Motzki, "Oder Fiqh des Zahiri," 1-44, especially 28-44.

[8] Günther, "Due Results in the Theory of Source-Criticism," 6.

[9] Motzki, "The Prophet and the Cat."

[10] Motzki, "The Prophet and the Cat."

[11] For the sake of brevity, we could not attach the full Arabic edition of MS. Berlin 9409. Only the traditions that are discussed here have been excerpted from the Arabic edition; they are included in Appendix 3.

[12] Hadith scholars often add more isnads of the same text without repeating the text each time.

[13] Due to the difficulty of incorporating all transmission lines in one page, I made six diagrams—one for each student of Anas ibn Mālik.

[14] Partial common links are, according to Juynboll:
Transmitters who receive something from a common link or any other sort of transmitter from a generation after the common link and pass it on to two or more of their pupils. See Juynboll, "Some Isnad-Analytical Methods," 352.

[15] Ibn Abi Shaybah, *Muṣannaf*, 7:333 (36570).

[16] Aḥmad ibn Ḥanbal, *al-Musnad*, 3:148 (12528).

[17] Ibn Mandah, *Kitāb al-Īmān*, 2:708.

[18] Abu 'Awānah, *Musnad Abu 'Awānah*, 1:113.

[19] Abu Ya'lā, *Musnad Abi Ya'lā*, 6:217.

[20] Abu Nu'aym, *al-Musnad al-Mustakhraj*, 1:227.

[21] Muslim, *Ṣaḥīḥ Muslim*, 1:145 (162).

[22] Ibn Mandah, *Kitāb al-Īmān*, 2:711.

[23] aṭ-Ṭabari, *Tafsīr aṭ-Ṭabari*, 27:54.

[24] Sharīk ibn 'Abdullāh is Madani. Ibn Ḥajar al-'Asqalāni, *Tahdhīb at-Tahdhīb*, 4:296.

25 Abu Nu‘aym, *al-Musnad al-Mustakhraj*, 1:230.

26 His version is included in the following: Muslim, *Ṣaḥīh Muslim*, 1:148 (162); Abu ‘Awānah, *Mustakhraj*, 1:135; aṭ-Ṭabari, *Tahdhīb al-Āthār*, 1:419; al-Bayhaqi, *as-Sunan al-Kubrā*, 1:360.

27 His version is contained in Bukhari’s *al-Jāmi‘ aṣ-Ṣaḥīḥ*, 6:237 (7079), Ibn Mandah’s *Kitāb al-Īmān*, and al-Fākihi’s *Akhbār Makkah*, 2:27, no. 719.

28 His version is included in Bukhari, 3:1308 (3377); Ibn Mandah, *Kitāb al-Īmān,* 2:719; Abu Nu‘aym, *al-Musnad al-Mustakhraj*, 1:229.

29 an-Nasā’i, *as-Sunan al-Kubrā*, 1:221.

30 Ibn ‘Asākir, *Tārīkh Madīnah Dimashq*, 65:281.

31 aṭ-Ṭabarāni, *Musnad as-Shāmiyyīn*, 1:195.

32 Ibn Kathīr, *Tafsīr Ibn Kathīr*, 3:7.

33 Ibn Kathīr, *Tafsīr Ibn Kathīr*, 3:7.

34 aṭ-Ṭabari, *Tafsīr aṭ-Ṭabari*, 15:6.

35 aṭ-Ṭabari, *Tahdhīb al-Āthār*, 1:410.

36 al-Bayhaqi, *Dalā’il an-Nubuwwah*, 2:248.

37 aṭ-Ṭabari, *Tafsīr aṭ-Ṭabari*, 27:35.

38 Aḥmad ibn Ḥanbal, *Musnad*, 3:138 (12333).

39 Ibn Abi Shaybah, *al-Muṣannaf*, 6:315 (31717).

40 Ibn Ḥajar al-‘Asqalāni, *Tahdhīb at-Tahdhīb*, 3:34.

41 It is included in al-Qaṭī‘i, *Juz’ al-Alf Dīnār*, 2:441.

42 aṣ-Ṣan‘āni, *Tafsīr aṣ-Ṣan‘āni*, 2:372.

43 aṭ-Ṭabari, *Tafsīr aṭ-Ṭabari*, 15:15.

44 al-Ḥumaydi, *Musnad al-Ḥumaydi*, 1:357.

45 Aḥmad ibn Ḥanbal, *al-Musnad*, 3:164 (1185).

46 Ibn Ḥibbān, *Ṣaḥīḥ Ibn Ḥibbān*, 1:234.

47 al-Bayhaqi, *Dalā’il an-Nubuwwah*, 2:249.

48 Ibn al-‘Arābi, *Mu‘jam*, 2:375.

49 al-Khaṭīb al-Baghdādi, *Tārīkh Baghdād*, 3:436.

50 These numbers were introduced to divide the text into segments in order to facilitate comparison. (Author)

51 al-Bayt al-Ma‘mūr: the house of worship in the seventh heaven that is frequented by angels; it is comparable to the Kaaba on Earth

52 sidrat al-muntahā: a lote tree that marks the end of the seventh heaven; it is a boundary which none of the creation can pass

53 Zamzam: the blessed spring of water that Allah caused to gush out at baby Ishmael’s feet; located near the Kaaba in Makkah.

54 This version is totally different from the previous short version, which is attributed to Ḥammād ibn Salamah.

55 Ibn Ḥajar al-‘Asqalāni, *Tahdhīb at-Tahdhīb*, 3:13.

56 I have used Muhammad Muhsin Khan’s English translation of *Sahih al-Bukhari*, with a few changes to the translated text. (Author)

57 aṭ-Ṭabari, *Tahdhīb al-Āthār*, 1:428.

58 By aural, I mean the interaction of the oral and the written language as a characteristic of the medieval Arabic-Islamic system of transmission. See Günther, "Due Results in the Theory of Source-Criticism," 13.
59 Ibn 'Abdul-Barr, *Al-Istī'āb*, 1:126.
60 Ḥammād ibn Usāmah is from Kufa and is one of the teachers of Ibn Abi Shaybah. He is known as a narrator of historical accounts, and he received traditions from Hishām ibn 'Urwah ibn az-Zubayr. According to Ibn Ḥajar, he is trustworthy with a firm memory. Ibn Ḥajr, *Tahdhīb at-Tahdhīb*, 3:3.
61 Ibn Abi Shaybah, *Muṣannaf*, 7:333 (36571).
62 He lived in Basra. Ibn Ḥajar al-'Asqalāni, *Tahdhīb at-Tahdhīb*, 9:67.
63 Aḥmad ibn Ḥanbal, *al-Musnad*, 3:8 (17870).
64 aṭ-Ṭabari, *Tafsīr aṭ-Ṭabari*, 15:3.
65 aṭ-Ṭabari, *Tafsīr aṭ-Ṭabari*, 27:35.
66 al-Marwazi, *Ṣalāt al-Witr*, 1:9.
67 Bukhari, *al-Jāmi' aṣ-Ṣaḥīḥ*, 3:1173 (3035).
68 Abu 'Awānah, *Musnad*, 1:109.
69 an-Nasā'i, *as-Sunan al-Kubrā*, 1:138 (313).
70 Ibn 'Asākir, *Tārīkh Madīnah Dimashq*, 3:483.
71 Though he is 'not strong (*laysa biqawi*)' according to Bukhari and an-Nasā'i, he is well-known for transmitting the traditions of Sa'īd ibn Abi 'Arūbah. Al-Mizzi, *Tahdhīb al-Kamāl*, 18:509.
72 Ibn Mandah, *Kitāb al-Īmān*, 2:726. It is included in Diagram 8.
73 al-Bayhaqi, *Dalā'il an-Nubuwwah*, 2:266.
74 Abu 'Awānah, *Mustakhraj*, 1:150.
75 Aḥmad ibn Ḥanbal, *al-Musnad*, 3:8.
76 Ibn Mandah, *Kitāb at-Tawḥīd*, 1:29.
77 Ibn 'Asākir, *Tārīkh Madīnah Dimashq*, 3:480.
78 aṭ-Ṭabari, *Tafsīr aṭ-Ṭabari*, 27:35.
79 Ibn Mandah, *Kitāb al-Īmān*, 2:722.
80 Ibn 'Asākir, *Tārīkh Madīnah Dimashq*, 3:483.
81 Ibn Mandah, *Kitāb al-Īmān*, 2:722.
82 Muslim, *Ṣaḥīḥ Muslim*, 1:150 (164).
83 Bukhari, *al-Jāmi' aṣ-Ṣaḥīḥ*, 3:1173 (3035).
84 an-Nasā'i, *as-Sunan al-Kubrā*, 1:138.
85 Abu 'Awānah, *Mustakhraj*, 1:109.
86 Ibn Mandah, *Kitāb al-Īmān*, 2:722.
87 Abu 'Awānah, *Mustakhraj*, 1:109.
88 Ibn 'Asākir, *Tārīkh Madīnah Dimashq*, 3:483.
89 Ibn Mandah, *Kitāb al-Īmān*, 2:728.
90 Ibn Ḥibbān, *Ṣaḥīḥ Ibn Ḥibbān*, 1:236.
91 Bukhari, *al-Jāmi' aṣ-Ṣaḥīḥ*, 3:1410 (3674).
92 Aḥmad ibn Ḥanbal, *al-Musnad*, 4:208 (17868).
93 Ibn 'Asākir, *Tārīkh Madīnah Dimashq*, 3:483.

94 Abu Nu'aym, *Ma'rifat aṣ-Ṣaḥābah*, 17:188.
95 aṭ-Ṭabarāni, *al-Mu'jam al-Kabīr*, 19:271.
96 Abu 'Awānah, *Mustakhraj*, 1:124.
97 See Diagram 7 in Appendix 1.
98 See Diagram 8 in Appendix 1.
99 See Diagram 9 in Appendix 1.
100 Ibn Ḥajar al-'Asqalāni, *Fatḥ al-Bāri*, 7:303.
101 Bayhaqi, *Dalā'il*, 2:377.
102 Ibn Mandah, *Kitāb al-Īmān*, 2:707.
103 aṭ-Ṭabari, *Tafsīr aṭ-Ṭabari*, 27:54.
104 Bukhari, *al-Jāmi' aṣ-Ṣaḥīḥ*, 3:1410 (3674).
105 See Diagrams 7, 8 and 9 in Appendix 1 for transmission details of the various narrations by Qatādah of this hadith.
106 'Aqīl's version is contained in Abu 'Awanah, *Mustakhraj*, 1:300; al-Fākihi, *Akhbār Makkah*, 2:24; al-Firyābi, *al-Qadar*, 1:279. This variant has an abridged text.
107 A 'dive', according to G. H. A. Juynboll, is a single strand that goes parallel to the common link and connects back to the Prophet (ﷺ). He views these as certain fabrications, although other scholars, such as Motzki, have cast serious doubt on the validity of this conclusion.
108 His version is included in al-Bayhaqi, *Dalā'il an-Nubuwwah*, 2:267; Bukhari, *Ṣaḥīḥ al-Bukhāri*, 1:135; Abu Nu'aym, *al-Musnad al-Mustakhraj*, 2:231; al-Bazzār's *Musnad al-Bazzār*, 9:337.
109 His version is included in al-Firyābi, *al-Qadar*, 1:280; Muslim, *Ṣaḥīḥ Muslim*, 1:148; Abu 'Awānah, *Musnad*, 2:231; Ibn Ḥibbān, *Ṣaḥīḥ Ibn Ḥibbān*, 16:420; Ibn Mandah, *Kitāb al-Īmān*, 1:720, al-'Ājurri, *ash-Sharī'ah*, 3:131; Abu Nu'aym, *al-Musnad al-Mustakhraj*, 2:231; an-Nasā'i, *as-Sunan al-Kubrā*, 1:140; al-Bayhaqi, *Dalā'il an-Nubuwwah*, 2:267; Ibn 'Asākir, *Tārīkh Madīnah Dimashq*, 3:489.
110 His version is included in Bukhari, *Ṣaḥīḥ al-Bukhāri*, 2:589.
111 His version is contained in Bukhari, *Ṣaḥīḥ al-Bukhāri*, 3:1217.
112 His version is included in Ibn 'Asākir, *Tārīkh Madīnah Dimashq*, 3:462.
113 This conclusion is drawn by an-Nasā'i, *as-Sunan al-Kubrā*, 1:140.

Chapter Four:
Origin of early biographical sources about the life of Prophet Muhammad (ﷺ)

1 Schacht, "Revaluation of Islamic Traditions," 144.
2 Schacht, "Revaluation of Islamic Traditions," 145.
3 Schacht, "Revaluation of Islamic Traditions," 145. Imam ash-Shāfi'i died in 204 AH/ 820 CE. (Editor)
4 Schacht, "Revaluation of Islamic Traditions," 145.
5 Schacht, "Revaluation of Islamic Traditions," 145.

[6] Schacht, "Revaluation of Islamic Traditions," 145.
[7] Schacht, "Revaluation of Islamic Traditions," 145.
[8] Schacht, "Revaluation of Islamic Traditions," 147.
[9] Schacht, "Revaluation of Islamic Traditions," 151.
[10] Schacht, "Revaluation of Islamic Traditions," 150.
[11] Schacht, "Revaluation of Islamic Traditions," 151.
[12] Schacht, "On Musa ibn Uqba's Kitab al-Maghazi," 288-300.
[13] This method was elaborated by Schoeler in *Charakter und Authentie*. Further refinements were introduced by Motzki in "The Murder of Ibn Abī l-Huqayq" and *The Biography of Muhammad*.
[14] Arabic texts of all the traditions reported by Ibn Abi Shaybah are included in Appendix 3.
[15] Schacht, "On Musa ibn Uqba's Kitab al-Maghazi," 288-300.
[16] Schacht, "On Musa ibn Uqba's Kitab al-Maghazi," 292.
[17] Schoeler, "Musa ibn Uqba's Maghazi," 67-97.
[18] Schoeler, "Musa ibn Uqba's Maghazi," 67-97.
[19] al-Ḥākim an-Naysābūri, *al-Mustadrak*, 3:71.
[20] al-Ḥākim an-Naysābūri, *al-Mustadrak*, 3:7.
[21] aṣ-Ṣan'āni, *al-Muṣannaf*, 5:392.
[22] Aḥmad ibn Ḥanbal, *Musnad*, 4:175 (17627).
[23] His variant is included in Ibn Ḥibbān, *Ṣaḥīḥ Ibn Ḥibbān*, 14:185.
[24] His variant is included in Ibn al-Mundhir, *al-Awsaṭ*, 10:253 and aṭ-Ṭabarāni, *al-Mu'jam al-Kabīr*, 7:133.
[25] It is contained in Ibn Abi 'Āṣim, *al-Āḥād wal-Mathāni*, 2:274 and aṭ-Ṭabarāni, *al-Mu'jam al-Kabīr*, 7:133.
[26] His variant is provided in Ibn 'Uqbah, *Dalā'il*, 2:349.
[27] Ibn Hishām, *Sīrah*, 1:489. This variant is also included in Abu Nu'aym, *Dalā'il*, 1:274.
[28] al-Ḥārith, *Bughyah,* 1:213.
[29] Ibn Abi Shaybah, *Muṣannaf*, 7:334.
[30] Juynboll, "Some Isnad-Analytical Methods," 369.
[31] See Sachau, "Das Berliner Fragment des Musa ibn 'Uqba," 445-70; Salmān, *Aḥādīth Muntakhabah min Maghāzi*, iii.
[32] I refer to a copy of the Berliner fragment, which exists in the library of the Jāmi'at al-Islāmiyah in Madinah. A copy is available here: http://al-mostafa.info/data/arabic/depot3/gap.php?file=m001361.pdf.
[33] Anṣār: 'helpers'; the Muslim citizens of Madinah who gave refuge to the Prophet (ﷺ) and the other Muslim emigrants from Makkah.
[34] The meaning here is: if they turn on you with aggression; see *(Qur'an 4: 91)*.
[35] Ibn Ḥajar al-'Asqalāni, *Tahdhīb at-Tahdhīb*, 2:232.
[36] Ibn Ḥajar al-'Asqalāni, *al-Iṣābah*, 6:257.
[37] Ibn Ḥibbān, *ath-Thiqāt*, 5:382.

[38] His version is not included in diagram 12 because it has an interrupted chain of transmission beyond Ibn Is-ḥāq.
[39] Abu Is-ḥāq ʻAmr ibn ʻAbdullāh as-Sabīʻi was Kufan, according to Ibn Ḥajar al-ʻAsqalāni, *Tahdhīb at-Tahdhīb*, 8:63-67 and adh-Dhahabi, *Tadhkirat al-Ḥuffāẓ*, 1:114-116.
[40] Bukhari, *Ṣaḥīḥ al-Bukhāri*, 3:1336 (3452).
[41] Ibn Abi Ḥātim ar-Rāzi, *Tafsīr Ibn Abi Ḥātim*, 6:1798.
[42] Ibn Ḥibbān, *Ṣaḥīḥ Ibn Ḥibbān*, 15:288.
[43] Abu Nuʻaym, *Dalā'il*, 1:272.
[44] al-Bayhaqi, *Dalā'il an-Nubuwwah*, 2:347.
[45] al-Bayhaqi, *Dalā'il an-Nubuwwah*, 2:46.
[46] Ibn Abi Shaybah, *Muṣannaf*, 7:343.
[47] Abu Yaʻlā, *Musnad*, 1:107.
[48] Aḥmad ibn Ḥanbal, *al-Musnad*, 1:2.
[49] Bukhari, *Ṣaḥīḥ al-Bukhāri*, 3:1323 (3419).
[50] al-Bayhaqi, *Dalā'il an-Nubuwwah*, 2:347.
[51] Muslim, *Ṣaḥīḥ Muslim*, 4:3209 (2009).
[52] Bukhari, *Ṣaḥīḥ al-Bukhāri*, 5:2127 (5284).
[53] ar-Rūyāni, *Musnad*, 1:211.
[54] Muslim, *Ṣaḥīḥ Muslim*, 3:1592 (2009).
[55] Abu Yaʻlā, *Musnad*, 1:106.
[56] Abu Bakr al-Marwazi, *Musnad Abi Bakr*, 1:91.
[57] Aḥmad ibn Ḥanbal, *al-Musnad*, 4:280 (8133).
[58] ar-Rūyāni, *Musnad*, 1:231.
[59] Abu Bakr al-Marwazi, *Musnad Abi Bakr*, 1:78.
[60] al-Lūwayn, *Juz'*, 1:2.
[61] The mosque in Makkah was beloved to the Prophet (ﷺ), and he hoped to receive a revelation instructing him to make it his prayer direction.

Bibliography

Abbott, Nabia. "An Arabic Papyrus in the Oriental Institute: Stories of the Prophets." *Journal of Near Eastern Studies* 5 (1946): 169-80.

______. *Hadith Literature-II: Collection and Transmission of Hadith, Cambridge History of Arabic Literature I.* Cambridge, 1983: 289-98.

______. *Studies in Arabic Literary Papyri, vol. 1: Historical Texts.* Chicago: Chicago University Press, 1957.

______. *Studies in Arabic Literary Papyri, vol. 2: Qur'anic Commentary and Tradition.* Chicago: University of Chicago Press, 1967.

'Abd Ibn Ḥumayd ibn Naṣr, Abu Muhammad. *Musnad 'Abd Ibn Ḥumayd.* Edited by Ṣubḥi al-Badri as-Sāmarrā'i and Maḥmūd Khalīl aṣ-Ṣa'īdi. Cairo: Maktabat as-Sunnah, 1988.

Abdel Haleem, M. A. S. *The Qur'an.* Oxford, UK: Oxford University Press.

'Abdul-Malik, Muhammad Baqshīsh. *Kitāb al-Maghāzi lī Mūsā ibn 'Uqbah.* Agadir, 1994.

Abu 'Awānah, Ya'qūb ibn Is-ḥāq al-Isfrā'īni. *Musnad Abu 'Awānah,* 5 vols. Beirut: Dār al-Ma'rifah.

______. *Mustakhraj.*

Abu Awfā, Yaḥyā ibn Muhammad ibn Ṣā'id Abu Muhammad. *Musnad Ibn Abi Awfā.* Edited by Sa'd ibn 'Abdullāh Āl al-Ḥumayd. Riyadh, 1408.

Abu Bakr al-Marwazi, Aḥmad ibn 'Ali ibn Sa'īd al-Umawi. *Musnad Abi Bakr.* Edited by Shu'ayb al-Arnā'*ūṭ*. Beirut: al-Maktab al-Islāmi.

Abu Dāwūd, Sulaymān ibn al-Ash'ath as-Sijistāni al-Azdi. *Al-Marāsīl.* Edited by Shu'ayb al-Arnā'ūṭ. Beirut: ar-Risālah, 1408 AH.

______. *Sunan Abi Dāwūd,* 4 vols. Edited by Muhammad Muḥyi ad-Dīn 'Abdul-Ḥamīd. Beirut: Dār al-Fikr.

Abu Dāwūd aṭ-Ṭayālisi, Sulaymān ibn Dāwūd al-Fārisi al-Baṣri. *Musnad Abi Dāwūd.* Beirut: Dār al-Ma'rifah.

Abu Nu'aym, Aḥmad ibn 'Abdullāh ibn Aḥmad ibn Is-ḥāq ibn Mūsā ibn Mahrān al-Aṣbahāni. *Dalā'il.*

______. *Ḥilyat al-Awliyā'*, 10 vols. Beirut: Dār al-Kitāb al-'Arabi, 1405 AH.

______. *Kitāb aḍ-Ḍu'afā'.* Edited by Fārūq Ḥamadah. Dār ath-Thaqāfah; ad-Dār al-Bayḍā', 1984.

______. *Ma'rifat aṣ-Ṣaḥābah.* Edited by 'Ādil Yūsuf al-'Azzāzi. Riyadh: Dār al-Waṭan, 1419 AH.

______. *Musnad Abi Ḥanīfah.* Edited by Nadhr Muhammad al-Fāryābi. Riyadh: Maktabat al-Kawthar, 1415 AH.

______. *Al-Musnad al-Mustakhraj 'alā Ṣaḥīḥ Muslim,* 4 vols. Edited by Muhammad Ḥasan Muhammad Ḥasan Ibrāhīm ash-Shāfi'i. Beirut: Dār al-Kutub al-'Ilmiyah, 1417 AH.

______. *Tārīkh Aṣbahān.* Edited by Sayyid Kasrawi Ḥasan. Beirut: Dār al-Kutub al-'Ilmiyah, 1990.

Abu Ya'lā, Aḥmad ibn 'Ali ibn al-Muthanna al-Mūṣili at-Tamīmi. *Al-Mafārīd.* Edited by 'Abdullāh Yūsuf al-Juday'. Kuwait: Maktabah Dār al-Aqṣā, 1405 AH.

______. *Mu'jam Abi Ya'lā.* Edited by Irshād al-Ḥaqq al-Athari. Faisalabad: Idārat al-'Ulūm al-Athariyah, 1407 AH.

______. *Musnad Abi Ya'lā,* 13 vols. Edited by Ḥusayn Salīm Asad. Damascus: Dār al-Ma'mūn, 1984.

Abu Yūsuf, Ya'qūb ibn Ibrāhīm al-Anṣāri. *Kitāb al-Āthār.* Edited by Abul-Wafā. Beirut: Dār al-Kutub al-'Ilmiyah, 1355 AH.

al-'Adani, Muhammad ibn Yaḥyā ibn Abi 'Āmir. *Al-Īmān.* Edited by Ḥamad ibn Ḥamdi ibn Ḥamdi al-Jābiril. Kuwait: ad-Dār as-Salafiyah, 1987.

Aḥmad ibn Ḥanbal, Abu 'Abdullāh ash-Shaybāni. *Al-Asāmi wal-Kunā.* Edited by 'Abdullāh Yūsuf al-Juday'. Kuwait: Maktabah Dār al-Aqṣā, 1985.

______. *Faḍā'il aṣ-Ṣaḥābah,* 2 vols. Edited by Waṣiyatullāh ibn Muhammad 'Abbās. Beirut: Mu'sasat ar-Risālah, 1983.

______. *Al-'Ilal wa Ma'rifat ar-Rijāl.* Edited by Waṣiyatullāh ibn Muhammad 'Abbās. 3 vols. Beirut: al-Maktab al-Islāmi, 1988.

______. *Al-Musnad,* 6 vols. Egypt: Mu'sasah Qurṭubah.

______. *Ar-Radd 'alā az-Zanādiqah wal-Jahmiyah.* Edited by Muhammad Ḥasan Rāshid. Cairo: al-Maṭba'at as-Salafiyah, 1393 AH.

______. *Uṣūl as-Sunnah*. Saudi Arabia: Dār al-Manār.

______. *Az-Zuhd*. Edited by 'Abdul-'Ali 'Abdul-Ḥamīd Ḥāmid. Cairo: Dār ar-Rayyān, 1408 AH.

al-'Ajlūni, Ismā'īl ibn Muhammad al-Jaraḥi. *Kashf al-Khafā'*, 2 vols. Edited by Aḥmad al-Qallāsh. Beirut: Mu'sasat ar-Risālah, 1405 AH.

al-*Ājurri*, Muhammad ibn al-Ḥusayn ibn 'Abdullāh al-Baghdādi. *Ash-Sharī'ah*. Edited by Muhammad Ḥāmid al-Fiqqi. Cairo: Maktabat Anṣār as-Sunnah al-Muḥammadiyah, 1950.

Ahlwardt. *A Catalogue of the Bibliotheca Orientalis Sprengeriana*. Giessen, 1857.

al-Albāni, Muhammad Nāṣir ad-Dīn. *Ḍa'īf at-Targhīb wat-Tarhīb,* 2 vols. Riyadh: Maktabat al-Ma'ārif.

______. *Irwā' al-Ghalīl fī Takhrīj Aḥādīth Manār as-Sabīl,* 9 vols. Beirut: al-Maktab al-Islāmi, 1985.

______. *Ṣaḥīḥ at-Targhīb wat-Tarhīb,* 3 vols. Riyadh: Maktabat al-Ma'ārif.

______. *Ṣaḥīḥ wa Ḍa'īf al-Jāmi' aṣ-Ṣaghīr wa Ziyādatih*. Beirut: al-Maktab al-Islāmi.

______. *As-Silsilat aḍ-Ḍa'īfah,* 11 vols. Riyadh: Maktabat al-Ma'ārif.

______. *As-Silsilat aṣ-Ṣaḥīḥah,* 7 vols. Riyadh: Maktabat al-Ma'ārif.

______. *Ẓilāl al-Jannah fī Takhrīj as-Sunnah lī Ibn Abi 'Āṣim*. Beirut: al-Maktab al-Islāmi, 1985.

Ansari, Zafar Ishaq. "The Authenticity of Traditions: a Critique of Joseph Schacht's Argument *E Silentio*", *Hamdard Islamicus* 7, 2 (1984): 51-61.

al-Arzaqi, Abul-Walīd Muhammad ibn 'Abdullāh ibn Aḥmad. *Akhbār Makkah,* 2 vols. Edited by Rushdi aṣ-Ṣāliḥ Maḥlas. Beirut: Dār al-Andalus, 1999.

Aslam ibn Sahl ar-Razaz al-Wāṣiṭi. *Tārīkh Wāṣiṭ*. Edited by Kūkays 'Awwād. Beirut: 'Ālam al-Kutub, 1406 AH.

Azami, Muhammad Mustafa. *On Schacht's Origins of Muhammadan Jurisprudence*. Oxford, 1996.

______. *Studies in Early Hadith Literature,* 2nd ed. Indianapolis, 1978.

al-Bābāni, Ismā'īl ibn Muhammad Amīn Bashā al-Baghdādi. *Hadiyat al-'Ārifīn ilā Asmā' al-Mu'alifīn wa Āthār al-Muṣanifīn*. Istanbul, 1951.

Badr ad-Dīn al-'Ayni, Maḥmūd ibn Aḥmad. *'Umdat al-Qāri*. Beirut: Dār Iḥyā' at-Turāth al-'Arabi.

al-Baghawi, 'Abdullāh ibn Muhammad ibn 'Abdul-'Azīz ibn al-Marzibān Abul-Qāsim. *Musnad Usāmah*. Edited by Ḥasan Amīn ibn al-Mandūh. Riyadh: Dār aḍ-Ḍiyā', 1409 AH.

al-Bayhaqi, Abu Bakr Aḥmad ibn al-Ḥusayn ibn 'Ali ibn 'Abdullāh ibn Mūsā. *Dalā'il an-Nubuwwah*. Edited by 'Abdul-Mu'ṭi Amīn Qal'aji. Cairo: Dār ar-Rayyān lit-Turāth, 1408 AH.

______. *Faḍā'il al-Awqāt*. Edited by 'Adnān 'Abdur-Raḥmān Majīd al-Qaysi. Makkah: Maktabat al-Manārah, 1410 AH.

______. *Ithbāt 'Adhāb al-Qabr.* Edited by Sharaf Maḥmūd al-Quḍāh. Amman: Dār al-Furqān, 1405 AH.

______. *Al-I'tiqād*. Edited by Aḥmad 'Iṣām al-Kātib. Beirut: Dār al-Āfāq al-Jadīdah, 1401 AH.

______. *Al-Jihād*. Edited by Musā'id ibn Sulaymān ar-Rāshid al-Jumayd. Madinah: Maktabat al-'Ulūm wal-Ḥikam, 1409 AH.

______. *Kitāb az-Zuhd al-Kabīr.* Edited by 'Āmir Aḥmad Ḥaydar. Beirut: Mu'sasat al-Kitāb, 1996.

______. *Shu'ab al-Īmān,* 7 vols. Edited by Muhammad as-Sa'īd Basyūni Zaghlūl. Beirut: Dār al-Kutub al-'Ilmiyah, 1410 AH.

______. *Sunan al-Bayhaqi*, 10 vols. Edited by Muhammad 'Abdul-Qādir 'Aṭā. Makkah: Maktabah Dār al-Bāz, 1994.

______. *As-Sunan al-Kubrā.*

______. *As-Sunan aṣ-Ṣughrā*. Edited by Muhammad Ḍiyā' ar-Raḥmān al-A'ẓami. Madinah: Maktabat ad-Dār, 1989.

______. *Az-Zuhd.* Edited by 'Abdul-'Ali 'Abdul-Ḥakīm Ḥāmid. Cairo: Dār ar-Rayyān lit-Turāth, 1408 AH.

al-Bazzār, Abu Bakr Aḥmad ibn 'Amr ibn 'Abdul-Khāliq. *Musnad al-Bazzār,* 10 vols. Edited by Maḥfūẓ ar-Raḥmān Zaynullāh. Beirut and Madinah: Mu'sasat 'Ulūm al-Qur'ān, 1409 AH.

Becker, Heinrich. *Islamstudien vom Werden und Wessen der islamischen Welt*, vol. i. Leipzig, 1924-32.

Bell, Richard. *The Origin of Islam in its Christian Environment*. London, 1926.

Blachère, Regis. *La Problème de Mahomet*. Paris: Presses Universitaires de France, 1952.

Brockelmann, Carl. *Gesschichte der Arabischen Literatur*, 2 vols. 2nd edition. Leiden, 1943-1949; 3 supplementary vols. Leiden, 1937-42.

Bukhari, Muhammad ibn Ismā'īl Abu 'Abdullāh al-Ja'fi. *Al-Adab al-Mufrad*. Edited by Muhammad Fu'ād 'Abdul-Bāqi. Beirut: Dār al-Bashā'ir al-Islāmiyah, 1998.

______. *Aḍ-Ḍu'afā' aṣ-Ṣaghīr.* Edited by Maḥmūd Ibrāhīm Zāyid. Aleppo: Dār al-Wa'i, 1396 AH.

______. *Al-Jāmi' aṣ-Ṣaḥīḥ*.

______. *Khalq Af'āl al-'Ibād*. Edited by 'Abdur-Raḥmān 'Amīrah. Riyadh: Dār al-Ma'ārif, 1978.

______. *Al-Kunā*, 8 vols. Edited by as-Sayyid Hāshim an-Nadawi. Beirut: Dār al-Fikr.

______. *Ṣaḥīḥ al-Bukhāri,* 6 vols. Edited by Muṣṭafā Dīb al-Bughā. Beirut: Dār Ibn Kathīr and al-Yamāmah, 1987.

______. *Sahih al-Bukhari*, 9 vols. Translated by Muhammad Muhsin Khan. Alexandria, VA: Al-Saadawi Publications, 1996.

______. *At-Tārīkh al-Awsaṭ*, 2 vols. Edited by Maḥmūd Ibrāhīm Zāyid. Aleppo: Dār al-Wa'i, 1977.

______. *At-Tārīkh al-Kabīr*, 8 vols. Edited by as-Sayyid Hāshim an-Nadawi. Beirut: Dār al-Fikr.

Burton, John. *An Introduction to the Hadith*. Edinburgh, 1992.

Caetani, L. *Annali dell' Islam*. Milan, 1905.

Chabbi, J. "Historie et Tradition Sacrée—la biographie impossible de Mahomet." *Arabica* 43 (1996): 189-205.

Cook, Michael. *Early Muslim Dogma: A Source Critical Study*. Cambridge: Cambridge University Press, 1981.

______. *Muhammad.* Oxford, 1983.

Cook, Michael and Patricia Crone. *Hagarism, The Making of the Islamic World.* Cambridge, 1980.

Coulson, N. J. *A History of Islamic Law*. Edinburgh, 1964.

Crone, Patricia. *Meccan Trade and the Rise of Islam*. Princeton, 1987.

______. *Slaves on Horses, the Evolution of Islamic Polity*. Cambridge: Cambridge University Press, 1980.

ad-Dāraquṭni, 'Ali ibn 'Umar Abul-Ḥasan. *Sunan ad-Dāraquṭni,* 4 vols. Edited by as-Sayyid 'Abdullāh Hāshim Yamāni al-Madani. Beirut: Dār al-Ma'rifah, 1966.

ad-Dārimi, 'Abdullāh ibn 'Abdur-Raḥmān Abu Muhammad. *Sunan ad-Dārimi.* Edited by Fawwāz Aḥmad Zumurli and Khālid as-Sab' al-'Alamami. Beirut: Dār al-Kitāb al-'Arabi.

ad-Dawlābi, Abu Bishr Muhammad ibn Aḥmad ibn Ḥammād. *Adh-Dhuriyyah aṭ-Ṭāhirah.* Edited by Sa'd al-Mubārāk al-Ḥasan. Kuwait: ad-Dār as-Salafiyah, 1407 AH.

ad-Dawraqi, Aḥmad ibn Ibrāhīm ibn Kathīr Abu 'Abdullāh. *Musnad Sa'd.* Edited by 'Āmir Ḥasan Ṣabri. Beirut: Dār al-Bashā'ir, 1407 AH.

adh-Dhahabi, Abu 'Abdullāh Muhammad ibn Aḥmad ibn 'Uthmān. *Al-'Ibar fī Khabar min Ghabar.* Beirut: Dār al-Kutub al-'Ilmiyah, 1985.

______. *Mīzān al-I'itidāl fī Naqd ar-Rijāl.* Edited by 'Ali Muhammad 'Awaḍ and 'Ādil Aḥmad 'Abdul-Mawjūd. Beirut: Dār al-Kutub al-'Ilmiyah, 1995.

______. *Ar-Ruwat ath-Thiqāt al-Mutakallim fī him bi mā lā Yujib Raddahum.* Edited by Muhammad Ibrāhīm al-Mūṣili. Beirut: Dār al-Bashā'ir al-Islāmiyah, 1412 AH.

______. *Sayr A'lām an-Nubalā',* 23 vols. Edited by Shu'ayb al-Arnā'ūṭ, et al. Beirut: ar-Risālah, 1413 AH.

______. *Tadhkirat al-Ḥuffāẓ*, 4 vols. Beirut: Dār al-Kutub al-'Ilmiyah; Hyderabad, 1330 AH.

al-Fākihi, Muhammad ibn Is-ḥāq ibn al-'Abbās. *Akhbār Makkah*, 2 vols. Edited by 'Abdul-Malik 'Abdullāh Duhaysh. Beirut: Dār Khiḍr, 1414 AH.

Fares, Said. *The Collection of the Qur'ān: A Reconsideration of the Twentieth Century Orientalists' View*, unpublished MA thesis. Leiden, 1999.

al-Fasawi, Abu Yūsuf Ya'qūb ibn Sufyān. *Al-Ma'rifah wat-Tārikh,* 3 vols. Edited by Khalīl al-Manṣūr. Beirut: Dār al-Kutub al-'Ilmiyah, 1999.

Fierro, Maribel. "Review of Motzki's Die Anfänge der Islamischen Jurisprudenz." *Al-Qantara* 13 (1992): 604-6.

al-Firyābi, Ja'far ibn Muhammad ibn al-Ḥasan Abu Bakr. *Dalā'il an-Nubuwwah.* Edited by 'Āmir Ḥasan Ṣabri. Makkah: Dār Ḥirā, 1406 AH.

______. *Al-Qadar.* Edited by 'Abdullāh ibn Ḥamad al-Manṣūr. Riyadh: Aḍwā' as-Salaf.

Fleischhammer, Manfred. *Quellenuntersuchungen zum Kitāb al-Agāni.* Habilitationschrift, not published. Halle/Saale, 1965.

Fua, Albert. *La vie et la Morale de Mahomet*. Paris, 1905.

Fück, Johann W. "Die Rolle des Traditionalismus im Islam." *Zeitschrift der Deutschen Morgenländischen Geselschaft* 39 (1939).

______. "Review of Joseph Schacht's Origins of Muhammadan Jurisprudence." *Bibliotheca Orientalis* (1953): 196-9.

______. "The Role of Traditionalism in Islam", translated by Marlin L. Swartz in his (ed.) *Studies on Islam*. New York, 1981.

al-Ghazāli, Muhammad. *Fiqh as-Sīrah.* Edited by Naṣir ad-Dīn al-Albāni. Damascus: Dār al-Qalam.

Gilliot, Glaude. "Review of Motzki's Die Anfänge der Islamischen Jurisprudenz." *Journal of Economic and Social History of the Orient* 37: 75-80.

Gimaret, Daniel. "Review of Motzki's Die Anfänge der Islamischen Jurisprudenz." *Bulletin Critique des Annales Islamologioques* 10 (1993): 40-3.

Goldziher, Ignác. *Muhammedanische Studien*. Halle, 1889-90.

______. *Muslim Studies.* Translated by Samuel Stern. London, 1967.

______. *Introduction to Islamic Theology and Law.* Translated by Andrew and Ruth Hamori. Princeton, 1981.

______. *Vorlesungen über den Islam*. Heidelberg, 1910.

Görke, A. "The Historical Tradition about al-Hudaybiya. A Study of 'Urwa b. az-Zubayr's Account." In *The Biography of Muhammad: The Issue of the Sources*, edited by Harald Motzki, 240-275. Leiden: Brill, 2000.

Guillaume, Alfred. "Review of Joseph Schacht's Origins of Muhammadan Jurisprudence." *BSOAS* (1954).

Günther, Sebastian. "Due Results in the Theory of Source-Criticism in Medieval Arabic Literature." *Al-Abhath* 41 (1994).

______. *Quellenuntesuchungen zu den Maqātil aṭ-Ṭālibiyyîn des Abû 'l Farağ al-Iṣfahānî (gest. 356/967). Ein Beitrag zur mündlichen und schriflichen Überliefrung in der mittelalterlichen Arabischen Literatur*. Zürich: Hidlescheim, New York, 1991.

al-Ḥākim an-Naysābūri, Muhammad ibn 'Abdullāh Abu 'Abdullāh. *Al-Mustadrak 'alā aṣ-Ṣaḥīḥayn*, 4 vols. Edited by Muṣṭafā 'Abdul-Qādir 'Aṭā. Beirut: Dār al-Kutub al-'Ilmiyah, 1990.

Hallaq, Wael. "Was al-Shāfii the Master Architect of Islamic Jurisprudence." *JMES* 25 (1993): 75-90.

Hamidullah, Muhammad. "History of the Early Hadith Compilation." In *Sahifah Hammam Ibn Munabbih*, 10th ed. Luton, 1979.

______. "Muhammad Ibn Ishaq, the Biographer of the Holy Prophet." *Journal of the Pakistan Historical Society*, vol. xv, part ii (April 1967): 91.

al-Ḥārith. *Bughyah.*

Hawting, G. R. "Review of Motzki's Die Anfänge der Islamischen Jurisprudenz." *BSOAS* 59 (1996): 141-3.

al-Haythami, 'Ali ibn Abi Bakr Abu Bakr al-Ḥasan. *Majma' az-Zawā'id,* 10 vols. Dār ar-Rayyān lit-Turāth. Cairo, 1407 AH.

______. *Mawārid aẓ-Ẓam'ān.* Edited by Muhammad 'Abdur-Rāziq Ḥamzah. Beirut: Dār al-Kutub al-'Ilmiyah.

Hinds, Martin. "Maghāzi." In *Encyclopedia of Islam*, new edition, v. Leiden: Brill, 1986, 1161-1164.

______. "Maghāzi and Sira", in *La vie du Prophète Mahomet: colloque de Strasbourg,* October 1980. Paris: Presses Universitaries des France, 1983, 57-66.

Horovitz, J. "Salmān al-Fārisi." *Der Islam* 12 (1922): 178-80.

Horst, H. "Zur Überlieferung in Korankommentar at-Tabari." *ZDMG* 103 (1953): 290-306.

al-Ḥumawi, Yāqūt. *Mu'jam al-Buldān.* Beirut: Dār Beirut liṭ-Ṭibā'ah wan-Nashr, 1988.

al-Ḥumaydi, 'Abdullāh ibn az-Zubayr Abu Bakr. *Musnad al-Ḥumaydi*, 2 vols. Edited by Ḥabīb ar-Raḥmān al-A'ẓami. Beirut and Cairo: Dār al-Kutub al-'Ilmiyah.

Hunwick, J. O. "Ta'rikh." In *Encyclopedia of Islam,* new edition, x. Leiden: Brill, 2000: 271.

Ibn 'Abdul-Barr, Abu 'Umar Yūsuf ibn 'Abdullāh ibn 'Abdul-Barr an-Namiri al-Qurṭubi. *Al-Istī'āb*, 4 vols. Edited by 'Ali Muhammad al-Bajāwi. Beirut: Dār al-Jīl, 1412 AH.

______. *Al-Istidhkār.* Edited by Sālim Muhammad 'Aṭā and Muhammad 'Ali Mu'awwaḍ. Beirut: Dār al-Kutub al-'Ilmiyah, 2000.

Ibn Abi 'Āṣim, 'Amr ibn aḍ-Ḍaḥḥāk ash-Shaybāni. *Al-Āḥād wal-Mathāni,* 6 vols. Edited by Bāsim Fayṣal Aḥmad al-Jawābirah. Riyadh: Dār ar-Rāyah, 1991.

______. *Al-Awā'il*. Edited by Muhammad Nāṣir al-'Ajami. Kuwait: Dār al-Khulafā'.

______. *As-Sunnah,* 2 vols. Edited by Muhammad Naṣir ad-Dīn al-Albāni. Beirut: al-Maktab al-Islāmi, 1400 AH.

Ibn Abi Ḥātim ar-Rāzi, 'Abdur-Raḥmān ibn Muhammad ibn Idrīs. *Al-Jarḥ wat-Ta'dīl*, 9 vols. Beirut: Dār Iḥyā' at-Turāth, 1952.

______. *Al-Marāsīl.* Edited by Shukrullāh ibn Ni'matullāh. Beirut: Mu'sasat ar-Risālah, 1379.

______. *Tafsīr Ibn Abi Ḥātim.* Edited by As'ad Muhammad aṭ-Ṭayyib. Saydā: al-Maktabat al-'Aṣriyah.

Ibn Abi Shaybah, Abu Bakr 'Abdullāh ibn Muhammad. *Kitāb al-Īmān*. Edited by Muhammad Riḍā Qahwaji. Beirut: Dār al-Bashā'ir al-Islāmiyah, 1999.

______. *Kitāb al-Īmān.* Edited by Nāsir ad-Dīn al-Albāni. Beirut: al-Maktab al-Islāmi, 1982.

______. *Kitāb al-Muṣannaf fil-Aḥādīth wal-Āthār*, 15 vols. Edited by 'Abdul-Khāliq al-Afghāni, et al. Bombay, 1979-83.

______. *Kitāb al-Muṣannaf fil-Aḥādīth wal-Āthār*. Edited by 'Abdul-Khāliq al-Afghāni. Hyderabad, 1966.

______. *Kitāb al-Muṣannaf fil-Aḥādīth wal-Āthār*. Edited by Mukhtār Aḥmad an-Nadawi. Bombay: ad-Dār as-Salafiyah, 1979-1983.

______. *Al-Kitāb al-Muṣannaf, al-Qism al-Awwal min al-Juz' ar-Rābi'*. Edited by 'Umar ibn Gharāmah al-'Amrawi, 1988.

______. *Muṣannaf.* Edited by Kamāl Yūsuf al-Ḥūt. Beirut: Mu'sasat al-Kutub ath-Thaqāfiyah, 1985.

______. *Muṣannaf.* Edited by Muhammad 'Abdus-Salām Shāhīn. Beirut: Dār al-Kutub al-'Ilmiyah, 1995.

______. *Al-Musnad.* Edited by 'Ādil 'Azzāzi and Aḥmad Farīd al-Muzaydi. Riyadh: Dār al-Waṭan, 1988.

Ibn Abi Usāmah, al-Ḥārith and al-Ḥāfiẓ Nūr ad-Dīn al-Haythami. *Musnad al-Ḥārith bi Zawā'id al-Haythami,* 2 vols. Edited by Ḥusayn Aḥmad Ṣāliḥ al-Bākiri. Madinah: Markaz Khidmat as-Sunnah, 1410 AH.

Ibn al-'Arābi. *Mu'jam.*

Ibn 'Asākir, Abul-Qāsim 'Ali ibn al-Ḥasan ibn Ḥibatullāh ibn 'Abdullāh ash-Shāfi'i. *Tārīkh Madīnah Dimashq*, 70 vols. Edited by Muḥib ad-Dīn Abu Sa'īd 'Umar ibn Gharāmah al-'Umari. Beirut: Dār al-Fikr, 1995.

Ibn al-Athīr, Abul-Ḥasan 'Ali ibn Muhammad ibn 'Abdul-Karīm ash-Shaybāni. *Al-Kāmil fit-Tārīkh*. Beirut: Dār Ṣādir.

Ibn Ḥabīb, ar-Rabī'. *Musnad ar-Rabī'*. Edited by Muhammad Irdīs and 'Āshūr ibn Yūsuf. Beirut: Dār al-Ḥikmah, 1415 AH.

Ibn Ḥajar al-'Asqalāni, Aḥmad ibn 'Ali. *Ad-Dirāyah fī Takhrīj Aḥādīth al-Hidāyah,* 2 vols. Edited by as-Sayyid 'Abdullāh Hāshim al-Yamāni al-Madani. Beirut: Dār al-Ma'rifah.

______. *Fatḥ al-Bāri bi Sharḥ Ṣaḥīḥ al-Bukhāri,* 14 vols. Edited by Muḥib ad-Dīn al-Khaṭīb. Beirut: Dār al-Ma'rifah.

______. *Al-Iṣābah fī Tamyīz aṣ-Ṣaḥābah*, 8 vols. Edited by Muhammad 'Ali al-Bajāwi. Beirut: Dār al-Jīl, 1992.

______. *Lisān al-Mīzān,* 7 vols. Edited by Dā'irat al-Ma'ārif an-Niẓāmiyah bil-Hind. Beirut: Mu'sasat al-A'lami, 1986.

______. *Al-Maṭālib al-'Āliyah,* 10 vols. Edited by Sa'd ibn Nāṣir ibn 'Abdul-'Azīz ash-Shatri. Saudi Arabia: Dār al-'Āṣimah, 1419.

______. *Al-Mu'jam al-Mufahris / Tajrīd Asānīd al-Kutub al-Mashhūrah wal-Ajzā' al-Manthūrah*. Edited by Muhammad Shakūr Muhammad al-Ḥājj Amrīr al-Mayādīni. Beirut: ar-Risalāh, 1988.

______. *Taghlīq at-Ta'līq,* 5 vols. Edited by Sa'īd 'Abdur-Raḥmān Mūsā al-Qazqi. Beirut: al-Maktab al-Islāmi, 1405 AH.

______. *Tahdhīb at-Tahdhīb*. Beirut: Dār al-Fikr, 1984.

______. *Talkhīṣ al-Ḥabīr,* 4 vols. Edited by as-Sayyid 'Abdullāh Hāshim al-Yamāni al-Madani. Madinah, 1964.

______. *Taqrīb at-Tahdhīb*. Edited by Muhammad 'Awāmah. Syria: Dār ar-Rashīd, 1986.

Ibn Ḥazm, 'Ali ibn Aḥmad ibn Sa'īd aẓ-Ẓāhiri. *Al-Muḥalla,* 11 vols. Beirut: Dār al-Āfāq al-Jadīdah; Beirut: Dār al-Kutub al-'Ilmiyah, 1408 AH.

Ibn Ḥibbān, Muhammad ibn Ḥibbān ibn Aḥmad Abu Ḥātim at-Tamīmi al-Busti. *Al-'Ilal.*

______. *Al-Majrūḥīn*. Edited by Maḥmūd Ibrāhīm Zāyid. Aleppo: Dār al-Wa'i, 1396 AH.

______. *Ṣaḥīḥ Ibn Ḥibbān*, 18 vols. Edited by Shu'ayb al-Arnā'ūṭ. Beirut: ar-Risālah, 1993.

______. *Ath-Thiqāt*, 9 vols. Edited by as-Sayyid Sharaf ad-Dīn Aḥmad. Beirut: Dār al-Fikr, 1975.

Ibn Hishām. *Sīrah*.

Ibn al-Jarrāḥ, Wakī'. *Kitāb az-Zuhd*. Edited by 'Abdur-Raḥmān ibn 'Abdul-Jabbār al-Firywā'i. Madinah: Maktabat ad-Dār, 1404 AH.

Ibn al-Jārūd, 'Abdullāh ibn 'Ali Abu Muhammad an-Naysābūri. *Al-Muntaqā*. Edited by 'Abdullāh 'Umar al-Bārūdi. Beirut: Mu'sasat al-Kitāb, 1988.

Ibn Kathīr, Ismā'īl ibn 'Umar ad-Dimashqi Abul-Fidā'. *Tafsīr Ibn Kathīr*, 4 vols. Beirut: Dār al-Fikr, 1401 AH.

Ibn Khayr, Abu Bakr Muhammad ibn 'Umar ibn Khalīfah al-Umawi al-Ishbīli. *Fahrasat mā Rawāhu 'an Shuyūkhihi min ad-Dawāwīn al-Muṣannafah fī Ḍurūbi al-'Ilm wa-Anwā'i al-Ma'rifah*. Beirut: Dār al-Āfāq al-Jadīdah, 1979.

Ibn Khuzaymah, Muhammad ibn Is-ḥāq Abu Bakr as-Sulami an-Naysābūri. *Ṣaḥīḥ Ibn Khuzaymah,* 4 vols. Edited by Muhammad Muṣṭafā al-A'ẓami. Beirut: al-Maktab al-Islāmi, 1970.

Ibn Ma'īn. *Tārīkh*.

Ibn Mājah, Muhammad ibn Yazīd ibn 'Abdullāh al-Quzwīni. *Sunan Ibn Mājah,* 2 vols. Edited by Muhammad Fu'ād 'Abdul-Bāqi. Beirut: Dār al-Fikr.

Ibn Mandah, Muhammad ibn Is-ḥāq ibn Yaḥyā. *Kitāb al-Īmān*, 2 vols. Edited by 'Ali ibn Muhammad ibn Nāṣir al-Faqīhi. Beirut: Mu'sasat ar-Risālah, 1406 AH.

______. *Kitāb at-Tawḥīd wa Ma'rifat Asmā' Allāh 'Azza wa Jalla 'alā al-Itifāq wat-Tafarrud*. Edited by 'Ali ibn Nāṣir al-Faqīhi. Madinah: al-Jāmi'at al-Islāmiyah, 1409 AH.

Ibn Manṣūr, *Sa'īd. Sunan Sa'īd ibn Manṣūr,* 2 vols. Edited by Sa'd ibn 'Abdullāh ibn 'Abdul-'Azīz Āl Ḥumayd. Riyadh: Dār al-'Uṣaymi, 1414 AH.

Ibn al-Mubārak, 'Abdullāh ibn al-Mubārak ibn Wāḍiḥ. *Al-Jihād*. Tunisia: ad-Dār at-Tunusiyah.

______. *Musnad ibn al-Mubārak*. Edited by Ṣubḥi al-Badri as-Sāmarrā'i. Baghdad, Ministry of Waqfs.

______. *Az-Zuhd*. Edited by Ḥabīb ar-Raḥmān al-A'ẓami. Beirut: Dār al-Kutub al-'Ilmiyah.

Ibn al-Mundhir. *Al-Awsaṭ*.

Ibn an-Nadīm, Muhammad ibn Is-ḥāq Abul-Faraj. *Al-Fihrist*. Beirut: Dār al-Ma'rifah, 1978.

Ibn Rajab al-Ḥanbali. *Sharḥ 'Ilal at-Tirmidhi.* Edited by Hammām 'Abdur-Raḥīm Sa'īd. Jordon: Maktabat al-Manār, 1407 AH.

Ibn Sa'd, Muhammad ibn Sa'd ibn Munī' Abu 'Abdullāh al-Baṣri az-Zuhri. *Aṭ-Ṭabaqāt al-Kubrā: al-Juz' al-Mutamim*. Edited by Ziyād Maḥmūd Manṣūr. Madinah: Maktabat al-'Ulūm wal-Ḥikam, 1408 AH.

Ibn Shabbah, 'Umar. *Tārīkh al-Madīnah al-Munawwarah,* 4 vols. Jeddah.

Ibn as-Sunni, Aḥmad ibn Muhammad ibn Is-ḥāq ad-Dīnūri ash-Shāfi'i. *'Amal al-Yawm wal-Laylah.* Edited by Kawthar al-Barni. Jeddah and Beirut: Dār al-Qiblah lith-Thaqāfah.

Ibn 'Uqbah, Ismā'īl ibn Ibrāhīm. *Dalā'il.*

Ibn Warraq, ed. *The Quest for the Historical Muhammad*. Prometheus Books, 2000.

Ibrahim, Mahmood. "Review of Rubin's the Eye of the Beholder: the Life of Muhammad as Viewed by the Early Muslims (a Textual Analysis)." *MESAB* (2000).

Is-ḥāq ibn Rāhawayh, Is-ḥāq ibn Ibrāhīm ibn Makhlad ibn Rāhawayh al-Ḥanẓali. *Musnad Is-ḥāq ibn Rahawayh,* 5 vols. Edited by 'Abdul-Ghafūr ibn 'Abdul-Ḥaq al-Ballūshi. Madinah: Maktabat al-Īmān, 1991.

Jarrar, Maher. *Die Prophetenbiographie im Islamischen Spanien. Ein Beitrag zur Überliefrungs und Redaktionsgeschichte*. Frankfurt/Bern, 1989.

al-Jazari, Abus-Sa'adāt al-Mubārak ibn Muhammad. *An-Nīhāyah fī Gharīb al-Ḥadīth,* 5 vols. Edited by Ṭāhir Aḥmad az-Zāwi and Maḥmūd Muhammad aṭ-Ṭanāḥi. Beirut: al-Maktabat al-'Ilmiyah, 1399 AH.

Jeffery, Arthur. "The Quest of the Historical Muhammad." *Muslim World* 16 (1926): 327-48.

Johnstone, P. D. L. *Muhammad and his Power*. Edinburgh, 1901.

Juynboll, G. H. A. "Hadith." In *Encyclopedia of Islam,* first edition. Leiden/London, 1913-1936.

______. *Muslim Tradition: Studies in Chronology, Provenance and Authorship of Early Hadith.* Cambridge: Cambridge University Press, 1983.

______. "Nafi, the Mawla of Ibn Umar, and his position in Muslim Hadith literature." *Der Islam* 70, II (1993): 279-300.

______. "(Re)appraisal of Some Technical Terms in Hadith Science." *Islamic Law and Society* 8 (2001): 303-349.

______. "Review of Motzki's Die Anfänge der Islamischen Jurisprudenz." *Bibliotheca Orientalis* 49 (1992): 357-364.

______. "The Role of Mu'ammarun in the Early Development of the Isnad." *Wiener Zeitschrift fur die Kunde des Morgenlandes*, 1991.

______. "Some Isnad-Analytical Methods Illustrated on the Basis of Several Woman-Demeaning Sayings from Hadith Literature." *Al-Qantara* X (1989): 343-84.

______. "Some Notes on Earliest Fuqaha of Islam Distilled from Hadith Literature." *Arabica* 39, 3 (1992): 287-314.

al-Kanāni, Aḥmad ibn Abi Bakr ibn Ismā'īl. *Miṣbāḥ az-Zujājah,* 4 vols. Edited by Muhammad al-Muntaqi al-Kashnāwi. Beirut: Dār al-'Arabiyah, 1403 AH.

Khalīfah ibn Khayyāṭ, Abu 'Amr al-Laythi al-'Asfūri. *Aṭ-Ṭabaqāt.* Edited by Akram Ḍiyā' al-'Umari. Riyadh: Dār Ṭībah, 1982.

al-Khaṭīb, Muhammad 'Ajāj. *As-Sunnah Qabla at-Tadwīn*. Cairo, 1963.

al-Khaṭīb al-Baghdādi, Aḥmad ibn 'Ali Abu Bakr. *Īḍaḥ al-Maknūn.*

______. *Taqyīd al-'Ilm*. Dār Iḥyā' as-Sunnah.

______. *Tārīkh Baghdād*, 14 vols. Beirut: Dār al-Kutub al-'Ilmiyah.

al-Kittāni, Muhammad ibn Ja'far. *Ar-Risālat al-Mustaṭrafah.* Edited by Muhammad al-Muntaṣir. Beirut: Dār al-Bashā'ir al-Islāmiyah, 1986.

Koren, J. and Y. D. Nevo. "Methodological Approaches to Islamic Studies." *Der Islam* 68 (1991).

Kramers, Johannes H. "A Tradition of Manichaen Tendency." In *Hadith: Origin and Developments*, edited by Harald Motzki. Ashgate Variorum, 2004.

______. "Une tradition á tendance manichéenne." *Acta Orientalia* 21 (1950-53): 10-22.

al-Lalālkā'i, Ḥibatullāh ibn al-Ḥasan ibn Manṣūr Abul-Qāsim. *I'tiqād Ahl as-Sunnah,* 4 vols. Edited by Aḥmad Sa'd Ḥimdān. Riyadh: Dār Ṭībah, 1402.

Lammens, Henri. "The Age of Muhammad and the Chronology of the Sira." In *The Quest for the Historical Muhammad,* edited by Ibn Warraq, 188-217. Prometheus Books, 2000.

______. *Fatima et les filles de Mahomet*. Rome, 1912; "Fatima and the Daughters of Muhammad." In *The Quest for the Historical Muhammad,* edited by Ibn Warraq, 218-329. Prometheus Books, 2000.

______. "The Koran and Tradition, how the Life of Muhammad was Composed." In *The Quest for the Historical Muhammad,* edited by Ibn Warraq. Prometheus Books, 2000.

______. "Qoran et tradition. Comment fut Compsee la vie de Mahomet." *Recherches de Science Religieuse* I (1910): 275.

Lecker, M. "The Death of the Prophet Muhammad's Father. Did al-Waqidi invent some of the evidence?" *Zeitschrift der Deutschen Morgenländischen Geselschaft* 145 (1995): 9-27.

Leites, Adrien. "Sira and the Question of Tradition." In *The Biography of Muhammad: The Issue of the Sources*, edited by Harald Motzki. Leiden: Brill, 2000.

Lekkegaard, F. "Review of Motzki's Die Anfänge der Islamischen Jurisprudenz." *Orentalische Literaturzeitung* 87 (1992): 552-554.

Lucey, William. *History: Methods and Interpretation*. Chicago: Loyola, 1958.

al-Lūwayn. *Juz'*.

MacDonald, D. B. *The Development of Muslim Theology, Jurisprudence and Constitutional Theory*. New York, 1903.

Madelung, Wilferd. "Review of Motzki's Die Anfänge der Islamischen Jurisprudenz." *Der Islam* 74 (1997): 171-3.

Mālik ibn Anas, Abu 'Abdullāh al-Aṣbaḥi. *Al-Mudawwanah al-Kubrā,* 6 vols. Beirut: Dār Ṣādir.

______. *Al-Muwaṭṭā'*, 2 vols. Beirut: Dār Iḥyā' at-Turāth.

al-Manāwi, 'Abdur-Ra'ūf. *Al-Fatḥ as-Samāwi*. Edited by Aḥmad Mujtabā. Riyadh: Dār al-'Āṣimah.

______. *Fayḍ al-Qadīr*. Egypt: al-Maktabat at-Tujāriyah, 1356 AH.

al-Maqdisi, Abu 'Abdullāh Muhammad ibn 'Abdul-Wāḥid ibn Aḥmad al-Ḥanbali. *Al-Aḥādīth al-Mukhtārah*, 10 vols. Edited by 'Abdul-Malik ibn 'Abdullāh ibn Duhaysh. Makkah: Maktabat an-Nahḍah al-Ḥadīthah, 1410 AH.

al-Marwazi, Muhammad ibn Naṣr. *Ikhtilāf al-'Ulamā'*. Edited by Ṣubḥi as-Sāmirrā'i. Beirut: 'Ālam al-Kutub, 1406 AH.

______. *Ṣalāt al-Witr*. Edited by Muhammad Aḥmad ʻĀshūr and Jamāl ʻAbdul-Mun'im al-Kūmi. Cairo: Dār al-I'tiṣām, 1993.

______. *As-Sunnah*. Edited by Sālim Aḥmad as-Salafi. Beirut: Mu'sasat al-Kitāb, 1408 AH.

al-Mizzi, Yūsuf ibn az-Zaki 'Abdur-Raḥmān Abul-Ḥajjāj. *Tahdhīb al-Kamāl*, 35 vols. Edited by Bashshār 'Awwād Ma'rūf. Beirut: Mu'sasat ar-Risālah, 1980.

Motzki, Harald, ed. *The Biography of Muhammad: The Issue of the Sources*. Leiden: Brill, 2000.

______. "The Collection of the Qur'an. A Reconsideration of Western Views in Light of Recent Methodological Developments." *Der Islam* 78 (2001): 1-34.

______. "Dating Muslim Traditions: A Survey." *Arabica* 52, 2 (2005): 204-253.

______. *Die Anfänge der Islamischen Jurisprudenz*. Stuttgart, 1991.

______, ed. *Hadith: Origin and Developments*. Ashgate Variorum, 2004.

______. "The Murder of Ibn Abī l-Huqayq: On the Origin and Reliability of Some Maghazi Reports." In *The Biography of Muhammad: The Issue of the Sources*, edited by Harald Motzki, 170-239. Leiden: Brill, 2000.

______. "The Musannaf of 'Abd al-Razzaq Al-San'ani as a Source of Authentic Ahadith of the First Century A. H." *JNES* 50 (January 1991): 1-21.

______. "Oder Fiqh des Zahiri: Die Quellenproblematik." *Der Islam* 68 (1991): 1-44.

______. *The Origins of Islamic Jurisprudence. Makkan Fiqh before the Classical Schools*. Translated by M. H. Katz. Leiden: E. J. Brill, 2002.

______. "The Prophet and the Cat: On Dating Malik's Muwatta' and Legal Traditions." *JSAI* 22 (1988).

______. "Quo vadis, Hadit Forshung? Eine kritische Untersuchung von G. H. A. Juynboll: Nafi the Mawla of Ibn Umar and his Position in Muslim Hadith Literature." *Der Islam* 73, I (1996): 43-47.

al-Mubārakfūri, Muhammad 'Abdur-Raḥmān ibn 'Abdur-Raḥīm Abul-'Ilā. *Tuḥfat al-Aḥwadhi,* 10 vols. Beirut: Dār al-Kutub al-'Ilmiyah.

Muir, Sir William. *The Life of Mahomet*. London: Smith, Elder, & Co., 1861.

______. *The Life of Mohammad*. Edited by T. H. W. Weir. Edinburgh, 1912.

______. "Value of Early Mahometan Historical Sources." In *The Mohammedan Controversy*. Edinburgh, 1897.

al-Mundhiri, ʻAbdul-ʻAẓīm ibn ʻAbdul-Qawwi. *At-Targhīb wat-Tarhīb,* 4 vols. Edited by Ibrāhīm Shams ad-Dīn. Beirut: Dār al-Kutub al-ʻIlmiyah, 1417 AH.

Muranyi, Bonn Miklos. "Review of Motzki's Die Anfänge der Islamischen Jurisprudenz." *ZDMG* 143 (1993): 408-10.

Muslim, Abul-Ḥusayn al-Qushayri an-Naysābūri. *Al-Kunā wal-Asmā',* 2 vols. Edited by ʻAbdur-Raḥīm Muhammad Aḥmad al-Qushayri. Madinah: al-Jāmiʻat al-Islāmiyah, 1404 AH.

______. *Ṣaḥīḥ Muslim*, 5 vols. Edited by Muhammad Fu'ād ʻAbdul-Bāqi. Beirut: Dār Iḥyā' at-Turāth.

an-Nasā'i, Aḥmad ibn Shuʻayb Abu ʻAbdur-Raḥmān. *ʻAmal al-Yawm wal-Laylah.* Edited by Fārūq Ḥamādah. Beirut: ar-Risālah, 1406 AH.

______. *Aḍ-Ḍuʻafā' wal-Matrūkīn*. Edited by Maḥmūd Ibrāhīm Zāyid. Aleppo: Dār al-Waʻi, 1396 AH.

______. *Khaṣā'iṣ ʻAli*. Edited by Aḥmad Mīrīn al-Ballūshi. Kuwait: Maktabat al-Muʻallah, 1406 AH.

______. *Al-Mujtabā,* 8 vols. Edited by ʻAbdul-Fattāḥ Abu Ghuddah. Aleppo: Maktabat al-Maṭbūʻāt, 1986.

______. *As-Sunan al-Kubrā,* 6 vols. Edited by ʻAbdul-Ghaffār Sulaymān al-Bindāri and Sayyid Kasrawi Ḥasan. Beirut: Dār al-Kutub al-ʻIlmiyah, 1991.

______. *Aṭ-Ṭabaqāt*. Edited by Mashūr Ḥasan and ʻAbdul-Karīm al-Waraykāt. Jordan: Maktabat al-Manār, 1987.

an-Nawawi, Imam. *Mā Tamussu Ilayhi Ḥājat al-Qāri lī Ṣaḥīḥ Imām al-Bukhāri.* Beirut: Dār al-Kutub al-ʻIlmiyah.

Nöldeke, T. *Das Leben Muhammads nach den Quellen populär dargestelt*. Hanover, 1863.

______. "Zur tendenziösen Gestaltung der Urgeschichte der Islam's." *Zeitschrift der Deutschen Morgenländischen Geselschaft* 52 (1898): 16-33.

Paret, Rudi. *Muhammad und der Koran*. Stuttgart, 1957.

Perceval, Causin de. *Essai sur l'Historie des Arabes,* 3 vols. Paris, 1847.

Peters, F. E. "The Quest of the Historical Muhammad." *International Journal of Middle Eastern Studies* 23 (1991): 291-315.

al-Qaṭīʻi, Abu Bakr Aḥmad ibn Jaʻfar ibn Ḥimdān ibn Mālik ibn Shabīb al-Baghdādi. *Juz' al-Alf Dīnār.* Edited by Badr ibn ʻAbdullāh al-Badr. Kuwait: Dār an-Nafā'is, 1414 AH.

al-Quḍā'i, Muhammad ibn Salamah ibn Ja'far Abu 'Abdullāh. *Musnad ash-Shihāb,* 2 vols. Edited by Ḥamdi ibn 'Abdul-Majīd as-Salafi. Beirut: Mu'sasat ar-Risālah, 1986.

ar-Rahawan, Mohammad Said Mitwally. "Ḥadith Textual Criticism in Muslim and Modern Western Studies." Master's diss., al-Azhar University, 2001.

ar-Rāmahurmuzi. *Al-Muḥaddith al-Fāṣil.* Edited by Muhammad 'Ajjāj al-Khaṭīb. Beirut, 1971.

Raven, W. "*Sira.*" In *Encyclopedia of Islam*, new edition, 662-3. Leiden: Brill, 1971.

ar-Rāzi, 'Abdur-Raḥmān ibn Muhammad ibn Idrīs ibn Mahrān ar-Rāzi Abu Muhammad. *'Ilal al-Ḥadīth*. Edited by Muḥib ad-Dīn al-Khaṭīb. Beirut: Dār al-Ma'rifah, 1405 AH.

Reckendorf, Hermann. *Mohammed und die Seinen*. Leipzig, 1907.

Reiner. *Muhammad und der Islam.* Leipzig, 1905.

Rippin, Andrew. *"The Functions of Asbab an-Nuzul in Qur'anic Exegesis."* *BSOAS* 51, I (1988):1-20.

______. "Literary Analysis of Qur'an, Tafsir, and Sira: The Methodologies of John Wansbrough." In *Approaches to Islam in Religious Studies*, edited by Richard Martin. Tuscan, 1985.

Robson, J. "Hadith." In *Encyclopedia of Islam*, second edition, iii. Leiden: Brill, 1965.

______. "Muslim Tradition: The Question of Authenticity." *Memoirs and Proceedings, Manchester Literary and Philosophical Society* 93, 7 (1951-2): 84-102.

______. "Review of Schacht's Origins of Muhammadan Jurisprudence." *Muslim World* 42 (1952).

Rodinson, Maxime. *Mahomet,* Paris, 1961.

______. *Mohammad.* Translated by Anne Carter. Penguin Press, 1971.

Rubin, Uri. *The Eye of the Beholder: the Life of Muhammad as Viewed by the Early Muslims (a Textual Analysis)*. Princeton, 1995.

ar-Rūyāni. *Musnad.*

aṣ-Ṣabāḥ, Abu 'Ali al-Ḥasan ibn 'Ali. *Musnad Bilāl.* Edited by Majdi Fatḥi as-Sayyid. Egypt: Dār aṣ-Ṣaḥābah, 1989.

Sachau, Edward. "Das Berliner Fragment des Musa ibn 'Uqba." *SPAW* (1904): 445-70.

aṣ-Ṣafaḍi. *Al-Wafi.*

Salmān, Mashhūr Ḥusayn. *Aḥādīth Muntakhabah min Maghāzi Mūsā ibn 'Uqbah.* Beirut, 1991.

aṣ-Ṣan'āni, 'Abdur-Razzāq ibn Hammām. *Al-Muṣannaf,* 11 vols. Beirut, 1972 and 1983.

______. *Al-Muṣannaf fil-Aḥādīth wal-Āthār*. Edited by Ḥabīb ar-Raḥmān al-A'ẓami, 11 vols. Beirut, 1970-2.

______. *Tafsīr aṣ-Ṣan'āni*, 2 vols. Edited by Muṣṭafā Muslim Muhammad. Riyadh: Maktabat ar-Rushd, 1410 AH.

aṣ-Ṣan'āni, Ḥammām ibn Munabbih. *Ṣaḥīfat Hammām ibn Munabbih.* Edited by 'Ali Ḥasan 'Ali 'Abdul-Ḥamīd. Beirut: al-Maktab al-Islāmi, 1987.

Schacht, Joseph. *An Introduction to the Islamic Law*. London, 1964.

______. "On Musa ibn Uqba's Kitab al-Maghazi." *Acta Orientalia* (1953).

______. *The Origins of Muhammadan Jurisprudence*. Oxford: Clarendon Press, 1967.

______. "Pre-Islamic Background and Early Development of Jurisprudence" *Law in the Middle East* I (1959).

______. "Revaluation of Islamic Traditions." *JRAS* (1949): 143-54.

Schneider, Irene. "Review of Motzki's Die Anfänge der Islamischen Jurisprudenz." *JAOS* 114, 4 (1994): 684-5.

Schoeler, Gregor. *Charakter und Authentie der Muslimischen Überlieferung über das Leben Mohammeds*. Berlin, 1996.

______. "Die Frage der schriftlichen oder mündlichen Überlieferung der Wissenschaften im frühen Islam." *Der Islam* 62, 2 (1985): 201-230.

______. "Foundations for a New Biography of Muhammad: The Production and Evaluation of the Corpus of Traditions according to 'Urwah ibn az-Zubayr'." In *Method and Theory in the Study of Islamic Origins,* edited by Herbert Berg. Leiden: Brill, 2003.

______. "Mündliche Thora und Hadit. Überlieferung, Schreibverbot, Redaktion." *Der Islam* 66 (1989): 213-251.

______. "Musa ibn Uqba's Maghazi." In *The Biography of Muhammad: The Issue of the Sources*, edited by Harald Motzki, 67-97. Leiden: Brill, 2000.

______. "Schreiben und Veröffentlichen. Zu Verwendung und Funktion der Schrift in den ersten islamischen Jahrhunderten." *Der Islam* 69 (1992): 1-43.

______. "Weiteres zur Frage der schriftlichen oder mündlichen Überlieferung der Wissenschaften im Islam." *Der Islam* 66 (1989): 38-67.

______. "Writing and Publishing on the Use and Function of Writing in the First Centuries of Islam: Translated into English by C. Gilliot." *Arabica*, 44, 3, (1997).

Schützinger, H. "Ibn Abi Šaiba und sein Tari'x: Eine Untersuchung an Hand des Berlin 9409." *Oriens* 23-24 (1974): 134-46.

Sell, Edward. *The Life of Mohammed*. Madras, 1913.

Sezgin, Fuat. *Bukharinin Kaynaklarihakkinda Arştumarlar*. Istanbul, 1956.

______. *Geschichte der Arabischen Schrifttums*, vol. i. Leiden, 1967.

ash-Shāfi'i, Muhammad ibn 'Ali ibn al-Ḥasan al-Ḥusayni ad-Dimashqi. *Dhayl Tadhkirat al-Ḥuffāẓ*. Beirut: Dār al-Kutub al-'Ilmiyah.

ash-Shāfi'i, Muhammad ibn Idrīs Abu 'Abdullāh. *Ikhtilāf al-Ḥadīth*. Edited by 'Āmir Aḥmad Ḥaydar. Beirut: Mu'sasat al-Kitāb, 1985.

______. *Musnad ash-Shāfi'i*. Beirut: Dār al-Kutub al-'Ilmiyah.

______. *As-Sunan al-Ma'thūrah*. Edited by 'Abdul-Mu'ṭi Amīn Qal'aji. Beirut: Dār al-Ma'rifah, 1406 AH.

______. *Al-Umm*. Beirut: Dār al-Kutub al-'Ilmiyah, 1993.

ash-Shaybāni, Muhammad ibn al-Ḥasan. *Al-Ḥujjah*. Edited by Mahdi Ḥasan al-Kīlāni al-Qādiri. Beirut: 'Ālam al-Kutub, 1403 AH.

______. *Al-Jāmi' aṣ-Ṣaghīr*. Beirut: 'Ālam al-Kutub, 1406 AH.

______. *Al-Mabṣūṭ,* 5 vols. Edited by Abul-Wafā al-Afghāni. Karachi: Idārat al-'Ulūm wal-Qur'*ān*.

as-Sibā'i, Muṣṭafā. *As-Sunnah wa Makanatuhā fit-Tashrī' al-Islāmi*. Cairo, 1961.

Siddiqi, Muhammad Zubayr. *Hadith Literature: Its Origin, Development and Special Features*. Islamic Texts Society, 1993.

as-Sijistāni, Abu Bakr 'Abdullāh ibn Sulaymān ibn al-Ash'ath. *Musnad 'Ā'ishah*. Edited by 'Abdul-Ghafūr 'Abdul-Ḥaqq Ḥusayn. 1405 AH.

Sprenger, Aloys. *Das Leben und die Lehre des Mohammad*, 3 vols. Berlin, 1861-1865.

______. *The Life of Mohammed from Original Sources*. Allahabad Presbyterian Mission Press, 1851.

______. *Mohammed und der Koran: eine Psychologische Studie*. Hamburg, 1889.

Stauth, Georg. "Die Überlieferung des Korankommentars Muǧāhid ibn Ǧabrs." Diss., Giessen, 1969.

as-Suyūṭi, 'Abdur-Raḥmān ibn al-Kamāl Jalāl ad-Dīn. *Ad-Dībāj 'alā Muslim*, 5 vols. Edited by Abu Is-ḥāq al-Huwayni al-Athari. al-Khubur: Dār Ibn 'Affān, 1996.

______. *Ad-Durr al-Manthūr*, 8 vols. Beirut: Dār al-Fikr, 1993.

______. *Sharḥ Sunan Ibn Mājah,* 8 vols. Edited by 'Abdul-Fattāḥ Abu Ghuddah. Aleppo: Maktabat al-Maṭbū'āt, 1986.

______. *Ṭabaqāt al-Ḥuffāẓ*.

______. *Tanwīr al-Ḥawālik,* 2 vols. Egypt: al-Maktabat at-Tujāriyah, 1969.

aṭ-Ṭabarāni, Abul-Qāsim Sulaymān ibn Aḥmad ibn Ayyūb. *Al-Aḥādīth aṭ-Ṭiwāl,* 25 vols. Edited by Ḥamdi ibn 'Abdul-Majīd as-Salafi. Al-Mūṣil: Maktabat al-'Ulūm wal-Ḥikam, 1983.

______. *Al-Awā'il*. Edited by Maḥmūd Shakūr ibn Maḥmūd al-Ḥājj Amrīr. Beirut: ar-Risālah, 1403 AH.

______. *Al-Mu'jam al-Awsaṭ,* 10 vols. Edited by Ṭāriq ibn 'Awaḍullāh ibn Muhammad and 'Abdul-Muḥsin ibn Ibrāhīm al-Ḥusayni. Cairo: Dār al-Ḥaramayn, 1415 AH.

______. *Al-Mu'jam al-Kabīr*, 25 vols. Edited by Ḥamdi ibn 'Abdul-Majīd as-Salafi. Al-Mūṣil: Maktabat al-'Ulūm wal-Ḥikam, 1983.

______. *Al-Mu'jam aṣ-Ṣaghīr,* 2 vols. Edited by Muhammad Shakūr Maḥmūd al-Ḥājj Amrīr. Beirut: al-Maktab al-Islāmi, 1985.

______. *Musnad ash-Shāmiyyīn*, 4 vols. Edited by Ḥamdi ibn 'Abdul-Majīd as-Salafi. Beirut: ar-Risālah, 1984.

aṭ-Ṭabari, Muhammad ibn Jarīr ibn Yazīd ibn Khālid Abu Ja'far. *Ar-Riyāḍ an-Naḍirah,* 2 vols. Edited by 'Īsā 'Abdullāh Muhammad Māni' al-Ḥumayri. Beirut: Dār al-Maghrib al-Islāmi, 1996.

______. *Ṣarīḥ as-Sunnah*. Edited by Badr Yūsuf al-Ma'tūq. Kuwait: Dār al-Fayḥā', 1405 AH.

______. *Tafsīr aṭ-Ṭabari*, 30 vols. Beirut: Dār al-Fikr, 1405 AH.

______. *Tahdhīb al-Āthār Musnad 'Ali,* 3 vols. Edited by Maḥmūd Muhammad Shākir. Cairo: Maṭba'at al-Madani.

aṭ-Ṭaḥāwi, Aḥmad ibn Muhammad ibn Salamah ibn 'Abdul-Malik ibn Salamah Abu Ja'far. *Sharḥ Ma'āni al-Āthār,* 3 vols. Edited by Muhammad Zuhri an-Najjār. Beirut: Dār al-Kutub al-'Ilmiyah, 1339 AH.

ath-Thawri, Abu 'Abdullāh Sufyān ibn Sa'īd ibn Masrūq. *Tafsīr ath-Thawri*. Beirut: Dār al-Kutub al-'Ilmiyah, 1403 AH.

at-Tirmidhi, Muhammad ibn 'Ali ibn al-Ḥasan Abu 'Abdullāh al-Ḥakīm. *Nawādir al-Uṣūl fī Aḥādīth ar-Rasūl,* 4 vols. Edited by 'Abdur-Raḥmān 'Amīrah. Beirut: Dār al-Jīl, 1992.

at-Tirmidhi, Muhammad ibn 'Īsa Abu 'Īsa as-Sulami. *Al-'Ilal aṣ-Ṣaghīr.* Edited by Aḥmad Muhammad Shākir, et al. Beirut: *Dār Iḥyā' at-Turāth.*

______. *Ash-Shamā'il al-Muḥammadiyah*. Edited by Sayyid 'Abbās al-Jumayli. Beirut: Mu'sasat al-Kitāb, 1412 AH.

______. *Sunan at-Tirmidhi,* 5 vols. Edited by Aḥmad Muhammad Shākir, et al. Beirut: Dār Iḥyā' at-Turāth.

al-'Uqayli, Abu Ja'far Muhammad ibn 'Umar ibn Mūsā. *Ḍu'afā' al-'Uqayli,* 4 vols. Edited by 'Abdul-Mu'ṭi Amīn Qal'aji. Beirut: Dār al-Maktabat al-'Ilmiyah, 1404 AH.

Van Ess, Joseph. *Zwischen Hadith und Theologie, Studien zum Entstehn pradestinnaatianischer Überliefurung*. Berlin: Walter de Gruyter, 1975.

Vikør, Knut S. "The Truth about Cats and Dogs: the Historicity of Early Islamic Law." Paper presented at the 5th Nordic Middle East Conference, Lund, October 25-28, 2001.

al-Wādi'i, Muqbil ibn Hādi. *Aṣ-Ṣaḥīḥ al-Musnad mimmā laysa fiṣ-Ṣaḥīḥayn*. Beirut: Dār Ibn Ḥazm, 1411 AH.

Waldmann, M. R. *Toward a Theory of Historical Narrative: A Case Study in Perso-Islamicate Historiography*. Columbus: The Ohio State University Press, 1980.

Wansbrough, John. *Qur'anic Studies: Sources and Methods of Scriptural Interpretation*. Oxford, 1977.

______. *The Sectarian Milieu: Content and Composition of Islamic Salvation History*. Oxford, 1978.

Watt, William Montgomery. "The Condemnation of the Jews of Banu Qurayza." *Muslim World* XLII (1952).

______. *Muhammad at Mecca*. Oxford, 1953.

______. *Muhammad at Medina*. Oxford, 1956.

Weil, Gustav. *The Bible, the Koran and Talmud.* New York, 1863.

______. *Geschichte der Chalifen, nach handschriflichen, grössentheils noch unbenützten Quellen bearibn.* Osnabrück: Neudruck der Ausg, 1846-1862.

______. *A History of the Islamic Peoples*. Translated by S. K. Bakhsh. Darf Publishers, 1914; reprint 1986.

______. *Muhammad der Prophet, sein Leben und seine Lehre.* Kessinger Pub. Co., 1843.

______. *Muhammad: Prophet and Statesman*. London, 1961; reprint 1974.

Wellhausen, Julius. *Muhammed in Medina*. Berlin, 1882.

Wensinck, A. J. *The Muslim Creed: Its Genesis and Historical Development.* Cambridge, 1932.

Wollaston, Arthur N. *Muhammad, His Life and Doctrines.* London, 1904.

Wüstenfeld, Ferdinand. *Chariken der Stadt Mekka*. 4 vols. Leipzig 1861.

______. *Das Gebiet von Medina.* Göttingen, 1873.

______. *Das Leben Mohammeds*, 3 vols. Göttingen, 1857-1859.

______. *Das Leben Mohammeds.* 2 vols. Translated by Gustav Weil. Stuttgart, 1864.

______. *Die Geschichtsreiber der Araber und Ihre Werke.* Göttingen, 1882.

______. *Genealogische Tabellen der Arabishcen Stamme und Familien.* Göttingen, 1882.

Yūsuf ibn Mūsā, Abul-Maḥāsin al-Ḥanafi. *Mu'taṣar al-Mukhtaṣar*. Beirut: 'Ālam al-Kutub.

Zaidan, Jurji. *Tārīkh Adab al-Lughat al-'Arabiyah.* Cairo 1937.

Zaman, I. "The Science of Rijal as a Method in the Study of Hadiths." *Journal of Islamic Studies* 5 (1994).

Zaman, Muhammad Qasim. "Maghazi and the Muhadditthun: Reconsidering the treatment of historical materials in early collections of Hadith." *IJMES* 28 (1996).

az-Zurqāni, Muhammad ibn 'Abdul-Bāqi ibn Yūsuf. *Sharḥ az-Zurqāni,* 4 vols. Beirut: Dār al-Kutub al-'Ilmiyah, 1411 AH.

Appendix 1
Diagrams of isnād bundles

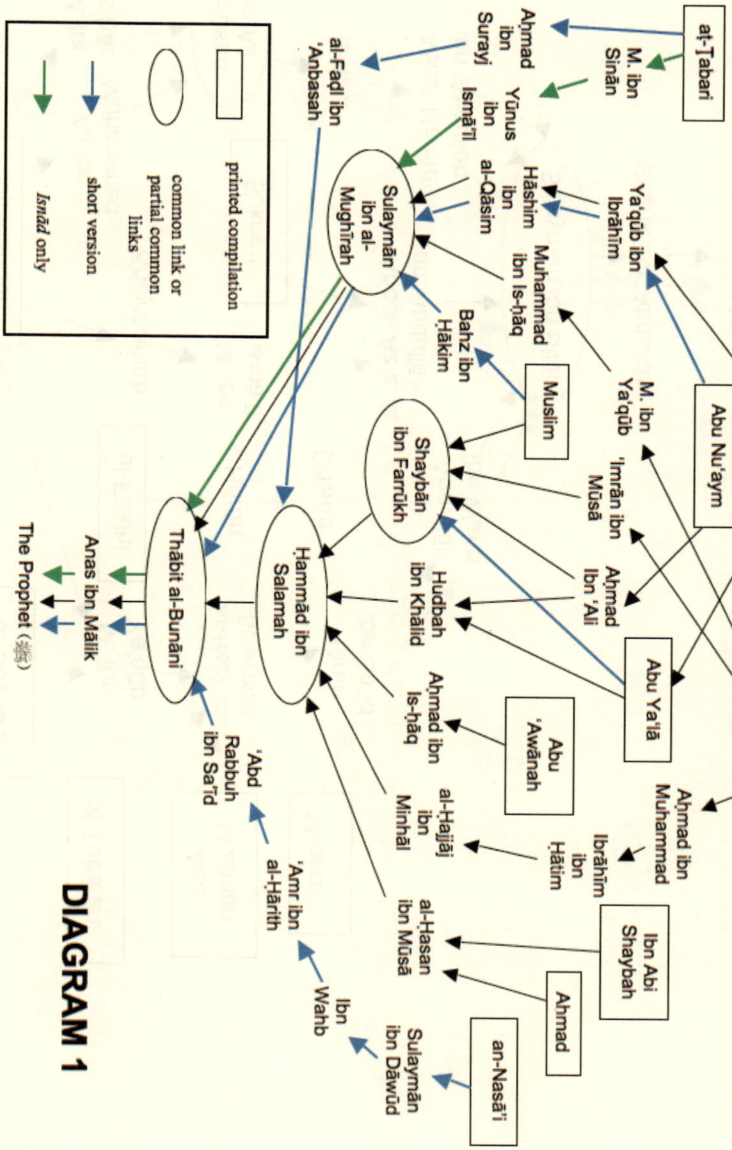

DIAGRAM 1

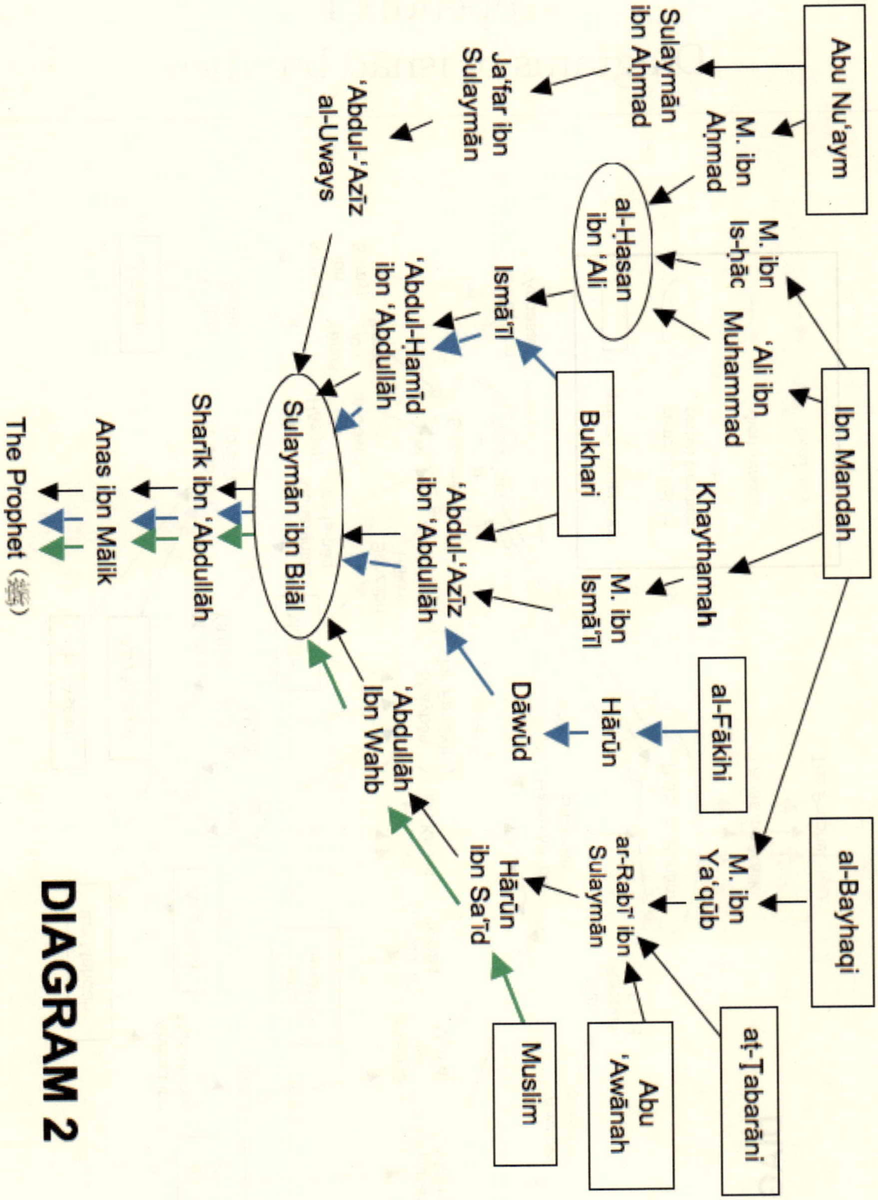
Abu Nu'aym
Ibn Mandah
al-Bayhaqi
aṭ-Ṭabarāni
Abu 'Awānah
Muslim
al-Fākihi
Bukhari
Sulaymān ibn Aḥmad
M. ibn Aḥmad
M. ibn Is-ḥāc
'Ali ibn Muhammad
Khaythamah
M. ibn Ya'qūb
ar-Rabī' ibn Sulaymān
al-Ḥasan ibn 'Ali
Ja'far ibn Sulaymān
Ismā'īl
'Abdul-'Azīz ibn 'Abdullāh
M. ibn Ismā'īl
Hārūn
Dāwūd
Hārūn ibn Sa'īd
'Abdul-'Azīz al-Uways
'Abdul-Ḥamīd ibn 'Abdullāh
'Abdullāh Ibn Wahb
Sulaymān ibn Bilāl
Sharīk ibn 'Abdullāh
Anas ibn Mālik
The Prophet (ﷺ)

DIAGRAM 2

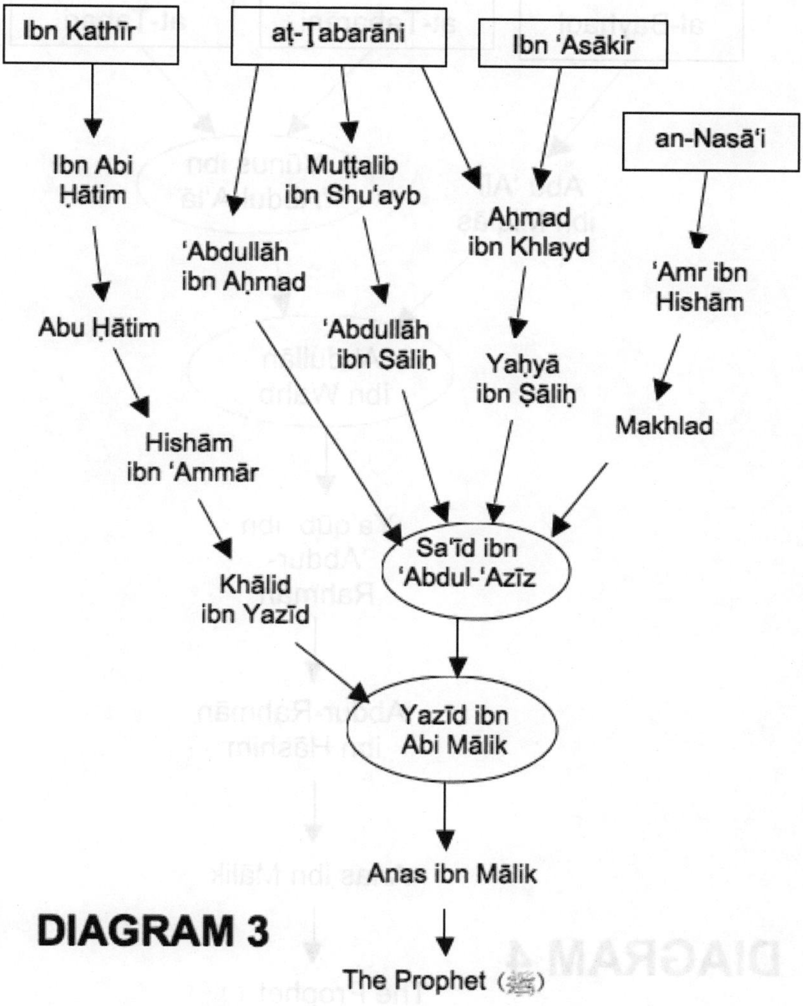
Ibn Kathīr
aṭ-Ṭabarāni
Ibn 'Asākir
an-Nasā'i
Ibn Abi Ḥātim
Muṭṭalib ibn Shu'ayb
Aḥmad ibn Khlayd
'Abdullāh ibn Aḥmad
'Amr ibn Hishām
Abu Ḥātim
'Abdullāh ibn Sālih
Yaḥyā ibn Ṣāliḥ
Makhlad
Hishām ibn 'Ammār
Sa'īd ibn 'Abdul-'Azīz
Khālid ibn Yazīd
Yazīd ibn Abi Mālik
Anas ibn Mālik
The Prophet (ﷺ)

DIAGRAM 3

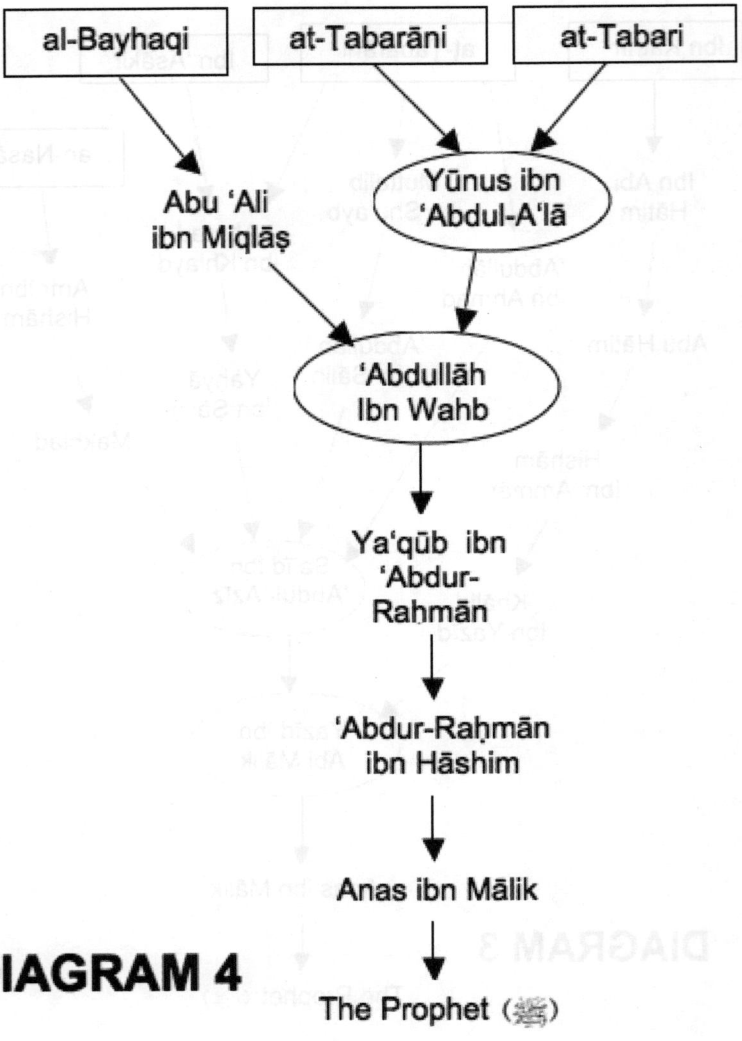
al-Bayhaqi
at-Ṭabarāni
at-Ṭabari
Abu 'Ali ibn Miqlāṣ
Yūnus ibn 'Abdul-A'lā
'Abdullāh Ibn Wahb
Ya'qūb ibn 'Abdur-Raḥmān
'Abdur-Raḥmān ibn Hāshim
Anas ibn Mālik
The Prophet (ﷺ)

DIAGRAM 4

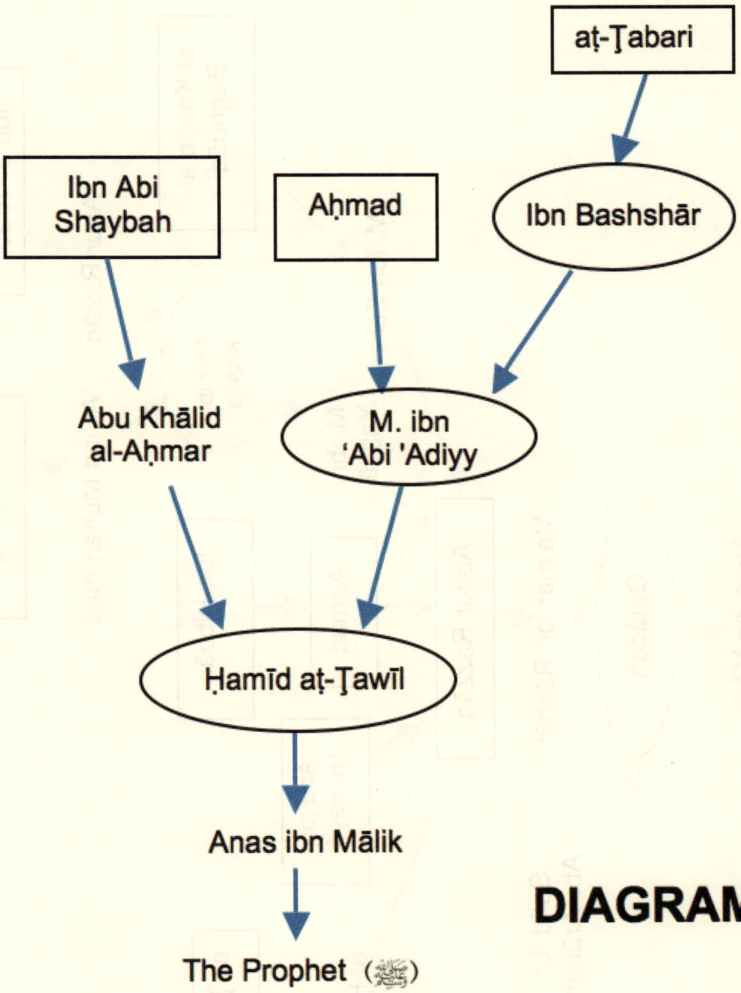
aṭ-Ṭabari
Ibn Abi Shaybah
Aḥmad
Ibn Bashshār
Abu Khālid al-Aḥmar
M. ibn 'Abi 'Adiyy
Ḥamīd aṭ-Ṭawīl
Anas ibn Mālik
The Prophet (ﷺ)

DIAGRAM 5

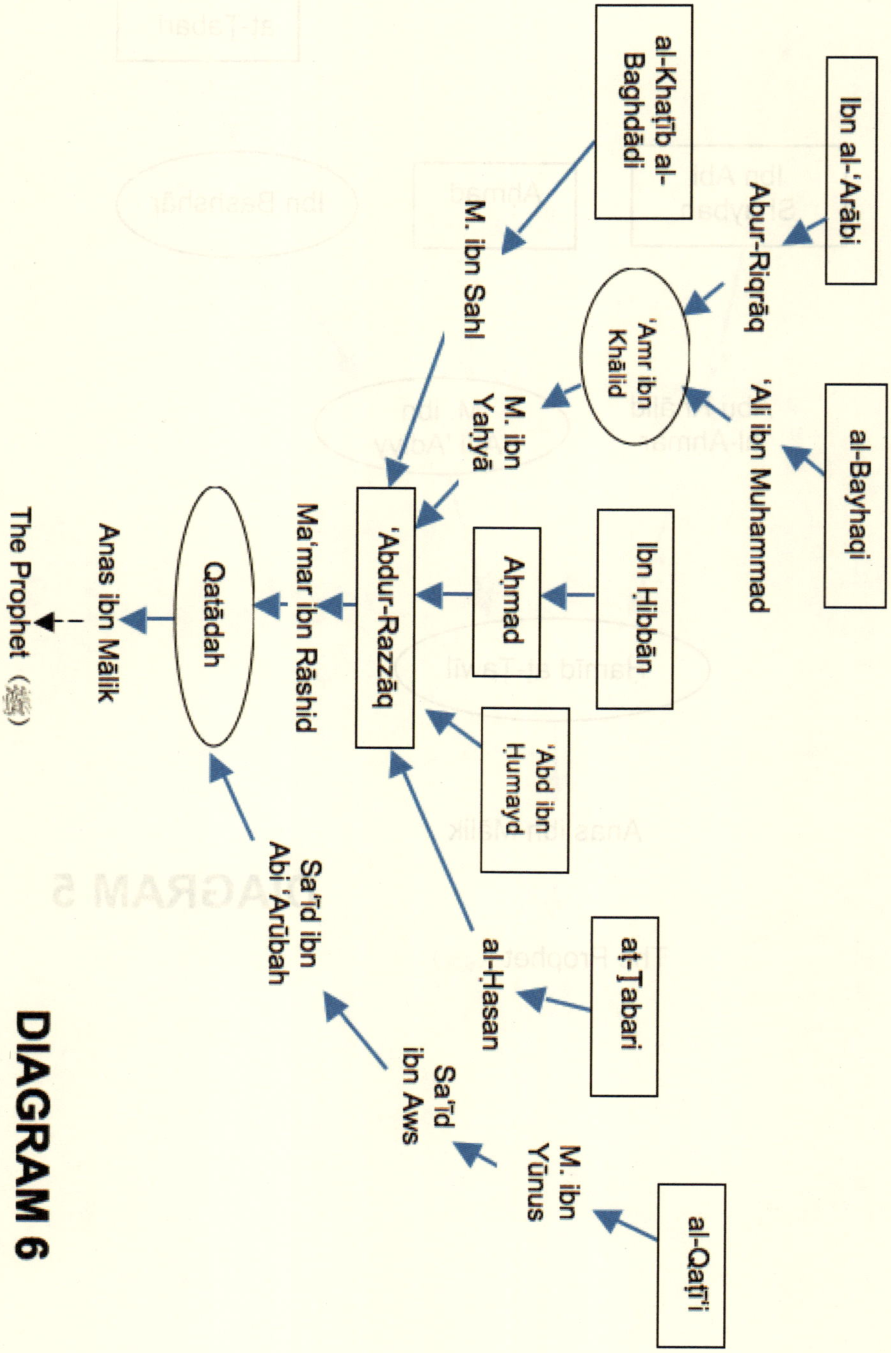
Ibn al-'Arābi
Abur-Riqrāq
al-Khaṭīb al-Baghdādi
M. ibn Sahl
'Amr ibn Khālid
al-Bayhaqi
'Ali ibn Muhammad
M. ibn Yaḥyā
Ibn Ḥibbān
Aḥmad
'Abdur-Razzāq
'Abd ibn Ḥumayd
Ma'mar ibn Rāshid
Qatādah
Anas ibn Mālik
The Prophet (ﷺ)
aṭ-Ṭabari
al-Ḥasan
Sa'īd ibn Abi 'Arūbah
Sa'īd ibn Aws
M. ibn Yūnus
al-Qaṭī'i

DIAGRAM 6

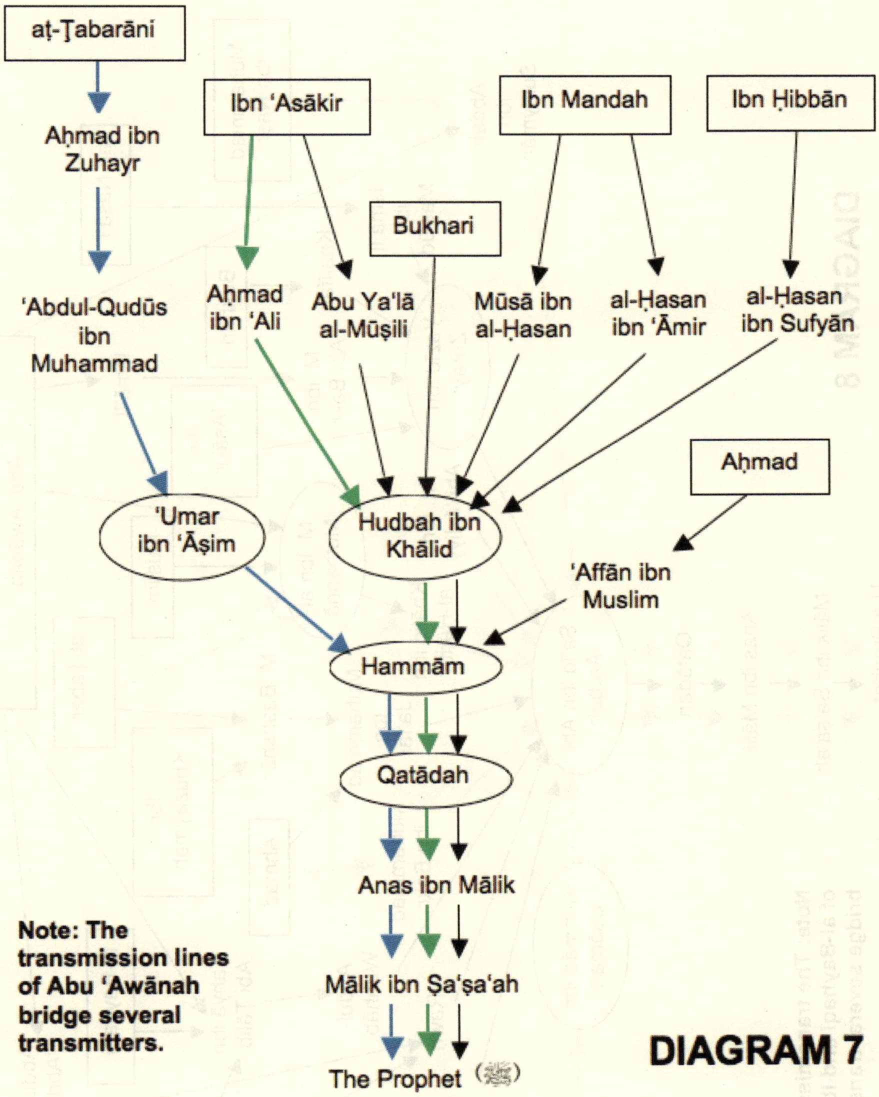
aṭ-Ṭabarānī
Ibn ʻAsākir
Ibn Mandah
Ibn Ḥibbān
Aḥmad ibn Zuhayr
Bukhari
ʻAbdul-Qudūs ibn Muhammad
Aḥmad ibn ʻAli
Abu Yaʻlā al-Mūṣili
Mūsā ibn al-Ḥasan
al-Ḥasan ibn ʻĀmir
al-Ḥasan ibn Sufyān
Aḥmad
ʻUmar ibn ʻĀṣim
Hudbah ibn Khālid
ʻAffān ibn Muslim
Hammām
Qatādah
Anas ibn Mālik
Mālik ibn Ṣaʻṣaʻah
The Prophet (ﷺ)
Note: The transmission lines of Abu ʻAwānah bridge several transmitters.

DIAGRAM 7

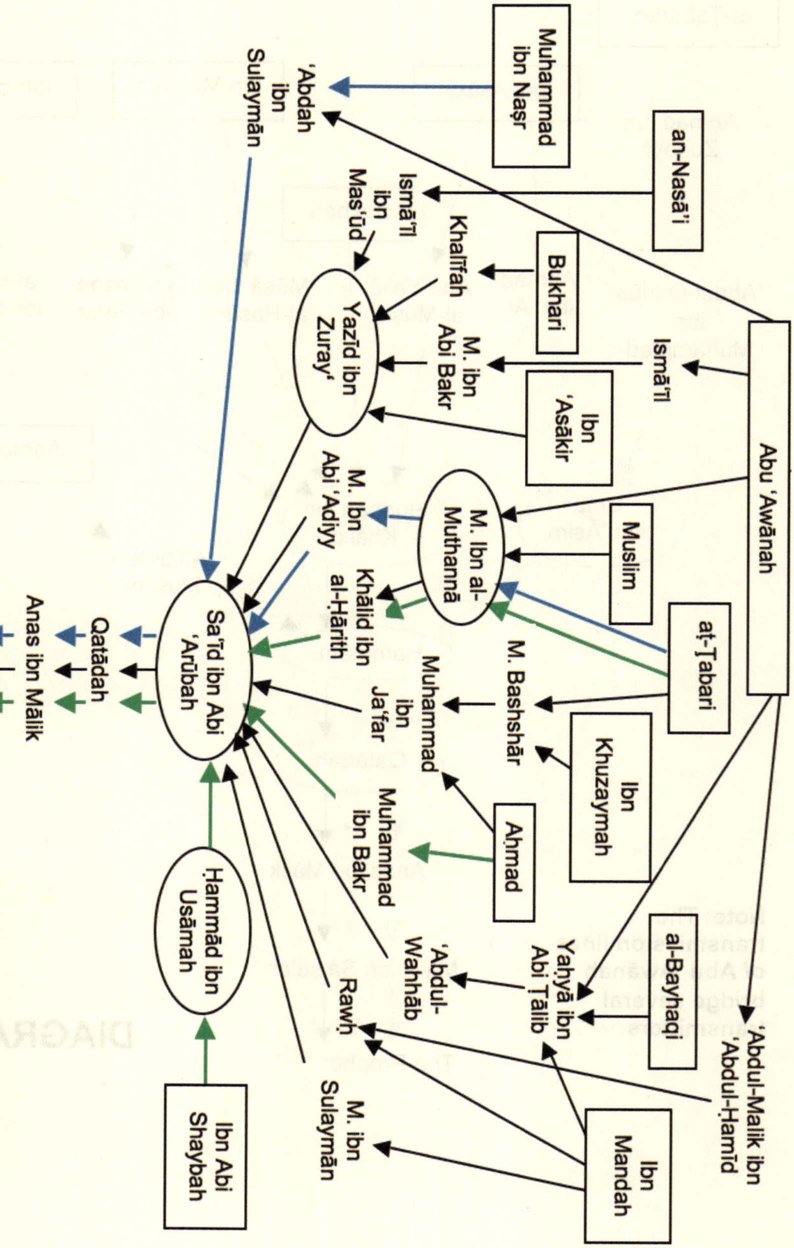

DIAGRAM 8

Note: The transmission lines of al-Bayhaqī and Ibn Mandah bridge several transmitters

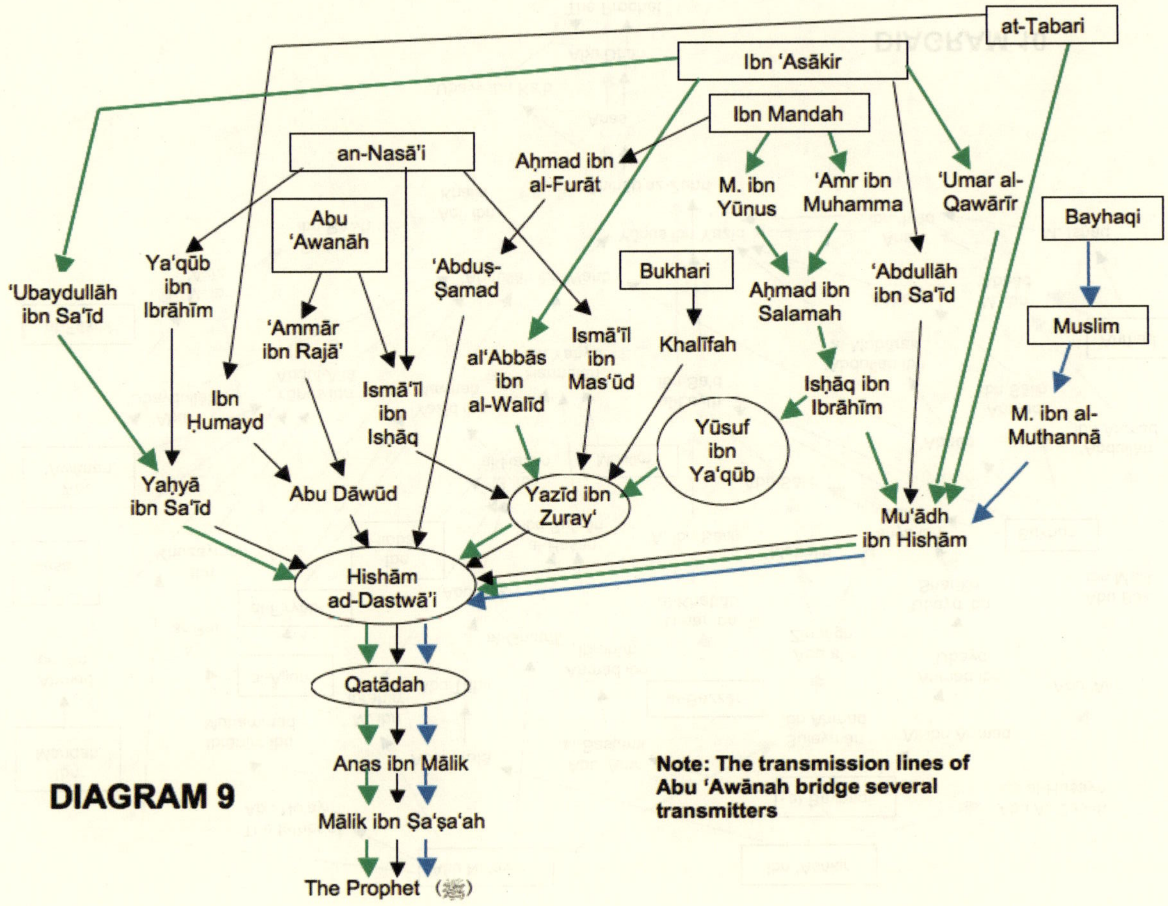

DIAGRAM 9

Note: The transmission lines of Abu ʻAwānah bridge several transmitters

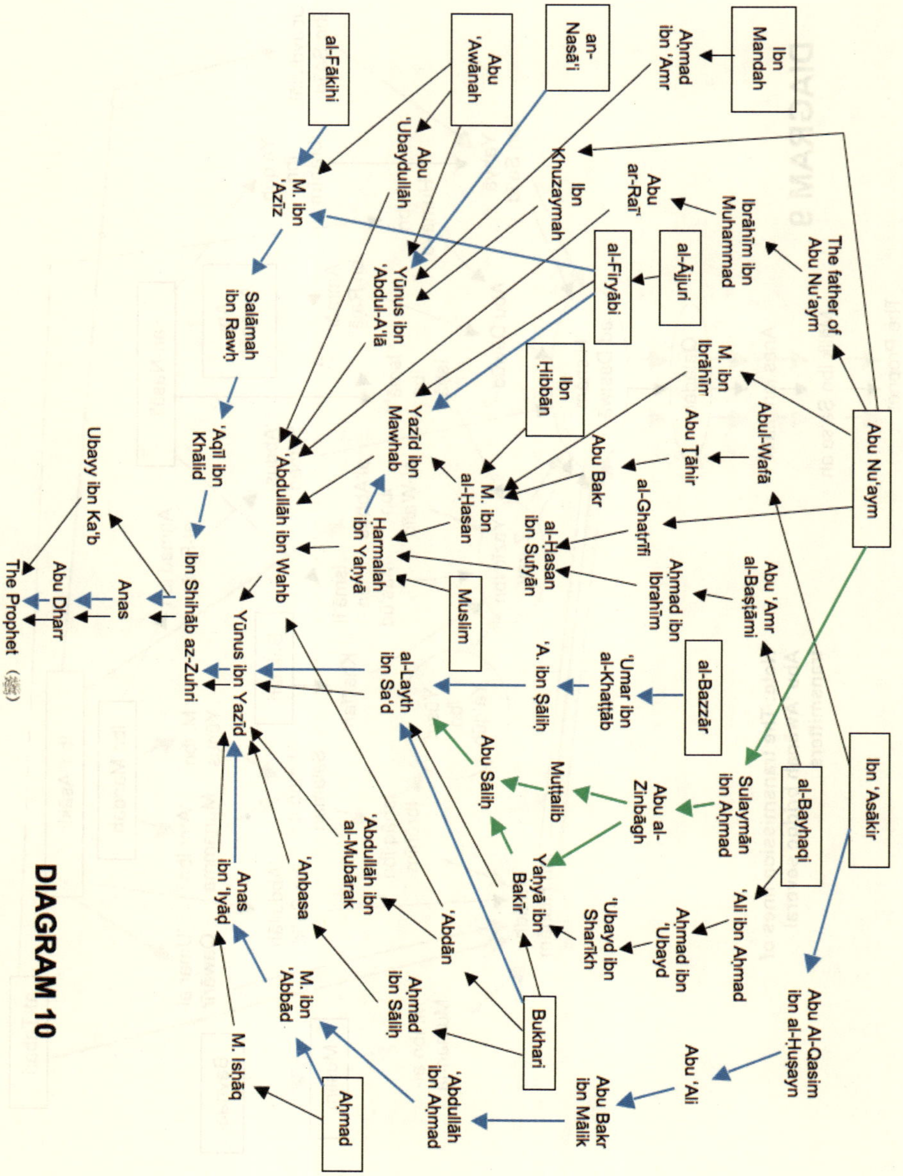
Ibn Mandah
Aḥmad ibn 'Amr
an-Nasā'i
Abu 'Awānah
al-Fākihi
The father of Abu Nu'aym
Ibrāhīm ibn Muhammad
Abu ar-Rai'
Ibn Khuzaymah
Abu 'Ubaydullāh
M. ibn 'Azīz
al-Ājuri
al-Firyābi
Yūnus ibn 'Abdul-A'lā
Salāmah ibn Rawḥ
Abu Nu'aym
M. ibn Ibrāhīm
Abul-Wafā
Abu Ṭāhir
Ibn Ḥibbān
Abu Bakr
Yazīd ibn Mawhab
M. ibn al-Ḥasan
'Aqīl ibn Khālid
'Abdullāh ibn Wahb
al-Ghaṭrīfi
al-Ḥasan ibn Sufyān
Harmalah ibn Yaḥyā
Ubayy ibn Ka'b
Abu 'Amr al-Basṭāmi
Aḥmad ibn Ibrahīm
Muslim
Ibn Shihāb az-Zuhri
Anas
Abu Dharr
The Prophet (ﷺ)
al-Bazzār
'Umar ibn al-Khaṭṭāb
'A. ibn Ṣāliḥ
al-Layth ibn Sa'd
Yūnus ibn Yazīd
Ibn 'Asākir
al-Bayhaqi
Sulaymān ibn Aḥmad
Abu al-Zinbāgh
Muṭṭalib
Abu Ṣāliḥ
Yaḥyā ibn Bakīr
'Ali ibn Aḥmad
Aḥmad ibn 'Ubayd
'Ubayd ibn Sharīkh
'Abdullāh ibn al-Mubārak
'Anbasa
Anas ibn 'Iyāḍ
'Abdān
Abu Al-Qasim ibn al-Ḥuṣayn
Abu 'Ali
Abu Bakr ibn Mālik
Bukhari
Aḥmad ibn Ṣāliḥ
M. ibn 'Abbād
'Abdullāh ibn Aḥmad
M. Isḥāq
Aḥmad

DIAGRAM 10

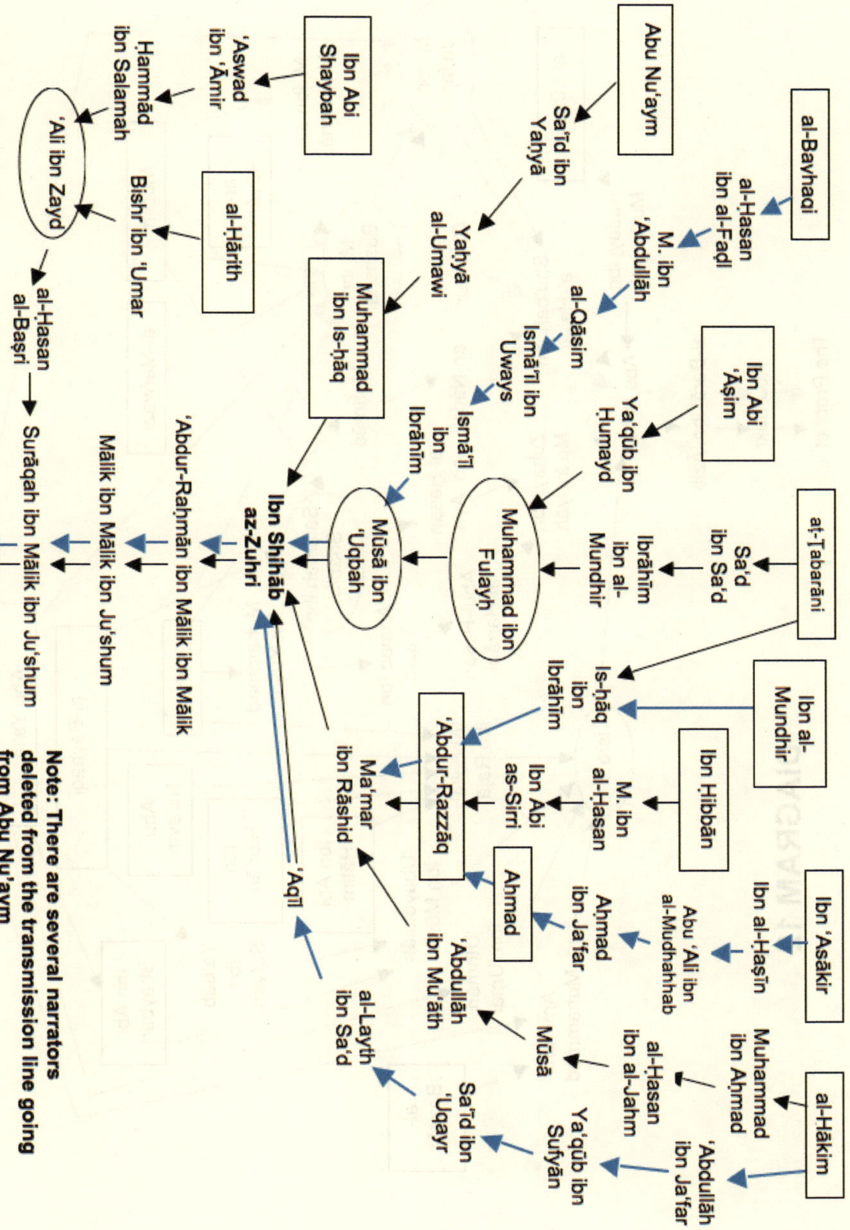
al-Bayhaqi
al-Ḥasan ibn al-Faḍl
M. ibn 'Abdullāh
al-Qāsim
Ismā'īl ibn Uways
Ismā'īl ibn Ibrāhīm
Abu Nu'aym
Sa'īd ibn Yaḥyā
Yaḥyā al-Umawi
Muhammad ibn Is-ḥāq
Ibn Abi Shaybah
'Aswad ibn 'Āmir
Ḥammād ibn Salamah
'Ali ibn Zayd
al-Ḥārith
Bishr ibn 'Umar
al-Ḥasan al-Baṣri
Ibn Abi 'Āṣim
Ya'qūb ibn Ḥumayd
Muhammad ibn Fulayḥ
Mūsā ibn 'Uqbah
aṭ-Ṭabarāni
Sa'd ibn Sa'd
Ibrāhīm ibn al-Mundhir
Is-ḥāq ibn Ibrāhīm
Ibn al-Mundhir
'Abdur-Razzāq
Ibn Ḥibbān
M. ibn al-Ḥasan
Ibn Abi as-Sirri
Ahmad
Ma'mar ibn Rāshid
Ibn 'Asākir
Ibn al-Ḥaṣīn
Abu 'Ali ibn al-Mudhahhab
Aḥmad ibn Ja'far
'Abdullāh ibn Mu'āth
al-Ḥākim
Muhammad ibn Aḥmad
al-Ḥasan ibn al-Jahm
Mūsā
'Abdullāh ibn Ja'far
Ya'qūb ibn Sufyān
Sa'īd ibn 'Uqayr
al-Layth ibn Sa'd
'Aqīl
Ibn Shihāb az-Zuhri
'Abdur-Raḥmān ibn Mālik ibn Mālik
Mālik ibn Mālik ibn Ju'shum
Surāqah ibn Mālik ibn Ju'shum
The Prophet (ﷺ)
Note: There are several narrators deleted from the transmission line going from Abu Nu'aym

DIAGRAM 11

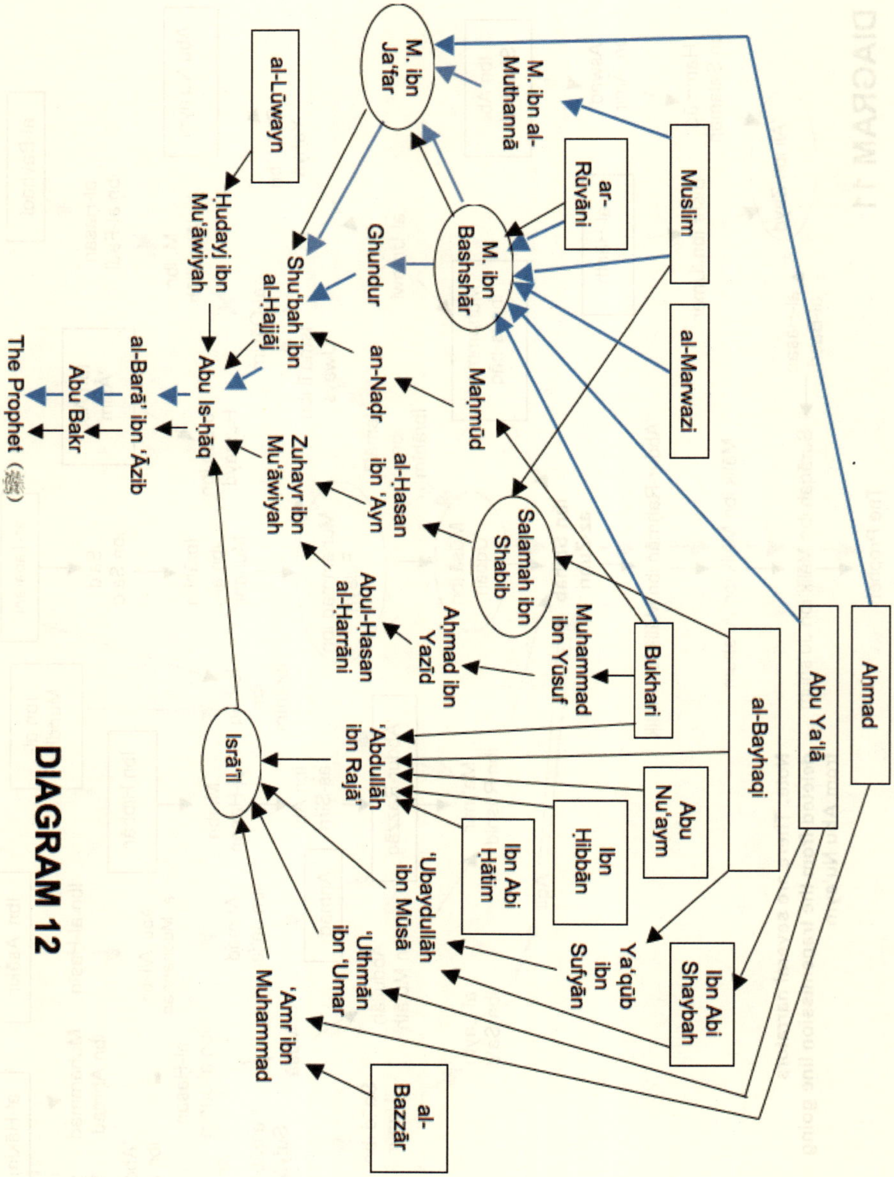

Ahmad
Abu Ya'lā
al-Bayhaqi
Bukhari
al-Marwazi
Muslim
ar-Rūyāni
M. ibn al-Muthannā
M. ibn Ja'far
al-Lūwayn
M. ibn Bashshār
Maḥmūd
Salamah ibn Shabib
Muhammad ibn Yūsuf
Aḥmad ibn Yazīd
Abul-Hasan al-Harrāni
al-Ḥasan ibn 'Ayn
an-Naḍr
Ghundur
Shu'bah ibn al-Ḥajjāj
Zuhayr ibn Mu'āwiyah
Hudayj ibn Mu'āwiyah
Abu Is-ḥāq
al-Barā' ibn 'Āzib
Abu Bakr
The Prophet
Abu Nu'aym
Ibn Ḥibbān
Ibn Abi Ḥātim
Ibn Abi Shaybah
Ya'qūb ibn Sufyān
'Abdullāh ibn Rajā'
'Ubaydullāh ibn Mūsā
'Uthmān ibn 'Umar
'Amr ibn Muhammad
al-Bazzār
Isrā'īl

DIAGRAM 12

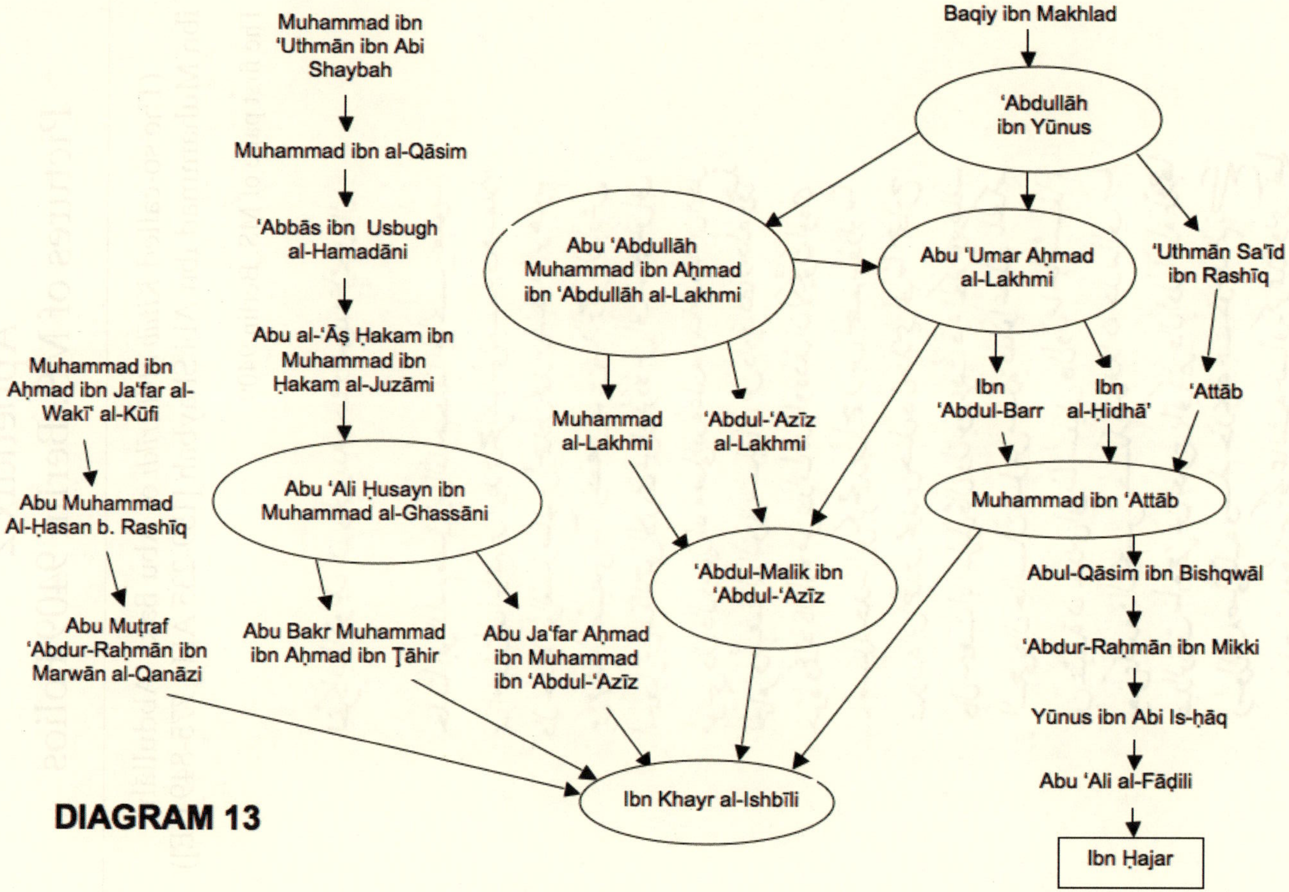
Muhammad ibn 'Uthmān ibn Abi Shaybah
Muhammad ibn al-Qāsim
'Abbās ibn Usbugh al-Hamadāni
Abu al-'Āṣ Ḥakam ibn Muhammad ibn Ḥakam al-Juzāmi
Abu 'Ali Ḥusayn ibn Muhammad al-Ghassāni
Abu Bakr Muhammad ibn Aḥmad ibn Ṭāhir
Abu Ja'far Aḥmad ibn Muhammad ibn 'Abdul-'Azīz
Muhammad ibn Aḥmad ibn Ja'far al-Wakī' al-Kūfi
Abu Muhammad Al-Ḥasan b. Rashīq
Abu Muṭraf 'Abdur-Raḥmān ibn Marwān al-Qanāzi
Baqiy ibn Makhlad
'Abdullāh ibn Yūnus
Abu 'Abdullāh Muhammad ibn Aḥmad ibn 'Abdullāh al-Lakhmi
Abu 'Umar Aḥmad al-Lakhmi
'Uthmān Sa'īd ibn Rashīq
Muhammad al-Lakhmi
'Abdul-'Azīz al-Lakhmi
Ibn 'Abdul-Barr
Ibn al-Ḥidhā'
'Attāb
Muhammad ibn 'Attāb
'Abdul-Malik ibn 'Abdul-'Azīz
Abul-Qāsim ibn Bishqwāl
'Abdur-Raḥmān ibn Mikki
Yūnus ibn Abi Is-ḥāq
Abu 'Ali al-Fāḍili
Ibn Ḥajar
Ibn Khayr al-Ishbīli

DIAGRAM 13

Appendix 2
Pictures of MS. Berlin 9409 Folios

(The so-called *Kitāb at-Tārīkh* of Abu Bakr 'Abdullāh ibn Muhammad ibn Abi Shaybah [159-235 AH/ 775-849 CE])

The first page of MS. Berlin 9409

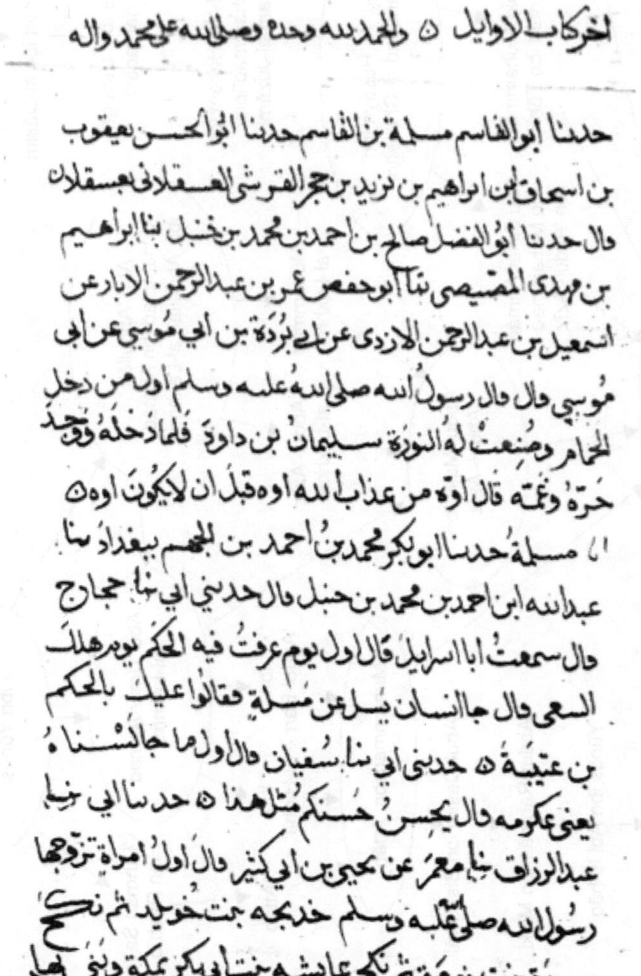
اخر كتاب الاوايل ٥ والحمد لله وحده وصلى الله على محمد واله

حدثنا ابو القاسم مسلمة بن القاسم حدثنا ابو الحسن يعقوب
بن اسحاق بن ابراهيم بن يزيد بن حجر القرشي العسقلاني بعسقلان
قال حدثنا ابو الفضل صالح بن احمد بن محمد بن حنبل نا ابراهيم
بن مهدي المصيصي نا ابو حفص عمر بن عبد الرحمن الابار عن
اسمعيل بن عبد الرحمن الازدي عن ابي بردة بن ابي موسى عن ابي
موسى قال قال رسول الله صلى الله عليه وسلم اول من دخل
الحمام وصنعت له النورة سليمان بن داود فلما دخله وجد
حره وغمه قال اوه من عذاب الله اوه قبل ان لا يكون اوه ٥
نا مسلمة حدثنا ابو بكر محمد بن احمد بن الجهم ببغداد نا
عبد الله بن احمد بن محمد بن حنبل قال حدثني ابي نا حجاج
قال سمعت ابا اسرايل قال اول يوم عرفت فيه الحكم يوم هلك
الشعبي قال جا انسان يسل عن مسلة فقالوا عليك بالحكم
بن عتيبة ٥ حدثني ابي نا سفيان قال اول ما جالسنا
يعني عكرمه قال يجلس حسنكم مثل هذا ٥ حدثنا ابي نا
عبد الرزاق نا معمر عن يحيى بن ابي كثير قال اول امراة تزوجها
رسول الله صلى الله عليه وسلم خديجه بنت خويلد ثم نكح
سودة بنت زمعة ثم نكح عايشه بنت ابي بكر بمكة وبنى بها
بالمدينة

The second page of MS. Berlin 9409

بالمدينه ثم نكح بالمدينه زينب بنت خزيمه الهلاليه ثم نكح ام
سلمة بنت ابي اميه ثم نكح جويريه بنت الحرث من بني المصطلق وكانت
مما افا الله عليه ثم نكح ميمونة بنت الحرث وهي التي وهبت نفسها
للنبي صلي الله عليه وسلم ثم نكح صفية بنت حيي وهي مما
افا الله عليه ثم نكح زينب بنت جحش وكانت امراة زيد بن
حارثه توفيت زينب بنت خزيمه قبل النبي صلى الله عليه وسلم
ونكح حفصه بنت عمر وام حبيبه بنت ابي سفيان والكنديه
وامراه من كلب وكان جميع من تزوج اربع عشرة امراه انا
مسلمة حدثنا يعقوب بن اسحاق بن حجر نا ابو موسى نا ضمرة
عن يزيد بن ابي يزيد عن رجل قد سماه قال اول من عقد
الالوية ابراهيم خليل الرحمن عليه السلام بلغه ان قوما اغاروا
على لوط فسبوه فعقد لواء وسار اليهم بعبيده ومواليه حتى
ادركهم فاستنقذه واهله انا مسلمة حدثنا ابو جعفر احمد
بن ابراهيم بن عبد الله بن محمد بن يحيى المعافري المصري المعروف
بابن حموية بالفسطاط في الجامع املاه من كتابه في ذي القعدة
سنة اثنتين وعشرين وثلثمايه قال نا الربيع بن سليمان
المرادي نا اسد بن موسى نا حماد بن سلمة عن ابي قزعه عن
حكيم بن معويه قال سمعت رسول الله صلى الله عليه وسلم
يقول تحشرون مشاة وركبانا وعلى وجوهكم تعرضون على

The last page of MS. Berlin 9409

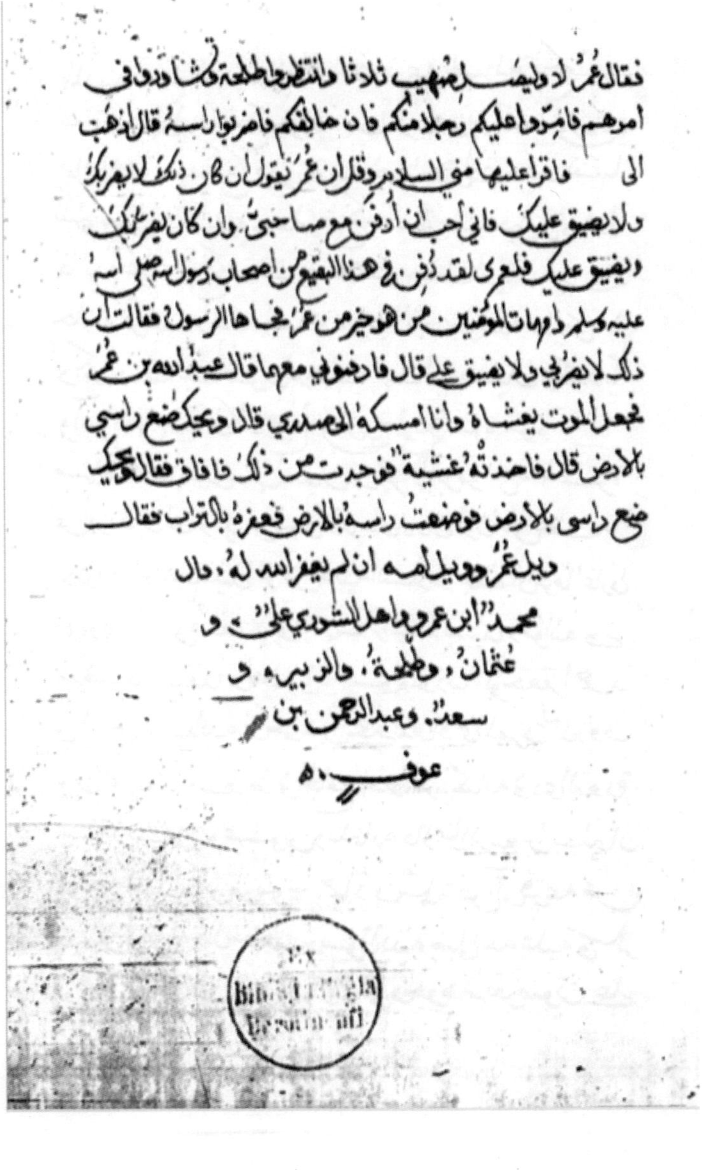

فقال عمر له وليصل صهيب ثلاثا وانتظروا طلحة وشاوروا في
امرهم فامّروا عليكم رجلا منكم فان خالفكم فاضربوا راسه قال اذهب
الى فاقرا عليها مني السلام وقل ان عمر يقول ان كان ذلك لا يضر بك
ولا يضيق عليك فاني احب ان ادفن مع صاحبيّ وان كان يضر بك
ويضيق عليك فلعمري لقد دفن في هذا البقيع من اصحاب رسول الله صلى الله
عليه وسلم وامهات المؤمنين من هو خير من عمر فجاءها الرسول فقالت ان
ذلك لا يضر بي ولا يضيق علي قال فادفنوني معهما قال عبد الله بن عمر
فجعل الموت يغشاه وانا امسكه الى صدري قال ويحك ضع راسي
بالارض قال فاخذته غشية فوجدت من ذلك فافاق فقال ويحك
ضع راسي بالارض فوضعت راسه بالارض فعفره بالتراب فقال
ويل عمر وويل امه ان لم يغفر الله له . قال
محمد ابن عمرو واهل الشورى علي و
عثمان وطلحة والزبير و
سعد وعبد الرحمن بن
عوف

Appendix 3
Traditions quoted from the Arabic edition of MS. Berlin 9409

(The so-called *Kitāb at-Tārīkh* of Abu Bakr ʻAbdullāh ibn Muhammad ibn Abi Shaybah [159-235 AH/ 775-849 CE]):

Traditions discussed in Chapter Three concerning the Prophet's ascension, as excerpted from MS. Berlin 9409

حَدِيثُ الْمِعْرَاجِ حِينَ أُسْرِيَ بِالنَّبِيِّ ﵇

٤٩. حَدَّثَنَا الْحَسَنُ بْنُ مُوسَى بْنُ الأَشْيَبِ[١]، قَالَ: حَدَّثَنَا حَمَّادُ بْنُ سَلَمَةَ، قَالَ: أَخْبَرَنَا ثَابِتٌ، عَنْ أَنَسٍ، أَنَّ رَسُولَ اللَّهِ ﷺ، قَالَ: أُتِيتُ بِالْبُرَاقِ -وَهُوَ دَابَّةٌ أَبْيَض فَوْقَ الْحِمَارِ وَدُونَ الْبَغْلِ، يَضَعُ حَافِرَهُ عِنْدَ مُنْتَهَى طَرَفِهِ- فَرَكِبْتُهُ فَسَارَ بِي حَتَّى أَتَيْتُ بَيْتَ الْمَقْدِسِ، فَرَبَطْتُ الدَّابَّةَ بِالْحَلَقَةِ الَّتِي كَانَ يَرْبِطُ[٢] بِهَا الأَنْبِيَاءُ عليهم السلام[٣]، ثُمَّ دَخَلْتُ فَصَلَّيْتُ فِيهِ رَكْعَتَيْنِ، ثُمَّ خَرَجْتُ فَجَاءَنِي جِبْرِيلُ بِإِنَاءٍ مِنْ خَمْرٍ وَإِنَاءٍ مِنْ لَبَنٍ، فَاخْتَرْتُ اللَّبَنَ، فَقَالَ جِبْرِيلُ: أَصَبْتَ الْفِطْرَةَ، قَالَ: ثُمَّ عَرَجَ بِنَا إِلَى السَّمَاءِ الدُّنْيَا، فَاسْتَفْتَحَ جِبْرِيلُ، فَقِيلَ: مَنْ أَنْتَ؟ فَقَالَ: جِبْرِيلُ، قِيلَ: وَمَنْ مَعَكَ؟ قَالَ: مُحَمَّدٌ ﷺ[٤]، فَقِيلَ[٥]: وَقَدْ أُرْسِلَ إِلَيْهِ؟ فَقَالَ: قَدْ أُرْسِلَ إِلَيْهِ، فَفُتِحَ لَنَا، فَإِذَا أَنَا بِآدَمَ، فَرَحَّبَ وَدَعَا لِي بِخَيْرٍ، ثُمَّ عَرَجَ بِنَا إِلَى السَّمَاءِ الثَّانِيَةِ، فَاسْتَفْتَحَ جِبْرِيلُ، فَقِيلَ: وَمَنْ أَنْتَ؟ قَالَ: جِبْرِيلُ، فَقِيلَ: وَمَنْ مَعَكَ؟ قَالَ: مُحَمَّدٌ ﷺ[٦]، فَقِيلَ: وَقَدْ أُرْسِلَ إِلَيْهِ؟ قَالَ: قَدْ أُرْسِلَ إِلَيْهِ، فَفُتِحَ لَنَا، فَإِذَا أَنَا بِابْنَيِ الْخَالَةِ: يَحْيَى

---

١ المصنف: حَدَّثَنَا حَدَّثَنَا أَبُو بَكْرٍ، قَالَ: حَدَّثَنَا الْحَسَنُ بْنُ مُوسَى بْنُ الأَشْيَبِ.

٢ برلين: تربط.

٣ المصنف: الأنبيا.

٤ المصنف: محمد.

٥ برلين: فقال.

٦ المصنف: محمد.

وَعِيسَى، فَرَحَّبَا وَدَعَوَا لِي بِخَيْرٍ، ثُمَّ عَرَجَ بِنَا إِلَى السَّمَاءِ الثَّالِثَةِ، فَاسْتَفْتَحَ جِبْرِيلُ، فَقِيلَ: وَمَنْ أَنْتَ؟ فَقَالَ: جِبْرِيلُ، فَقِيلَ: وَمَنْ مَعَكَ؟ قَالَ: مُحَمَّدٌ، قَالُوا: وَقَدْ أُرْسِلَ إِلَيْهِ؟ قَالَ: قَدْ أُرْسِلَ إِلَيْهِ، فَفُتِحَ لَنَا، فَإِذَا أَنَا بِيُوسُفَ، وَإِذَا هُوَ قَدْ أُعْطِيَ شَطْرَ الْحُسْنِ، فَرَحَّبَ وَدَعَا لِي بِخَيْرٍ، ثُمَّ عَرَجَ بِنَا إِلَى السَّمَاءِ الرَّابِعَةِ، فَاسْتَفْتَحَ جِبْرِيلُ، فَقِيلَ: وَمَنْ أَنْتَ؟ فَقَالَ: جِبْرِيلُ، فَقِيلَ: وَمَنْ مَعَكَ؟ قَالَ: مُحَمَّدٌ ﷺ فَقِيلَ: وَقَدْ أُرْسِلَ إِلَيْهِ؟ فَقَالَ: قَدْ أُرْسِلَ إِلَيْهِ، فَفُتِحَ لَنَا، فَإِذَا أَنَا بِإِدْرِيسَ، فَرَحَّبَ وَدَعَا لِي بِخَيْرٍ، ثُمَّ قَالَ: يَقُولُ اللَّهُ: ﴿وَرَفَعْنَٰهُ مَكَانًا عَلِيًّا ۝٥٧﴾[٧]، ثُمَّ عَرَجَ بِنَا إِلَى السَّمَاءِ الْخَامِسَةِ، فَاسْتَفْتَحَ جِبْرِيلُ، فَقِيلَ: مَنْ أَنْتَ؟ قَالَ: جِبْرِيلُ، فَقِيلَ: وَمَنْ مَعَكَ؟ فَقَالَ: مُحَمَّدٌ ﷺ فَقِيلَ: وَقَدْ بُعِثَ إِلَيْهِ؟ قَالَ: قَدْ بُعِثَ إِلَيْهِ، فَفُتِحَ لَنَا، فَإِذَا أَنَا بِهَارُونَ، فَرَحَّبَ بِي، وَدَعَا لِي بِخَيْرٍ، ثُمَّ عَرَجَ بِنَا إِلَى السَّمَاءِ السَّادِسَةِ، فَاسْتَفْتَحَ جِبْرِيلُ، فَقِيلَ: مَنْ أَنْتَ؟ قَالَ: جِبْرِيلُ، فَقِيلَ: وَمَنْ مَعَكَ؟ قَالَ: مُحَمَّدٌ، فَقِيلَ: وَقَدْ بُعِثَ إِلَيْهِ؟ قَالَ: قَدْ بُعِثَ إِلَيْهِ، (فَفُتِحَ لَنَا)[٨]، فَإِذَا أَنَا بِمُوسَى، فَرَحَّبَ وَدَعَا لِي بِخَيْرٍ، ثُمَّ عَرَجَ بِنَا إِلَى السَّمَاءِ السَّابِعَةِ، فَاسْتَفْتَحَ جِبْرِيلُ، فَقِيلَ: مَنْ أَنْتَ؟ قَالَ: جِبْرِيلُ، فَقِيلَ: وَمَنْ مَعَكَ؟ قَالَ: مُحَمَّدٌ، فَقِيلَ: وَقَدْ بُعِثَ إِلَيْهِ؟ قَالَ: قَدْ بُعِثَ إِلَيْهِ، فَفُتِحَ لَنَا، فَإِذَا أَنَا بِإِبْرَاهِيمَ عليه السلام وَإِذَا هُوَ مُسْنِدٌ[٩] إِلَى الْبَيْتِ الْمَعْمُورِ، وَإِذَا هُوَ يَدْخُلُهُ كُلَّ يَوْمٍ سَبْعُونَ أَلْفَ مَلَكٍ لَا يَعُودُونَ إِلَيْهِ، ثُمَّ ذَهَبَ بِي إِلَى سِدْرَةِ الْمُنْتَهَى، فَإِذَا وَرَقُهَا كَآذَانِ الْفِيَلَةِ، وَإِذَا ثَمَرُهَا أَمْثَالُ الْقِلَالِ، فَلَمَّا غَشِيَهَا مِنْ أَمْرِ اللَّهِ مَا غَشِيَهَا تَغَيَّرَتْ، فَمَا أَحَدٌ مِنْ خَلْقِ اللَّهِ يَسْتَطِيعُ أَنْ يَصِفَهَا مِنْ حُسْنِهَا، قَالَ: فَأَوْحَى اللَّهُ إِلَيَّ مَا أَوْحَى، وَفَرَضَ عَلَيَّ فِي كُلِّ يَوْمٍ وَلَيْلَةٍ خَمْسِينَ صَلَاةً، فَنَزَلْتُ حَتَّى انْتَهَيْتُ إِلَى مُوسَى، فَقَالَ: مَا فَرَضَ رَبُّكَ عَلَى أُمَّتِكَ؟ قَالَ: قُلْتُ: خَمْسِينَ صَلَاةً فِي كُلِّ يَوْمٍ وَلَيْلَةٍ، فَقَالَ: ارْجِعْ إِلَى رَبِّكَ فَاسْأَلْهُ التَّخْفِيفَ؛ فَإِنَّ أُمَّتَكَ لَا تُطِيقُ ذَلِكَ؛ فَإِنِّي[١٠] قَدْ بَلَوْتُ بَنِي إِسْرَائِيلَ وَخَبَرْتُهُمْ، قَالَ: فَرَجَعْتُ إِلَى رَبِّي، فَقُلْتُ لَهُ: رَبِّ، خَفِّفْ عَنْ أُمَّتِي، فَحَطَّ عَنِّي خَمْسًا، فَرَجَعْتُ إِلَى مُوسَى، فَقَالَ: مَا فَعَلْتَ؟ فَقُلْتُ: حَطَّ عَنِّي خَمْسًا، قَالَ: إِنَّ أُمَّتَكَ

---

٧ سورة مريم: ٥٧.

٨ ساقطة من برلين.

٩ برلين: مستند.

١٠ برلين: فإني وإني.

لَا تُطِيقُ ذَلِكَ، فَارْجِعْ إِلَى رَبِّكَ فَاسْأَلْهُ التَّخْفِيفَ لِأُمَّتِكَ، فَلَمْ أَزَلْ أَرْجِعُ بَيْنَ رَبِّي وَبَيْنَ مُوسَى عليه السلام، فَيَحُطُّ عَنِّي خَمْسًا خَمْسًا، حَتَّى قَالَ: يَا مُحَمَّدُ، هِيَ خَمْسُ صَلَوَاتٍ فِي كُلِّ يَوْمٍ وَلَيْلَةٍ، بِكُلِّ صَلَاةٍ عَشْرٌ؛ فَتِلْكَ خَمْسُونَ صَلَاةً، وَمَنْ هَمَّ بِحَسَنَةٍ فَلَمْ يَعْمَلْهَا كُتِبَتْ لَهُ حَسَنَةً، فَإِنْ عَمِلَهَا كُتِبَتْ لَهُ عَشْرًا، وَمَنْ هَمَّ بِسَيِّئَةٍ وَلَمْ يَعْمَلْهَا لَمْ تُكْتَبْ لَهُ شَيْئًا، فَإِنْ عَمِلَهَا كُتِبَتْ سَيِّئَةً وَاحِدَةً، فَنَزَلْتُ حَتَّى انْتَهَيْتُ إِلَى مُوسَى فَأَخْبَرْتُهُ، فَقَالَ: ارْجِعْ إِلَى رَبِّكَ فَاسْأَلْهُ التَّخْفِيفَ لِأُمَّتِكَ؛ فَإِنَّ أُمَّتَكَ لَا تُطِيقُ ذَلِكَ، فَقَالَ رَسُولُ اللَّهِ ﷺ: لَقَدْ رَجَعْتُ إِلَى رَبِّي حَتَّى اسْتَحْيَيْتُ[١١].

---

١١ ابن أبي شيبة (٣٦٥٧٠) وأحمد (١٢٥٢٧) قالا: حدثنا حسن بن موسى، ومسلم (١٦٢) وأبو يعلى (٦/ ١٠٩) قالا: حدثنا شيبان بن فرُّوخ، وأبو عوانة (١/ ١١٤)، وابن منده في الإيمان (٢/ ٧٠٩) قال: أخبرنا عبد الواحد بن أحمد بن عبد الرحمن، ثنا علي بن الحسن بن أبي عيسى، ح، وأنبأ محمد بن محمد بن الأزهر، ثنا علي بن عبد العزيز، ح، وأنبأ أحمد بن محمد بن إبراهيم، ثنا أحمد بن يحيى بن إبراهيم، ح، وأنبأ أحمد بن إسحاق، ثنا إبراهيم بن حاتم البصري، قالوا: ثنا حجاج بن منهال؛ ثلاثتُهم (الحسن وشيبان وحجاج بن منهال) عن ثابتٍ البُناني، عن أنس بن مالك، قال شعيب الأرناؤوط: إسناده صحيح على شرط مسلم.

وأخرجه الحاكم (٤/ ٦٤٨)، وأبو يعلى (٨/ ٤٤٩)، والبزار (٥/ ١٤)، والوادعي في الصحيح المسند (٨٧٤) وحسَّنه عن عبد اللَّه بن مسعود، قال الهيثمي في مجمع الزوائد (١/ ٧٤): رجاله رجال الصحيح، قال ابن حجر (مختصر البزار ١/ ٩٣): فيه أبو حمزة -وهو ميمون الأعور- متروك.

وأخرجه أحمد (٢٣٣٨٠)، وأبو داود في مسنده (٤١١)، والطبري في تهذيب الآثار (١/ ٤٤٦)، عن حذيفة بن اليمان: أن رسول اللَّه ﷺ قال: أتيتُ بالبراق، وهو دابة طويل، حافره عند منتهى طَرَفِه، فلم يزل على ظهره هو وجبريل حتى أتى بيت المقدس، وفُتحت لهما أبواب السماء، ورأيا الجنة والنار.

وأخرجه ابن أبي شيبة (٣١٦٩٨)، و(٣٦٥٧٣)، وأحمد (٢٣٣٨٠)، وأبو داود الطيالسي في مسنده (٤١١) عن حذيفة بن اليمان، قال شعيب الأرناؤوط: إسناده حسن؛ لأن فيه عاصم بن بهدلة.

٥٠ . حَدَّثَنَا أَبُو أُسَامَةَ، عَنْ سَعِيدٍ، عَنْ قَتَادَةَ، عَنْ أَنَسِ بْنِ مَالِكِ بْنِ صَعْصَعَةَ[١٢]، عَنِ النَّبِيِّ ﷺ بِنَحْوٍ مِنْهُ، أَوْ شَبِيهٍ بِهِ[١٣].

٥١ . حَدَّثنا هَوْذَةُ بْنُ خَلِيفَةَ، قَالَ: حَدَّثَنَا عَوْفٌ[١٤]، عَنْ زُرَارَةَ بْنِ أَوْفَى، قَالَ: قَالَ ابْنُ عَبَّاسٍ: قَالَ رَسُولُ اللَّهِ ﷺ: لَمَّا كَانَ لَيْلَةَ أُسْرِيَ بِي أَصْبَحْتُ بِمَكَّةَ، قَالَ: فَظِعْتُ بِأَمْرِي، وَعَرَفْتُ أَنَّ النَّاسَ مُكَذِّبِيَّ، فَقَعَدَ رَسُولُ اللَّهِ ﷺ مُعْتَزِلًا حَزِينًا، فَمَرَّ بِهِ أَبُو جَهْلٍ، فَجَاءَ حَتَّى جَلَسَ إِلَيْهِ، فَقَالَ كَالْمُسْتَهْزِئِ: هَلْ كَانَ مِنْ شَيْءٍ؟ قَالَ: نَعَمْ، قَالَ: وَمَا هُوَ؟ قَالَ: أُسْرِيَ بِيَ اللَّيْلَةَ، قَالَ: إِلَى أَيْنَ؟ قَالَ: إِلَى بَيْتِ الْمَقْدِسِ، قَالَ: ثُمَّ أَصْبَحْتَ بَيْنَ أَظْهُرِنَا؟! قَالَ: نَعَمْ، فَلَمْ يُرِهِ أَنَّهُ يُكَذِّبُهُ؛ مَخَافَةَ أَنْ يَجْحَدَ الْحَدِيثَ إِنْ دَعَا قَوْمَهُ إِلَيْهِ، قَالَ: أَتُحَدِّثُ قَوْمَكَ مَا حَدَّثْتَنِي إِنْ دَعَوْتُهُمْ إِلَيْكَ؟ قَالَ: نَعَمْ، قَالَ: هَيَّا مَعْشَرَ بَنِي كَعْبِ بْنِ لُؤَيٍّ، هَلُمَّ، قَالَ: فَتَنَفَّضَتِ الْمَجَالِسُ، فَجَاؤُوا حَتَّى جَلَسُوا إِلَيْهِمَا، فَقَالَ: حَدِّثْ قَوْمَكَ مَا حَدَّثْتَنِي، قَالَ رَسُولُ اللَّهِ ﷺ: إِنِّي أُسْرِيَ بِيَ اللَّيْلَةَ، قَالُوا: إِلَى أَيْنَ؟ قَالَ: إِلَى بَيْتِ الْمَقْدِسِ، قَالُوا: ثُمَّ أَصْبَحْتَ بَيْنَ ظَهْرَانَيْنَا؟! قَالَ: نَعَمْ، قَالَ: فَمِنْ بَيْنِ مُصَفِّقٍ، وَمِنْ بَيْنِ وَاضِعٍ يَدَهُ عَلَى رَأْسِهِ مُتَعَجِّبًا لِلْكَذِبِ - زَعَمَ، وَقَالُوا: أَتَسْتَطِيعُ أَنْ تَنْعَتَ لَنَا الْمَسْجِدَ؟ قَالَ: وَفِي الْقَوْمِ مَنْ سَافَرَ إِلَى ذَلِكَ الْبَلَدِ وَرَأَى الْمَسْجِدَ، قَالَ رَسُولُ اللَّهِ ﷺ: فَذَهَبْتُ أَنْعَتُ لَهُمْ، فَمَا زِلْتُ أَنْعَتُ حَتَّى الْتَبَسَ عَلَيَّ بَعْضُ النَّعْتِ، فَجِيءَ بِالْمَسْجِدِ وَأَنَا أَنْظُرُ إِلَيْهِ حَتَّى وُضِعَ دُونَ دَارِ عَقِيلٍ، أَوْ دَارِ عِقَالٍ، فَنَعَتُّهُ وَأَنَا أَنْظُرُ إِلَيْهِ، فَقَالَ الْقَوْمُ: أَمَّا النَّعْتُ فَوَاللَّهِ لَقَدْ أَصَابَ[١٥].

---

١٢ لعله خطأ من الناسخ، والصواب: عن أنس بن مالك عن مالك بن صعصعة، كما هو عند البخاري ومسلم والترمذي وأبي داود والنسائي وأحمد وغيرهم.

١٣ ابن أبي شيبة (٣٦٥٧١)، والبخاري (٣٠٣٥)، ومسلم (١٦٤)، والترمذي (٣١٧٢)، وأبو داود (٣١٣)، والنسائي (٤٤٨)، وأحمد (١٧٨٦٧)، وأبو عوانة (١/ ١١٦)، عن قتادة رضي اللّه عنه، عن أنس بن مالك رضي اللّه عنه، عن مالك بن صعصعة.

١٤ برلين: قال عوف.

١٥ ابن أبي شيبة (٣١٧٠٠) و(٣٦٥٧٢)، وأحمد (٢٨٢٠)، والنسائي في الكبرى (١١٢٨٥)، قال: أخبرنا محمد بن عبد الأعلى في حديثه عن معتمر بن سليمان، والطبراني في الكبير (١٢٧٨٢)، والحارث في المسند (٢١)، والأصبهاني في الدلائل (١/ ٨٤)، والضياء في المختارة (٣٤)، وابن عساكر (٤١/ ٢٣٥)، بسند صحيح عن ابن عباس رضي اللّه عنهما.

٥٢. حَدَّثَنَا عَفَّانُ، قَالَ: حَدَّثَنَا حَمَّادُ بْنُ سَلَمَةَ، عَنْ عَاصِمٍ، عَنْ زِرٍّ[١٦]، عَنْ حُذَيْفَةَ بْنِ الْيَمَانِ، أَنَّ رَسُولَ اللَّهِ ﷺ أُتِيَ بِالْبُرَاقِ، هُوَ دَابَّةٌ أَبْيَض طَوِيلٌ، يَضَعُ حَافِرَهُ عِنْدَ مُنْتَهَى طَرَفِهِ، قَالَ: فَلَمْ يُزَايِلْ ظَهْرَهُ هُوَ وَجِبْرِيلُ حَتَّى أَتَيَا بَيْتَ الْمَقْدِسِ، وَفُتِحَتْ لَهُمَا أَبْوَابُ السَّمَاءِ، ورَأَى[١٧] الْجَنَّةَ وَالنَّارَ، قَالَ: وَقَالَ حُذَيْفَةُ: وَلَمْ يُصَلِّ فِي بَيْتِ الْمَقْدِسِ، قَالَ زِرٌّ: فَقُلْتُ: بَلَى قَدْ صَلَّى، قَالَ حُذَيْفَةُ: مَا اسْمُكَ يَا أَصْلَعُ؟ فَإِنِّي أَعْرِفُ وَجْهَكَ، وَلَا أَدْرِي مَا اسْمُكَ، قَالَ[١٨]: زِرُّ بْنُ حُبَيْشٍ، قَالَ: فَقَالَ: وَمَا يُدْرِيكَ؟ وَهَلْ تَجِدُهُ صَلَّى؟ قَالَ: قُلْتُ: يَقُولُ اللَّهُ: ﴿سُبْحَٰنَ ٱلَّذِىٓ أَسْرَىٰ بِعَبْدِهِۦ لَيْلًا مِّنَ ٱلْمَسْجِدِ ٱلْحَرَامِ إِلَى ٱلْمَسْجِدِ ٱلْأَقْصَا ٱلَّذِى بَٰرَكْنَا حَوْلَهُۥ لِنُرِيَهُۥ مِنْ ءَايَٰتِنَآ ۚ إِنَّهُۥ هُوَ ٱلسَّمِيعُ ٱلْبَصِيرُ ۝١﴾، قَالَ: وَهَلْ تَجِدُهُ صَلَّى؟ إِنَّهُ لَوْ صَلَّى فِيهِ صَلَّيْنَا مَعَهُ[١٩] كَمَا نُصَلِّي فِي الْمَسْجِدِ الْحَرَامِ، وَقِيلَ لِحُذَيْفَةَ: وَرَبَطَ الدَّابَّةَ بِالْحَلَقَةِ الَّتِي يَرْبِطُ[٢٠] بِهَا الْأَنْبِيَاءُ، فَقَالَ حُذَيْفَةُ: كَانَ يَخَافُ[٢١] أَنْ تَذْهَبَ وَقَدْ أَتَاهُ اللَّهُ بِهَا؟![٢٢].

قال الهيثمي: ورجال أحمد رجال الصحيح؛ (مجمع الزوائد، ج١، ص٦٥).

قال شعيب الأرناؤوط: إسناده صحيح على شرط الشيخين.

وأخرجه ابن حبان (٤٧) من حديث بريدة.

الدرجة: صحيح.

١٦ برلين: ذر، بالذال، والصحيح بالزاي، وهو زِرُّ بن حبيش؛ كما هو مصرَّح به عند أحمد وابن أبي شيبة في المصنف في متن الحديث.

١٧ المصنف: رأيا الجنة.

١٨ المصنف: قال: قلت: زر بن حبيش.

١٩ المصنف: صلينا فيه.

٢٠ برلين: تربط.

٢١ المصنف: أو كان يخاف.

٢٢ ابن أبي شيبة (٣١٦٩٨) و(٣٦٥٧٣)، وأحمد (٢٣٣٨٠)، وأبو داود في مسنده (٤١١) عن حذيفة ابن اليمان.

قال شعيب الأرناؤوط: إسناده حسن؛ لأن فيه عاصم بن بهدلة.

وأخرجه ابن أبي شيبة (٣٦٥٧٠)، ومسلم (١٦٢)، وأحمد (١٢٥٢٧)، وأبو عوانة (١/ ١١٤)، وابن منده في الإيمان (٢/ ٧٠٩)، وأبو يعلى (٦/ ١٠٩) عن ثابت البُناني، عن أنس بن مالك.

٥٣ . حَدَّثَنَا الْحَسَنُ بْنُ مُوسَى، قَالَ: حَدَّثَنَا حَمَّادُ بْنُ سَلَمَةَ، عَنْ عَلِيِّ بْنِ زَيْدِ بْنِ جُدْعَانَ، عَنْ أَبِي الصَّلْتِ، عَنْ أَبِي هُرَيْرَةَ، قَالَ: قَالَ رَسُولُ اللَّهِ ﷺ: رَأَيْتُ لَيْلَةَ أُسْرِيَ بِي لَمَّا انْتَهَيْنَا إِلَى السَّمَاءِ السَّابِعَةِ، فَنَظَرْتُ فَوْقِي، فَإِذَا أَنَا بِرَعْدٍ وَبَرْقٍ وَصَوَاعِقَ، قَالَ: وَأَتَيْتُ عَلَى قَوْمٍ بُطُونُهُمْ كَالْبُيُوتِ فِيهَا الْحَيَّاتُ تُرَى مِنْ خَارِجِ بُطُونِهِمْ، فَقُلْتُ: مَنْ هَؤُلَاءِ يَا جِبْرِيلُ؟ قَالَ: هَؤُلَاءِ أَكَلَةُ الرِّبَا، فَلَمَّا نَزَلْتُ إِلَى السَّمَاءِ الدُّنْيَا نَظَرْتُ أَسْفَلَ مِنِّي، فَإِذَا بِرَهْجٍ وَدُخَانٍ وَأَصْوَاتٍ، فَقُلْتُ: مَا هَذَا يَا جِبْرِيلُ؟ قَالَ: هَذِهِ الشَّيَاطِينُ يَحُومُونَ[٢٣] عَلَى أَعْيُنِ بَنِي آدَمَ لَا يَتَفَكَّرُوا فِي مَلَكُوتِ السَّمَوَاتِ وَالْأَرْضِ، وَلَوْلَا ذَاكَ لَرَأَوُا الْعَجَائِبَ[٢٤].

قال شعيب الأرناؤوط: إسناده صحيح على شرط مسلم.

وأخرجه الحاكم (٤/ ٦٤٨)، وأبو يعلى (٨/ ٤٤٩)، والبزار (٥/ ١٤)، والوادعي في الصحيح المسند (٨٧٤) وحسنه عن عبد اللّه بن مسعود، قال الهيثمي في مجمع الزوائد (١/ ٧٤): رجاله رجال الصحيح، قال ابن حجر (مختصر البزار ١/ ٩٣): فيه أبو حمزة -وهو ميمون الأعور- متروك.

وأخرجه أحمد (٢٣٣٨٠)، وأبو داود في مسنده (٤١١)، والطبري في تهذيب الآثار (١/ ٤٤٦)، عن حذيفة بن اليمان: أن رسول اللّه ﷺ قال: أتيتُ بالبراق، وهو دابة طويل، حافره عند منتهى طرَفه، فلم يزل على ظهره هو وجبريل حتى أتى بيت المقدس، وفُتحت لهما أبواب السماء، ورأيا الجنة والنار.

وأخرجه الهيثمي في زوائده على مسند الحارث (١/ ١٧٠)، عن أبي سعيد الخدري.

الدرجة: حسن.

٢٣ برلين: يحرقون.

٢٤ ابن أبي شيبة في المصنف (٣٦٥٧٤)، وأحمد (٨٦٢٥)، وابن ماجه (٢٢٧٣)، والمنذري في الترغيب (٣/ ٧)، وابن كثير في التفسير (٣/ ٥١٩)، وضعَّفه؛ لأن به علي بن زيد بن جدعان، قال: وله منكَرات، وضعفه الألباني (ضعيف الترغيب: ١١٦٣)، وعقَّب شعيب الأرناؤوط على إسناد أحمد بأنه ضعيف.
الدرجة: ضعيف لأجل ابن أبي الصلت.

٥٤. حَدَّثَنَا الْحَسَنُ بْنُ مُوسَى، قَالَ: حَدَّثَنَا حَمَّادُ بْنُ سَلَمَةَ، قَالَ: أَخْبَرَنَا سُلَيْمَانُ التَّيْمِيُّ وَثَابِتٌ الْبُنَانِيُّ، عَنْ أَنَسٍ، قَالَ: قَالَ رَسُولُ اللَّهِ ﷺ: أَتَيْتُ عَلَى مُوسَى لَيْلَةَ أُسْرِيَ بِي عِنْدَ الْكَثِيبِ الأَحْمَرِ وَهُوَ قَائِمٌ يُصَلِّي فِي قَبْرِهِ[٢٥].

٥٥. حَدَّثَنَا وَكِيعٌ، عَنْ حَمَّادِ بْنِ سَلَمَةَ، عَنْ عَلِيِّ بْنِ زَيْدٍ، عَنْ أَنَسِ بْنِ مَالِكٍ، قَالَ: قَالَ رَسُولُ اللَّهِ ﷺ: مَرَرْتُ لَيْلَةَ أُسْرِيَ بِي عَلَى قَوْمٍ تُقْرَضُ شِفَاهُهُمْ بِمَقَارِيضَ مِنْ نَارٍ، فَقُلْتُ: مَنْ هَؤُلَاءِ؟ قِيلَ: هَؤُلَاءِ خُطَبَاءُ مِنْ أَهْلِ الدُّنْيَا مِمَّنْ كَانُوا[٢٦] يَأْمُرُونَ النَّاسَ بِالْبِرِّ وَيَنْسَوْنَ أَنْفُسَهُمْ وَهُمْ يَتْلُونَ الْكِتَابَ أَفَلَا يَعْقِلُونَ![٢٧].

٥٦ حَدَّثَنَا عَلِيُّ بْنُ مُسْهِرٍ، عَنْ أَبِي إِسْحَاقَ الشَّيْبَانِيِّ، عَنْ عَبْدِ اللَّهِ بْنِ شَدَّادٍ، قَالَ: لَمَّا أُسْرِيَ بِالنَّبِيِّ ﷺ أُتِيَ بِدَابَّةٍ فَوْقَ الْحِمَارِ وَدُونَ الْبَغْلِ، يَضَعُ حَافِرَهُ عِنْدَ مُنْتَهَى طَرَفِهِ، يُقَالُ لَهُ: بُرَاقٌ، فَمَرَّ رَسُولُ اللَّهِ ﷺ بِعِيرٍ لِلْمُشْرِكِينَ، فَنَفَرَتْ، فَقَالُوا: يَا هَؤُلَاءِ، مَا هَذَا؟ قَالُوا:

---

٢٥ ابن أبي شيبة في المصنف (٣٦٥٧٥)، ومسلم (٢٣٧٥)، والنسائي في الكبرى (١٣٢٨)، وفي المجتبى (٢٠٨٩)، وأحمد (١٢٥٢٦)، وابن حبان (١/ ٢٤٢)، وعبد بن حميد (١/ ٣٢٦)، وأبو نعيم في الحلية (٦/ ٢٥٣)، وأبو يعلى (٦/ ٧١)، وابن عساكر (٦١/ ١٨٤)، قال شعيب الأرناؤوط: إسناده صحيح على شرط مسلم.

وأخرجه الطبراني في الأوسط (٨/ ١٣)، عن أبي سعيد الخدري.

الدرجة: صحيح.

٢٦ برلين: كانا.

٢٧ ابن أبي شيبة (٣٦٥٧٦)، وأحمد (١٢٢٣٢)، وأبو داود الطيالسي في المسند (٢٠٦٠)، وأبو يعلى (٧/ ٦٩)، والحارث (١/ ١٧٠)، وعبد اللّه بن المبارك في مسنده (١/ ١٥)، وعبد بن حميد في مسنده (١/ ٣٦٧)، عن حماد بن سلمة، عن علي بن زيد، عن أنس، وأخرجه ابن حبان في صحيحه (١/ ٢٤٩)، وابن أبي حاتم، وابن مردويه، والطبراني في الأوسط (٨/ ١٤٤)، وأبو نعيم في الحلية (ج٢، ص٣٨٦)، من حديث هشام الدَّستوائي عن المغيرة -يعني ابن حبيب، خَتَن مالك بن دينار- عن مالك بن دينار، عن ثمامة، عن أنس بن مالك، وأخرجه عبد الرزاق في التفسير (٢/ ٣٧٣)، عن عمر بن نبهان، عن قتادة، عن أنس.

الدرجة: صحيح المتن، وهذا الإسناد ضعيف؛ لضعف علي بن زيد.

مَا نَرَى[٢٨] شَيْئًا، مَا هَذِهِ إِلَّا رِيحٌ، حَتَّى أَتَى بَيْتَ الْمَقْدِسِ، فَأُتِيَ بِإِنَاءَيْنِ، فِي وَاحِدٍ: خَمْرٌ، وَفِي الْآخَرِ: لَبَنٌ، فَأَخَذَ النَّبِيُّ ﷺ اللَّبَنَ، فَقَالَ لَهُ جِبْرِيلُ: هُدِيتَ وَهُدِيَتْ أُمَّتُكَ، ثُمَّ صَارَ إِلَى مُضَرَ[٢٩].

٥٧. حَدَّثَنَا أَبُو خَالِدٍ[٣٠]، عَنْ حُمَيْدٍ، عَنْ أَنَسٍ، قَالَ: قَالَ رَسُولُ اللَّهِ ﷺ: لَمَّا انْتَهَيْتُ إِلَى السِّدْرَةِ إِذَا وَرَقُهَا مِثْلُ آذَانِ الْفِيلَةِ، وَإِذَا نَبْقُهَا[٣١] أَمْثَالُ الْقِلَالِ، فَلَمَّا غَشِيَهَا مِنْ أَمْرِ اللَّهِ مَا غَشِيَ، تَحَوَّلَتْ، فَذَكَرَ الْيَاقُوتَ[٣٢].

٥٨. حَدَّثَنَا ابْنُ يَمَانٍ، عَنْ سُفْيَانَ، عَنْ سَلَمَةَ بْنِ كُهَيْلٍ، عَنْ[٣٣] غَزْوَانَ، قَالَ: سِدْرَةُ الْمُنْتَهَى: صُبْرُ[٣٤] الْجَنَّةِ[٣٥].

---

٢٨ برلين: ترى.

٢٩ ابن أبي شيبة (٣٦٥٧٧)، والطبري في تفسيره (١٥/ ١٥)، عن أنس رضي اللّه عنه.
الدرجة: مرسل صحيح.

٣٠ المصنف: أبو خالد الأحمر.

٣١ ثمر شجر السِّدر، وهو حَبٌّ أبيضُ صغير.

٣٢ أخرجه ابن أبي شيبة (٣٣٩٦٥)، وعبد الرزاق في التفسير (٣/ ٢٥١)، والدارقطني (٢٩) مختصرًا، والبخاري (٣٦٧٤)، وابن حبان (٤٨)، وابن خزيمة (٣٠١)، بطوله.
الدرجة: صحيح.

٣٣ برلين: بن غزوان، والصحيح: عن غزوان.

٣٤ المصنف: صَبْرُ بفتح الصاد، والصواب بالضم، كما هو عند هناد بن السري في الزهد، باب صفة أهل الجنة، حديث: (٤٩)، وعند الطبراني في الكبير، حديث: (٨٩٠٥٩).

٣٥ ابن أبي شيبة في المصنف (٣٦٥٨٠)، والطبري في التفسير (٢٧/ ٥٤)، عن غزوان عن عبد اللّه بن مسعود موقوفًا، وأخرجه الطبراني في الكبير (٩٠٥٦)، وابن السري في الزهد (٥٠)، عن هزيل بن شرحبيل عن عبد اللّه بن مسعود، وأخرجه ابن أبي شيبة في المصنف (٣٣٩٦٢)، من كلام غزوان. وصُبْرُ الْجَنَّةِ: أعلى نواحيها، وصُبرُ كل شيء: أعلاه؛ (النهاية ٣/ ٩)، وقيل: وسطها؛ كما في حديث عبد اللّه بن مسعود الذي يليه.
الدرجة: مقطوع، ورُوي موقوفًا.

٥٩. حَدَّثَنَا وَكِيعٌ، عَنْ سُفْيَانَ، عَنْ سَلَمَةَ بْنِ كُهَيْلٍ، عَنِ الْحَسَنِ الْعُرَنِيِّ، عَنْ هُزَيْلِ بْنِ شُرَحْبِيلَ، عَنْ عَبْدِ اللَّهِ فِي قَوْلِهِ: ﴿...سِدْرَةِ ٱلْمُنتَهَىٰ ﴿١٤﴾﴾، قَالَ: صُبْرُ الْجَنَّةِ، يَعْنِي: وَسَطَهَا، عَلَيْهَا فُضُولُ السُّنْدُسِ وَالإِسْتَبْرَقِ[٣٦].

٦٠. حَدَّثَنَا أَبُو خَالِدٍ، عَنْ يَحْيَى بْنِ مَيْسَرَةَ، عَنْ عَمْرِو بْنِ مُرَّةَ، عَنْ كَعْبٍ، قَالَ: سِدْرَةُ الْمُنْتَهَى: يَنْتَهِي إِلَيْهَا أَمْرُ كُلِّ نَبِيٍّ وَمَلَكٍ[٣٧].

Traditions discussed in Chapter Four concerning the Prophet's migration, as excerpted from MS. Berlin 9409

مَا قَالُوا فِي مُهَاجَرِ النَّبِيِّ عليه السلام وَأَبِي بَكْرٍ، وَقُدُومِ مَنْ قَدِمَ

٨٦. حَدَّثنا أَبُو أُسَامَةَ[٣٨]، قَالَ: حَدَّثَنَا هِشَامُ بْنُ عُرْوَةَ، عَنْ أَبِيهِ وَفَاطِمَةَ، عَنْ أَسْمَاءَ، قَالَتْ: صَنَعْتُ سُفْرَةَ النَّبِيِّ ﷺ فِي بَيْتِ أَبِي بَكْرٍ حِينَ أَرَادَ أَنْ يُهَاجِرَ إِلَى الْمَدِينَةِ، قَالَتْ: فَلَمْ نَجِدْ لِسُفْرَتِهِ وَلَا لِسِقَائِهِ مَا نَرْبِطُهُمَا بِهِ، فَقُلْتُ لِأَبِي بَكْرٍ: وَاللَّهِ مَا أَجِدُ شَيْئًا أَرْبِطُ بِهِ إِلَّا نِطَاقِي،

---

٣٦ ابن أبي شيبة في المصنف (٣٣٩٦٢)، هكذا من كلام غزوان، وأخرجه ابن أبي شيبة في المصنف (٣٦٥٨٠)، والطبري في التفسير (٢٧/ ٥٤)، عن غزوان عن عبد اللَّه بن مسعود موقوفًا، وأخرجه الطبراني في الكبير (٩/ ٢١٧)، وابن السَّري في الزهد (١/ ٦٧)، عن هزيل بن شرحبيل عن عبداللَّه ابن مسعود.

الدرجة: أثر موقوف.

٣٧ أخرجه ابن أبي شيبة في المصنف (٣٦٥٨١)، عن كعب.

وأخرجه الطبري في التفسير (٢٧/ ٥٢)، قال: حدثني جعفر بن محمد المروزي، قال: ثنا يعلى، عن الأجلح، قال: قلت للضحاك: لِمَ تسمَّى سدرةَ المنتهى؟ قال: لأنه ينتهي إليها كلُّ شيء من أمر اللَّه، لا يعْدُوها.

الدرجة: أثر موقوف.

٣٨ المصنف: حَدَّثَنَا أَبُو بَكْرٍ، قَالَ: حَدَّثَنَا أَبُو أُسَامَةَ.

قَالَتْ: فَقَالَ: شُقِّيهِ بِاثْنَيْنِ، فَارْبِطِي بِوَاحِدٍ السِّقَاءَ، وَبِالْآخَرِ [٣٩] السُّفْرَةَ؛ فَلِذَلِكَ سُمِّيَتْ: ذَاتَ النِّطَاقَيْنِ[٤٠].

٨٧. حَدَّثَنَا أَبُو أُسَامَةَ، عَنِ ابْنِ عَوْنٍ، عَنْ عُمَيْرِ بْنِ إِسْحَاقَ، قَالَ: لَمَّا خَرَجَ رَسُولُ اللَّهِ ﷺ، وَأَبُو بَكْرٍ، يَعْنِي إِلَى الْمَدِينَةِ، تَبِعَهُمَا سُرَاقَةُ بْنُ مَالِكٍ، فَلَمَّا أَتَاهُمَا قَالَ: هَذَانِ فَرَّا مِنْ قُرَيْشٍ، لَوْ رَدَدْتُ عَلَى قُرَيْشٍ فَرَّهَا، قَالَ: فَعَطَفَ[٤١] فَرَسَهُ عَلَيْهِمَا، فَسَاخَتِ الْفَرَسُ[٤٢]، فَقَالَ: اُدْعُوَا اللَّهَ أَنْ يُخْرِجَهَا، وَلَا أَقْرَبُكُمَا، قَالَ: فَخَرَجَتْ، (فَعَادَتْ)[٤٣] حَتَّى فَعَلَ ذَلِكَ مَرَّتَيْنِ، أَوْ ثَلَاثًا، قَالَ: فَكَفَّ، ثُمَّ قَالَ: هَلُمَّا إِلَى الزَّادِ وَالْحُمْلَانِ، فَقَالَا: لَا نُرِيدُ، وَلَا حَاجَةَ لَنَا فِي ذَلِكَ[٤٤].

٨٨. حَدَّثَنَا عُبَيْدُ اللَّهِ بْنُ مُوسَى، قَالَ: أَخْبَرَنَا إِسْرَائِيلُ، عَنْ أَبِي إِسْحَاقَ، عَنِ الْبَرَاءِ بْنِ عَازِبٍ، قَالَ: اشْتَرَى أَبُو بَكْرٍ مِنْ عَازِبٍ رَحْلًا بِثَلَاثَةَ عَشَرَ دِرْهَمًا، فَقَالَ أَبُو بَكْرٍ لِعَازِبٍ: مُرِ الْبَرَاءَ فَلْيَحْمِلْهُ إِلَى رَحْلِي، فَقَالَ لَهُ عَازِبٌ: لَا، حَتَّى تُحَدِّثَنَا كَيْفَ صَنَعْتَ أَنْتَ وَرَسُولُ اللَّهِ ﷺ حَيْثُ خَرَجْتُمَا وَالْمُشْرِكُونَ يَطْلُبُونَكُمَا، قَالَ: رَحَلْنَا مِنْ مَكَّةَ، فَأَحْيَيْنَا لَيْلَتَنَا وَيَوْمَنَا حَتَّى أَظْهَرْنَا وَقَامَ قَائِمُ الظَّهِيرَةِ، فَرَمَيْتُ بِبَصَرِي هَلْ أَرَى مِنْ ظِلٍّ نَأْوِي إِلَيْهِ، فَإِذَا أَنَا بِصَخْرَةٍ،

---

٣٩ المصنف: وبالآخرة.

٤٠ ابن أبي شيبة (٣٦٦٠٨)، والبخاري (٢٨١٧)، والطبراني في الكبير (٢٤/ ٧٩)، وأحمد (٢٦٩٧٣).
الدرجة: صحيح.

٤١ المصنف: فعطفت.

٤٢ غرقت رِجلاها في الرمل ولم تقدر على الوقوف.

٤٣ زيادة في المصنف.

٤٤ ابن أبي شيبة (٣١٧٧٧)، عن عمير بن إسحاق، وهو تابعي، ليَّنه ابنُ معين، وقوَّاه غيره، وهو مقبول عند ابن حجر.
وأخرجه الحاكم (٣/ ٧١)، وصححه عن ابن شهاب، عن عبد الرحمن بن مالك المُدلجي –وهو ابن أخي سراقة– عن سراقة.
وأخرجه البخاري (٥٢٨٤)، عن عمير بن إسحاق، عن البراء بن عازب.
الدرجة: مرسَل له شواهد في الصحيح.

فَانْتَهَيْنَا إِلَيْهَا، فَإِذَا بَقِيَّةُ ظِلٍّ لَهَا، فَنَظَرْتُ بَقِيَّةَ ظِلٍّ فَسَوَّيْتُهُ، ثُمَّ فَرَشْتُ لِرَسُولِ اللَّهِ ﷺ فِيهِ فَرْوَةً، ثُمَّ قُلْتُ: اضْطَجِعْ يَا رَسُولَ اللَّهِ، فَاضْطَجَعَ، ثُمَّ ذَهَبْتُ أَنْفُضُ مَا حَوْلِي هَلْ أَرَى مِنْ الطَّلَبِ أَحَدًا، فَإِذَا أَنَا بِرَاعِي غَنَمٍ يَسُوقُ غَنَمَهُ إِلَى الصَّخْرَةِ يُرِيدُ مِنْهَا الَّذِي أُرِيدُ، فَسَأَلْتُهُ، فَقُلْتُ: لِمَنْ أَنْتَ يَا غُلَامُ؟ فَقَالَ: لِرَجُلٍ مِنْ قُرَيْشٍ، قَالَ: فَسَمَّاهُ، فَعَرَفْتُهُ، فَقُلْتُ: هَلْ فِي غَنَمِكَ مِنْ لَبَنٍ؟ قَالَ: نَعَمْ، قُلْتُ: هَلْ أَنْتَ حَالِبٌ لِي؟ قَالَ: نَعَمْ، قَالَ: فَأَمَرْتُهُ فَاعْتَقَلَ شَاةً مِنْ غَنَمِهِ، فَأَمَرْتُهُ أَنْ يَنْفُضَ ضَرْعَهَا مِنَ الْغُبَارِ، ثُمَّ أَمَرْتُهُ أَنْ يَنْفُضَ كَفَّيْهِ، فَقَالَ هَكَذَا، فَضَرَبَ إِحْدَى يَدَيْهِ بِالْأُخْرَى، فَحَلَبَ كُثْبَةً مِنْ لَبَنٍ[٤٥]، وَمَعِي لِرَسُولِ اللَّهِ ﷺ إِدَاوَةٌ عَلَى فَمِهَا خِرْقَةٌ، فَصَبَبْتُ عَلَى اللَّبَنِ حَتَّى بَرَدَ أَسْفَلُهُ، فَأَتَيْتُ رَسُولَ اللَّهِ ﷺ فَوَافَقْتُهُ قَدِ اسْتَيْقَظَ، فَقُلْتُ: اشْرَبْ يَا رَسُولَ اللَّهِ، فَشَرِبَ رَسُولُ اللَّهِ ﷺ حَتَّى رَضِيتُ، ثُمَّ قُلْتُ: أَنَى الرَّحِيلُ يَا رَسُولَ اللَّهِ، فَارْتَحَلْنَا وَالْقَوْمُ يَطْلُبُونَنَا، فَلَمْ يُدْرِكْنَا أَحَدٌ مِنْهُمْ غَيْرُ سُرَاقَةَ بْنِ مَالِكِ بْنِ جُعْشُمٍ عَلَى فَرَسٍ لَهُ، فَقُلْتُ: هَذَا الطَّلَبُ قَدْ لَحِقَنَا يَا رَسُولَ اللَّهِ[٤٦]، (فَقَالَ: لَا تَحْزَنْ إِنَّ اللَّهَ مَعَنَا، حَتَّى إِذَا دَنَا مِنَّا فَكَانَ بَيْنَنَا وَبَيْنَهُ قَدْرُ رُمْحٍ[٤٧] أَوْ رُمْحَيْنِ أَوْ ثَلَاثَةٍ، قَالَ: قُلْتُ: يَا رَسُولَ اللَّهِ، هَذَا الطَّلَبُ قَدْ لَحِقَنَا)[٤٨]، وَبَكَيْتُ، فَقَالَ: مَا يُبْكِيكَ؟ فَقُلْتُ: أَمَا وَاللَّهِ مَا عَلَى نَفْسِي أَبْكِي، وَلَكِنِّي أَبْكِي عَلَيْكَ، قَالَ: فَدَعَا عَلَيْهِ رَسُولُ اللَّهِ ﷺ، فَقَالَ: اللَّهُمَّ اكْفِنَاهُ بِمَا شِئْتَ، قَالَ: فَسَاخَتْ بِهِ فَرَسُهُ فِي الْأَرْضِ إِلَى بَطْنِهَا، فَوَثَبَ عَنْهَا، ثُمَّ قَالَ: يَا مُحَمَّدُ، قَدْ عَلِمْتُ أَنَّ هَذَا عَمَلُكَ، فَادْعُ اللَّهَ أَنْ يُنْجِيَنِي مِمَّا أَنَا فِيهِ؛ فَوَاللَّهِ لَأُعَمِّيَنَّ عَلَى مَنْ وَرَائِي مِنَ الطَّلَبِ، وَهَذِهِ كِنَانَتِي، فَخُذْ سَهْمًا مِنْهَا؛ فَإِنَّكَ سَتَمُرُّ عَلَى إِبِلِي وَغَنَمِي بِمَكَانِ كَذَا وَكَذَا، فَخُذْ مِنْهَا حَاجَتَكَ، فَقَالَ رَسُولُ اللَّهِ ﷺ: لَا حَاجَةَ لَنَا فِي إِبِلِكَ، وَانْصَرَفَ عَنْ رَسُولِ اللَّهِ ﷺ، وَدَعَا لَهُ رَسُولُ اللَّهِ ﷺ، وَانْطَلَقَ رَاجِعًا إِلَى أَصْحَابِهِ، وَمَضَى رَسُولُ اللَّهِ ﷺ وَأَنَا مَعَهُ حَتَّى قَدِمْنَا الْمَدِينَةَ لَيْلًا، فَتَنَازَعَهُ الْقَوْمُ أَيُّهُمْ يَنْزِلُ عَلَيْهِ، فَقَالَ رَسُولُ اللَّهِ ﷺ: إِنِّي أَنْزِلُ اللَّيْلَةَ عَلَى بَنِي النَّجَّارِ أَخْوَالِ عَبْدِ الْمُطَّلِبِ؛ أُكْرِمُهُمْ بِذَلِكَ، فَخَرَجَ النَّاسُ

---

٤٥ قليلًا منه.

٤٦ زيادة في برلين.

٤٧ مسافة رمي الرمح.

٤٨ ما بين القوسين زيادة في نسخة المصنف.

حَتَّى دَخَلَ الْمَدِينَةَ، وَفِي الطَّرِيقِ وَعَلَى الْبُيُوتِ الْغِلْمَانُ وَالْخَدَمُ: جَاءَ مُحَمَّدٌ ﷺ، جَاءَ رَسُولُ اللَّهِ ﷺ، فَلَمَّا أَصْبَحَ انْطَلَقَ فَنَزَلَ حَيْثُ أَمَرَهُ اللَّهُ[٤٩]، وَكَانَ رَسُولُ اللَّهِ ﷺ قَدْ صَلَّى نَحْوَ بَيْتِ الْمَقْدِسِ سِتَّةَ عَشَرَ شَهْرًا، أَوْ سَبْعَةَ عَشَرَ شَهْرًا، وَكَانَ رَسُولُ اللَّهِ ﷺ يُحِبُّ أَنْ يُوَجَّهَ نَحْوَ الْكَعْبَةِ، فَأَنْزَلَ اللَّهُ: ﴿قَدْ نَرَىٰ تَقَلُّبَ وَجْهِكَ فِي ٱلسَّمَآءِ فَلَنُوَلِّيَنَّكَ قِبْلَةً تَرْضَىٰهَا فَوَلِّ وَجْهَكَ شَطْرَ ٱلْمَسْجِدِ ٱلْحَرَامِ﴾[٥٠]، قَالَ: فَوُجِّهَ نَحْوَ الْكَعْبَةِ، وَقَالَ السُّفَهَاءُ مِنَ النَّاسِ: ﴿سَيَقُولُ ٱلسُّفَهَآءُ مِنَ ٱلنَّاسِ مَا وَلَّىٰهُمْ عَن قِبْلَتِهِمُ ٱلَّتِي كَانُواْ عَلَيْهَا قُل لِّلَّهِ ٱلْمَشْرِقُ وَٱلْمَغْرِبُ يَهْدِي مَن يَشَآءُ إِلَىٰ صِرَٰطٍ مُّسْتَقِيمٍ ﴿١٤٢﴾﴾[٥١]، قَالَ: وَصَلَّى مَعَ النَّبِيِّ ﷺ[٥٢] رَجُلٌ، ثُمَّ خَرَجَ بَعْدَمَا صَلَّى، فَمَرَّ عَلَى قَوْمٍ مِنَ الْأَنْصَارِ وَهُمْ رُكُوعٌ فِي صَلَاةِ الْعَصْرِ نَحْوَ بَيْتِ الْمَقْدِسِ، فَقَالَ: هُوَ يَشْهَدُ أَنَّهُ صَلَّى مَعَ النَّبِيِّ ﷺ، وَأَنَّهُ قَدْ وُجِّهَ نَحْوَ الْكَعْبَةِ، قَالَ: فَانْحَرَفَ الْقَوْمُ حَتَّى وُجِّهُوا نَحْوَ الْكَعْبَةِ، قَالَ الْبَرَاءُ: وَكَانَ نَزَلَ عَلَيْنَا مِنَ الْمُهَاجِرِينَ مُصْعَبُ بْنُ عُمَيْرٍ أَخُو بَنِي عَبْدِ الدَّارِ بْنِ قُصَيٍّ، فَقُلْنَا لَهُ: مَا فَعَلَ رَسُولُ اللَّهِ ﷺ؟ فَقَالَ[٥٣]: هُوَ وَمَكَانُهُ[٥٤]، وَأَصْحَابُهُ عَلَى أَثَرِي، ثُمَّ أَتَانَا بَعْدُ عَمْرُو ابْنُ أُمِّ مَكْتُومٍ، أَخُو بَنِي فِهْرٍ، الْأَعْمَى، فَقُلْنَا لَهُ: مَا فَعَلَ مَنْ وَرَاءَكَ: رَسُولُ اللَّهِ وَأَصْحَابُهُ؟ فَقَالَ: هُمْ عَلَى أَثَرِي، ثُمَّ أَتَانَا (بَعْدَهُ عَمَّارُ بْنُ يَاسِرٍ وَسَعْدُ بْنُ أَبِي وَقَّاصٍ وَعَبْدُ اللَّهِ بْنُ مَسْعُودٍ وَبِلَالٌ، ثُمَّ أَتَانَا)[٥٥] عُمَرُ بْنُ الْخَطَّابِ مِنْ بَعْدِهِمْ فِي عِشْرِينَ

---

٤٩ برلين: فنزل حيث أمر، وكان رسول الله ﷺ.

٥٠ البقرة: ١٤٥.

٥١ البقرة: ١٤٣.

٥٢ المصنف: عليه الصلاة والسلام.

٥٣ برلين: فقلت.

٥٤ هكذا في نسخة برلين وفي معظم النسخ المطبوعة من المصنف، وقد أثبتها كمال الحوت (٧/ ٣٣٤)، والجمعة واللحيدان في تحقيقهما وعلّقا: هكذا في جميع الأصول، ولعل الصواب من غير الواو (ج١٣/ ٢٤٠)، وأثبتها أبو أسامة محمد بن إبراهيم في تحقيقه للمصنف، ط دار الفاروق (ج١٣/ ٣٩)، لكن لم يثبتها الشيخ محمد عوامة في تحقيقه للمصنف (٢٠/ ٢٧٠).

٥٥ ما بين القوسين زيادة في نسخة برلين.

رَاكِبًا، ثُمَّ أَتَانَا بَعْدَهُمْ رَسُولُ اللَّهِ ﷺ وَأَبُو بَكْرٍ مَعَهُ، فَلَمْ يَقْدَمْ عَلَيْنَا حَتَّى قَرَأْتُ سُوَرًا مِنْ سُوَرِ الْمُفَصَّلِ، ثُمَّ خَرَجْنَا حَتَّى نَتَلَقَّى الْعِيرَ، فَوَجَدْنَاهُمْ قَدْ حُذِّرُوا[٥٦].

٨٩. حَدَّثَنَا عَفَّانُ، قَالَ: حَدَّثَنَا شُعْبَةُ، عَنْ أَبِي إِسْحَاقَ، قَالَ: سَمِعْتُ الْبَرَاءَ يَقُولُ: أَوَّلُ مَنْ قَدِمَ عَلَيْنَا مِنْ أَصْحَابِ رَسُولِ اللَّهِ ﷺ مُصْعَبُ بْنُ عُمَيْرٍ وَابْنُ أُمِّ مَكْتُومٍ، فَجَعَلَا يُقْرِئَانِ النَّاسَ الْقُرْآنَ، ثُمَّ جَاءَ عَمَّارٌ وَبِلَالٌ وَسَعْدٌ، ثُمَّ جَاءَ عُمَرُ بْنُ الْخَطَّابِ فِي عِشْرِينَ رَاكِبًا، ثُمَّ جَاءَ رَسُولُ اللَّهِ ﷺ، قَالَ: فَمَا رَأَيْتُ أَهْلَ الْمَدِينَةِ فَرِحُوا بِشَيْءٍ قَطُّ فَرَحَهُمْ بِهِ، قَالَ: فَمَا قَدِمَ حَتَّى قَرَأْتُ: ﴿سَبِّحِ ٱسْمَ رَبِّكَ ٱلْأَعْلَى ۝١﴾ فِي سُوَرٍ مِنَ الْمُفَصَّلِ[٥٧].

٩٠. حَدَّثَنَا أَسْوَدُ بْنُ عَامِرٍ، قَالَ: حَدَّثَنَا حَمَّادُ بْنُ سَلَمَةَ، عَنْ عَلِيِّ بْنِ زَيْدٍ، عَنِ الْحَسَنِ، عَنْ سُرَاقَةَ بْنِ مَالِكٍ الْمُدْلِجِيِّ، حَدَّثَهُمْ أَنَّ قُرَيْشًا جَعَلَتْ فِي رَسُولِ اللَّهِ ﷺ وَأَبِي بَكْرٍ أَرْبَعِينَ أُوقِيَّةً، قَالَ: فَبَيْنَمَا أَنَا جَالِسٌ إِذْ جَاءَنِي رَجُلٌ، فَقَالَ: إِنَّ الرَّجُلَيْنِ اللَّذَيْنِ جَعَلَتْ قُرَيْشٌ فِيهِمَا مَا جَعَلَتْ قَرِيبٌ مِنْكَ بِمَكَانِ كَذَا وَكَذَا، فَأَتَيْتُ فَرَسِي وَهُوَ فِي الْمَرْعَى، فَنَفَرْتُ بِهِ، ثُمَّ أَخَذْتُ رُمْحِي، قَالَ فَرَكِبْتُهُ، قَالَ: فَجَعَلْتُ أَجُرُّ الرُّمْحَ مَخَافَةَ أَنْ يَشْرَكَنِي فِيهِمَا أَهْلُ الْمَاءِ، قَالَ: فَلَمَّا رَأَيْتُهُمَا قَالَ أَبُو بَكْرٍ: هَذَا بَاغٍ يَبْغِينَا، فَالْتَفَتَ إِلَيَّ النَّبِيُّ ﷺ، فَقَالَ: اللَّهُمَّ اكْفِنَاهُ بِمَا شِئْتَ، قَالَ: فَوَجِلَ[٥٨] فَرَسِي وَإِنِّي لَفِي جَلَدٍ مِنَ الْأَرْضِ! فَوَقَعْتُ عَلَى حَجَرٍ فَانْقَلَبْتُ، فَقُلْتُ: ادْعُ الَّذِي فَعَلَ بِفَرَسِي مَا أَرَى أَنْ يُخَلِّصَهُ، وَعَاهَدَهُ أَنْ لَا يَعْصِيَهُ، قَالَ:

---

٥٦ ابن أبي شيبة (٣٦٦١٠)، وأحمد (٣)، والبخاري (٣٤١٩) و(٣٤٥٢)، ومسلم (٢٠٠٩)، وابن حبان (١٤/ ١٩١)، والبزار (١/ ١١٩)، وأبو بكر المروزي في مسنده (١/ ١٢٣)، وابن سعد عن البراء بن عازب رضي الله عنه.

الدرجة: صحيح.

٥٧ ابن أبي شيبة (٣٦٦١١)، والبخاري (٣٧٠٩)، والنسائي في السنن الكبرى (١١٦٦٦)، وأبو داود الطيالسي في مسنده (٧٠٤)، وابن أبي عاصم في الأوائل (١/ ١٥٥)، وابن سعد (٤/ ٢٠٦).

الدرجة: صحيح.

٥٨ هكذا بالجيم (فوجِل) في نسخة برلين، وكذا الطبعة القديمة للمصنف، تحقيق كمال الحوت (٧/ ٣٤٥)، وكذلك في تحقيق الجمعة واللحيدان (١٣/ ٢٤١)، لكن الشيخ عوامة أثبتها بالحاء (٢٠/ ٢٧٦)، ولعله الصحيح.

فَدَعَا لَهُ، فَخُلِّصَ الْفَرَسُ، فَقَالَ رَسُولُ اللَّهِ ﷺ: أَوَاهِبُهُ أَنْتَ لِي؟ فَقُلْتُ: نَعَمْ، فَقَالَ: فَهَاهُنَا، قَالَ: فَعَمِّ عَنَّا النَّاسَ، وَأَخَذَ رَسُولُ اللَّهِ ﷺ طَرِيقَ السَّاحِلِ مِمَّا يَلِي الْبَحْرَ، قَالَ: فَكُنْتُ أَوَّلَ النَّهَارِ لَهُمْ طَالِبًا، وَآخِرَ النَّهَارِ[٥٩] لَهُمْ مَسْلَحَةً[٦٠]، وَقَالَ لِي: إِذَا اسْتَقْرَرْنَا بِالْمَدِينَةِ فَإِنْ رَأَيْتَ أَنْ تَأْتِيَنَا فَأْتِنَا، قَالَ: فَلَمَّا قَدِمَ الْمَدِينَةَ وَظَهَرَ عَلَى أَهْلِ بَدْرٍ وَأُحُدٍ، وَأَسْلَمَ النَّاسُ وَمَنْ حَوْلَهُمْ، قَالَ سُرَاقَةُ: بَلَغَنِي أَنَّهُ يُرِيدُ أَنْ يَبْعَثَ خَالِدَ بْنَ الْوَلِيدِ إِلَى بَنِي مُدْلِجٍ، قَالَ: فَأَتَيْتُهُ، فَقُلْتُ لَهُ: أَنْشُدُكَ النِّعْمَةَ، فَقَالَ الْقَوْمُ: مَهْ! فَقَالَ رَسُولُ اللَّهِ ﷺ: دَعُوهُ، فَقَالَ رَسُولُ اللَّهِ ﷺ: مَا تُرِيدُ؟ فَقُلْتُ: بَلَغَنِي أَنَّكَ تُرِيدُ أَنْ تَبْعَثَ خَالِدَ بْنَ الْوَلِيدِ إِلَى قَوْمِي، فَأَنَا أُحِبُّ أَنْ تُوَادِعَهُمْ؛ فَإِنْ أَسْلَمَ قَوْمُهُمْ أَسْلَمُوا مَعَهُمْ، وَإِنْ لَمْ يُسْلِمُوا لَمْ تَخْشُنْ صُدُورُ قَوْمِهِمْ عَلَيْهِمْ، فَأَخَذَ رَسُولُ اللَّهِ ﷺ بِيَدِ خَالِدِ بْنِ [إن كانت في أول السطر كما هي في البي دي إف، فترسم: ابنِ] الْوَلِيدِ، فَقَالَ لَهُ: اذْهَبْ مَعَهُ فَاصْنَعْ مَا أَرَادَ، فَذَهَبَ إِلَى بَنِي مُدْلِجٍ، فَأَخَذُوا عَلَيْهِمْ أَنْ لَا يُعِينُوا عَلَى رَسُولِ اللَّهِ ﷺ، فَإِنْ أَسْلَمَتْ قُرَيْشٌ أَسْلَمُوا مَعَهُمْ، فَأَنْزَلَ اللَّهُ: ﴿وَدُّواْ لَوۡ تَكۡفُرُونَ كَمَا كَفَرُواْ﴾ حَتَّى بَلَغَ: ﴿إِلَّا ٱلَّذِينَ يَصِلُونَ إِلَىٰ قَوۡمِۭ بَيۡنَكُمۡ وَبَيۡنَهُم مِّيثَٰقٌ أَوۡ جَآءُوكُمۡ حَصِرَتۡ صُدُورُهُمۡ أَن يُقَٰتِلُوكُمۡ أَوۡ يُقَٰتِلُواْ قَوۡمَهُمۡۚ وَلَوۡ شَآءَ ٱللَّهُ لَسَلَّطَهُمۡ عَلَيۡكُمۡ فَلَقَٰتَلُوكُمۡۚ﴾[٦١]، قَالَ الْحَسَنُ: فَالَّذِينَ حَصِرَتْ صُدُورُهُمْ: بَنُو مُدْلِجٍ، فَمَنْ وَصَلَ إِلَى بَنِي مُدْلِجٍ مِنْ غَيْرِهِمْ كَانَ فِي مِثْلِ عَهْدِهِمْ[٦٢].

---

٥٩ برلين: الليل.

٦٠ قوة حراسة وحماية.

٦١ النساء: ٩٠، ٩١، في نسخة برلين خطأ في الآية.

٦٢ ابن أبي شيبة (٣٦٦١٢)، والحارث وابن أبي حاتم (٣/ ١٠٢٦)، وابن مردويه، وأبو نعيم في الدلائل، كذا في الدر المنثور (٢/ ٦١٣).

الدرجة: ضعيف لأجل علي بن زيد.

٩١ . حَدَّثَنَا عَفَّانُ، قَالَ: حَدَّثَنَا هَمَّامٌ، قَالَ: أَخْبَرَنَا ثَابِتٌ، عَنْ أَنَسٍ، أَنَّ أَبَا بَكْرٍ حَدَّثَهُ، قَالَ: قُلْتُ لِلنَّبِيِّ ﷺ وَنَحْنُ فِي الْغَارِ: لَوْ أَنَّ أَحَدَهُمْ يَنْظُرُ إِلَى قَدَمَيْهِ لَأَبْصَرَنَا تَحْتَ قَدَمَيْهِ، قَالَ: يَا أَبَا بَكْرٍ، مَا ظَنُّكَ بِاثْنَيْنِ اللَّهُ ثَالِثُهُمَا؟![٦٣].

٩٢ . حَدَّثَنَا أَبُو أُسَامَةَ، قَالَ: حَدَّثَنَا هِشَامٌ، عَنْ أَبِيهِ، أَنَّ عَبْدَ اللَّهِ بْنَ أَبِي بَكْرٍ كَانَ الَّذِي يَخْتَلِفُ بِالطَّعَامِ إِلَى النَّبِيِّ عليه الصلاة والسلام وَأَبِي بَكْرٍ وَهُمَا فِي الْغَارِ[٦٤].

٩٣ . حَدَّثَنَا شَبَابَةُ، عَنْ وَرْقَاءَ، عَنِ ابْنِ أَبِي نَجِيحٍ، عَنْ مُجَاهِدٍ فِي قَوْلِهِ: ﴿إِلَّا تَنصُرُوهُ﴾، ثُمَّ ذَكَرَ مَا كَانَ مِنْ أَوَّلِ شَأْنِهِ حِينَ بُعِثَ، يَقُولُ: فَاللَّهُ فَاعِلٌ ذَلِكَ بِهِ؛ نَاصِرُهُ كَمَا نَصَرَهُ ثَانِيَ اثْنَيْنِ[٦٥].

٩٤ . حَدَّثَنَا وَكِيعٌ، عَنْ شَرِيكٍ، عَنْ إِبْرَاهِيمَ بْنِ مُهَاجِرٍ، عَنْ مُجَاهِدٍ، قَالَ: مَكَثَ أَبُو بَكْرٍ مَعَ النَّبِيِّ ﷺ فِي الْغَارِ ثَلَاثًا[٦٦].

---

٦٣ ابن أبي شيبة (٣٦٦١٣)، والبخاري (٣٤٥٣)، ومسلم (٢٣٨١)، وابن حبان (١٥/ ٢٨٧)، وأبو يعلى (١/ ٦٨)، وأحمد (١١)، والبزار (١/ ٩٦)، وعبد بن حميد (٢)، وغيرهم.
الدرجة: صحيح.

٦٤ ابن أبي شيبة (٣٦٦١٤)، والحاكم (٣/ ٥٤٣)، وابن سعد (٣/ ١٧٣)، عن هشام عن عروة، وأخرجه إسحاق بن راهويه في مسنده (٢/ ٥٨٤)، عن هشام عن عروة عن عائشة، وأخرجه ابن عساكر عن هشام عن عروة عن أسماء بنت أبي بكر.
وأخرجه البخاري (٣٦٩٢)، عن الزهري عن عروة عن عائشة.
الدرجة: صحيح.

٦٥ أخرجه ابن أبي شيبة (٣٦٦١٥)، والطبري في التفسير (١٠/ ١٣٦).
الدرجة: مقطوع.

٦٦ ابن أبي شيبة (٣٦٦١٦)، والطبري في التفسير (١٠/ ١٣٦).
الدرجة: مقطوع.

٩٥. حَدَّثَنَا وَكِيعٌ، عَنْ نَافِعِ بْنِ عُمَرَ، عَنْ رَجُلٍ، عَنْ أَبِي بَكْرٍ، أَنَّهُمَا لَمَّا انْتَهَيَا إِلَى الْغَارِ[٦٧]، قَالَ: إِذَا جُحْرٌ، قَالَ: فَأَلْقَمَهُ أَبُو بَكْرٍ رِجْلَهُ، فَقَالَ: يَا رَسُولَ اللَّهِ، إِنْ كَانَتْ لَدْغَةٌ أَوْ لَسْعَةٌ كَانَتْ بِي[٦٨].

٩٦. حَدَّثَنَا عَبْدُ الرَّحِيمِ بْنُ سُلَيْمَانَ، عَنْ إِسْرَائِيلَ، عَنْ سِمَاكٍ، عَنْ سَعِيدِ بْنِ جُبَيْرٍ[٦٩]، عَنِ ابْنِ عَبَّاسٍ: ﴿كُنتُمْ خَيْرَ أُمَّةٍ أُخْرِجَتْ لِلنَّاسِ﴾[٧٠]، قَالَ: هُمُ الَّذِينَ هَاجَرُوا مَعَ مُحَمَّدٍ ﷺ إِلَى الْمَدِينَةِ[٧١].

---

٦٧ المصنف: انتهيا، قال:

٦٨ ابن أبي شيبة (٣٦٦١٧)، وابن عساكر (٣٠/ ٨١)، عن نافع بن عمر عن رجل عن أبي بكر، وهذا الرجل هو أبو مليكة، كما عند اللالكائي في اعتقاد أهل السنة (٧/ ١٢٧٧)، وعند الفاكهي في أخبار مكة (٤/ ٧٩).

الدرجة: ضعيف؛ لانقطاعه.

وأورده ابن كثير في السيرة النبوية (٢/ ٢٥٨)، وقال: قال الحافظ أبو بكر البزار: حدثنا محمد بن معمر، حدثنا يعقوب بن محمد، حدثنا عبد الرحمن بن عقبة بن عبدالرحمن بن جابر بن عبدالله، حدثنا أبي، عن أبيه، عن جابر قال: لما خرج رسولُ اللَّه ﷺ وأبو بكر مهاجرين، فدخلا الغار، إذا في الغار جُحر، فألقمه أبو بكر عقِبَه حتى أصبح؛ مخافة أن يخرج على رسول اللَّه ﷺ منه شيء، قال البزار: لا نعلمه يروى إلا بهذا الإسناد، وعبدالرحمن بن عقبة لا نعلم أحدًا حدَّث عنه إلا يعقوب بن محمد، وإن كان معروفًا في النسب.

٦٩ المصنف: عن ابن جبير.

٧٠ آل عمران: ١١١.

٧١ ابن أبي شيبة (٣٢٣٤٩)، وعبد الرزاق الصنعاني في التفسير (١/ ١٣٠)، وأحمد (٢٤٦٣)، والحارث (٢/ ٧١٨)، والنسائي (١١٠٧٢)، وابن جرير، وابن أبي حاتم، وابن المنذر، والطبراني (١٢/ ٦)، والحاكم (٢/ ٣٢٣)، وصححه أبو بكر الشيباني في الآحاد والمثاني (١/ ٢٥٨).

قال شعيب الأرناؤوط: إسناده حسن.

الدرجة: حسن.

٩٧. حَدَّثَنَا وَكِيعٌ، عَنْ مُوسَى بْنِ عَلِيِّ بْنِ رَبَاحٍ، عَنْ أَبِيهِ، قَالَ: سَمِعْتُ مَسْلَمَةَ بْنَ مَخْلَدٍ يَقُولُ: وُلِدْتُ حِينَ قَدِمَ النَّبِيُّ ﷺ، وَقُبِضَ وَأَنَا ابْنُ عَشْرٍ[٧٢].

٩٨. حَدَّثَنَا ابْنُ عُيَيْنَةَ، عَنِ الزُّهْرِيِّ سَمِعَ أَنَسًا يَقُولُ: قَدِمَ رَسُولُ اللَّهِ ﷺ الْمَدِينَةَ وَأَنَا ابْنُ عَشْرٍ، وَقُبِضَ وَأَنَا ابْنُ عِشْرِينَ، وَكُنَّ أُمَّهَاتِي يَحْثُثْنَنِي عَلَى خِدْمَتِهِ[٧٣].

٩٩. حَدَّثَنَا يَزِيدُ بْنُ هَارُونَ، عَنْ حَمَّادِ بْنِ سَلَمَةَ، عَنْ هِشَامِ بْنِ عُرْوَةَ، عَنْ أَبِيهِ، أَنَّ رَسُولَ اللَّهِ ﷺ لَمَّا هَاجَرَ إِلَى الْمَدِينَةِ هُوَ وَأَبُو بَكْرٍ وَعَامِرُ بْنُ فُهَيْرَةَ، قَالَ: اسْتَقْبَلَتْهُمْ هَدِيَّةُ طَلْحَةَ إِلَى أَبِي بَكْرٍ فِي الطَّرِيقِ، فِيهَا ثِيَابٌ بِيضٌ، فَدَخَلَ رَسُولُ اللَّهِ ﷺ وَأَبُو بَكْرٍ فِيهَا الْمَدِينَةَ[٧٤].

١٠٠. حَدَّثَنَا خَالِدُ بْنُ مَخْلَدٍ، عَنْ عَلِيِّ بْنِ مُسْهِرٍ، عَنْ هِشَامِ بْنِ عُرْوَةَ، عَنْ أَبِيهِ، عَنْ أَسْمَاءَ ابْنَةِ أَبِي بَكْرٍ، (أَنَّهَا)[٧٥] هَاجَرَتْ إِلَى رَسُولِ اللَّهِ ﷺ وَهِيَ حُبْلَى بِعَبْدِاللَّهِ بْنِ الزُّبَيْرِ، فَوَضَعَتْهُ بِقُبَاءٍ، فَلَمْ تُرْضِعْهُ حَتَّى أَتَتْ بِهِ النَّبِيَّ ﷺ فَأَخَذَهُ فَوَضَعَهُ فِي حَجْرِهِ، فَطَلَبُوا تَمْرَةً لِيُحَنِّكُوهُ[٧٦]، حَتَّى وَجَدُوهَا، فَحَنَّكُوهُ، فَكَانَ أَوَّلَ شَيْءٍ دَخَلَ بَطْنَهُ رِيقُ رَسُولِ اللَّهِ ﷺ وَسَمَّاهُ عَبْدَ اللَّهِ[٧٧].

---

٧٢ ابن أبي شيبة (٣٣٨٥٧)، وأبو بكر الشيباني في الآحاد والمثاني (٥/ ٣٢٤)، والطبراني في الكبير (١٩/ ٤٣٧).

قال الهيثمي في مجمع الزوائد (١٠/ ٦): ورجاله رجال الصحيح.

الدرجة: صحيح.

٧٣ ابن أبي شيبة (٣٣٨٥٨)، وأبو عوانة (٥/ ١٥٥)، وابن عساكر (٩/ ٣٤٠)، وابن عبد البر في الاستيعاب (١/ ١١٠).

ومحمد بن الوليد البسري: صدوق، معروف بحَمْل العلم.

الدرجة: حسن.

٧٤ أخرجه ابن أبي شيبة (٣٦٦٢١).

٧٥ زيادة في المصنف.

٧٦ فركوا لِثَته بشيء، وهنا: بالتمرة.

٧٧ أخرجه ابن أبي شيبة (٣٦٦٢٢)، والبخاري (٣٦٩٧)، وأحمد (٢٦٩٨٣)، وغيرهم.

١٠١ . حَدَّثَنَا جَعْفَرُ بْنُ عَوْنٍ، عَنْ أَبِي الْعُمَيْسِ، عَنِ الْحَسَنِ بْنِ سَعْدٍ، عَنْ عَبْدِ الرَّحْمَنِ بْنِ عَبْدِ اللَّهِ، قَالَ: قَالَ عَبْدُ اللَّهِ: إِنَّ أَوَّلَ مَنْ هَاجَرَ مِنْ هَذِهِ الْأُمَّةِ غُلَامَانِ مِنْ قُرَيْشٍ[٧٨].

١٠٢ حَدَّثَنَا أَبُو أُسَامَةَ، عَنْ أَبِي هِلَالٍ، عَنْ قَتَادَةَ، عَنْ سَعِيدِ بْنِ الْمُسَيَّبِ، قَالَ: قُلْتُ لَهُ: مَا فَرْقُ مَا بَيْنَ الْمُهَاجِرِينَ الْأَوَّلِينَ وَالْآخِرِينَ؟ قَالَ: فَرْقُ مَا بَيْنَهُمَا الْقِبْلَتَانِ؛ فَمَنْ صَلَّى مَعَ رَسُولِ اللَّهِ ﷺ الْقِبْلَتَيْنِ فَهُوَ مِنَ الْمُهَاجِرِينَ الْأَوَّلِينَ[٧٩].

١٠٣ . حَدَّثَنَا عَفَّانُ، قَالَ: حَدَّثَنَا حَمَّادُ بْنُ سَلَمَةَ، قَالَ: أَخْبَرَنَا ثَابِتٌ، عَنْ أَنَسٍ، أَنَّ أَبَا بَكْرٍ كَانَ رَدِيفَ النَّبِيِّ ﷺ مِنْ مَكَّةَ إِلَى الْمَدِينَةِ، وَكَانَ أَبُو بَكْرٍ يَخْتَلِفُ إِلَى الشَّامِ؛ فَكَانَ يُعْرَفُ، وَكَانَ النَّبِيُّ -عليه الصلاة والسلام- لَا يُعْرَفُ، فَكَانُوا يَقُولُونَ: يَا أَبَا بَكْرٍ، مَنْ هَذَا الْغُلَامُ بَيْنَ يَدَيْكَ؟ قَالَ: هَادٍ يَهْدِينِي السَّبِيلَ، قَالَ: فَلَمَّا دَنَوْا مِنَ الْمَدِينَةِ نَزَلَا الْحَرَّةَ[٨٠]، وَبَعَثَا[٨١] إِلَى الْأَنْصَارِ فَجَاؤُوا، قَالَ: فَشَهِدْتُهُ يَوْمَ دَخَلَ الْمَدِينَةَ، فَمَا رَأَيْتُ يَوْمًا كَانَ أَحْسَنَ وَلَا أَضْوَأَ مِنْ يَوْمِ دَخَلَ عَلَيْنَا فِيهِ، وَشَهِدْتُ[٨٢] يَوْمَ مَاتَ، فَمَا رَأَيْتُ يَوْمًا كَانَ أَقْبَحَ وَلَا أَظْلَمَ مِنْ يَوْمِ مَاتَ فِيهِ ﷺ[٨٣].

---

٧٨ ابن أبي شيبة (٣٦٦٢٣)، عن عبد اللَّه بن مسعود، وأخرجه ابن عدي في الضعفاء (٥/ ٣٣٩)، عن عطاءٍ عن ابن عباس، قال: وفيه عبد اللَّه بن داود التمار، وهو ممَّن لا بأس به.
الدرجة: أثر موقوف.

٧٩ ابن أبي شيبة (٣٦٦٢٤)، عن سعيد بن المسيَّب.
الدرجة: أثر موقوف.

٨٠ برلين: الحيرة، وهو خطأ.

٨١ برلين: بعث.

٨٢ برلين: وشهدته.

٨٣ ابن أبي شيبة (٣٦٦٢٥)، وأحمد (١٢٢٥٦)، عن أنس رضي اللَّه عنه.
الدرجة: صحيح على شرط مسلم.

Glossary of Islamic Terms*

abu (or *abi*)	أبو، أبي	father (of)
āmīn	آمين	O Allah, accept our invocation; amen
Anṣār	أنصار	'helpers'; the Muslim citizens of Madinah who gave refuge to the Prophet (ﷺ) and the other Muslim emigrants from Makkah
'arḍ	عرض	presentation; a student's recitation of hadith to the teacher
*āyah (*pl. *āyāt)*	آيات	Qur'anic verses
banu (or *bani*)	بنو، بني	*lit.* 'children (of)'; *usu.* referring to a tribe that claims a common ancestor
Bayt al-Ma'mūr	بيت المعمور	the house of worship in the seventh heaven that is frequented by angels; it is comparable to the Kaaba on Earth
burāq	براق	a white animal smaller than a mule and bigger than a donkey. It carried the Prophet (ﷺ) from Makkah to Jerusalem in the first part of the night journey.
dirham	درهم	a silver coin; a unit of currency
fiṭrah	فطرة	the natural inclination (of humans) instilled by Allah
Hadith *(ḥadīth)*	حديث	the collected statements and actions of Prophet Muhammad (ﷺ) that with the Qur'an form the basis of Islamic law

* The Arabic words are transliterated according to the conventions of the Transliteration Chart found in this book. If a word has become part of the English language (that is, it is found in a dictionary of Standard English), that spelling is used in this book and appears first in this Glossary, with the transliterated form in brackets after it.

hadith *(ḥadīth)*	حديث	a statement or action of Prophet Muhammad (ﷺ) that was remembered and recorded by his Companions and followers. It constitutes the speech and traditions of the Prophet (ﷺ) along with the reports from or about the Prophet (ﷺ)
al-ḥaṭīm	الحطيم	a semi-circular wall of about one and a quarter metres, which represents the border of the Kaaba. It is located to its southwest.
al-ḥijr Ismāʻīl	الحجر إسماعيل [حِجْر]	the crescent-shaped area next to the Kaaba, which includes part of the original Kaaba as built by Abraham
Ḥijāz	حجاز	the Western region of the Arabian Peninsula that includes Makkah and Madinah
Hijrah	هجرة	migration: *esp.* the migration from Makkah to Madinah by Prophet Muhammad (ﷺ) and his Companions that marks the start of the Islamic calendar
imam (*imām*)	إمام	leader
isnād (or *sanad*, pl. *asānīd*)	إسناد	chain of narrators supporting and proving the authenticity of the text of a tradition
al-isrā wal-miʻrāj	الإسراء والمعراج	the night journey of the Prophet (ﷺ) from Makkah to Jerusalem and then up to visit heaven
al-jarḥ wat-taʻdīl	الجرح والتعديل	impugnment and validation of Hadith narrators
Kaaba (*Kaʻbah*)	الكعبة	the house of Allah in Makkah, originally built by Prophets Abraham and Ishmael, and which Muslims face wherever they pray
al-Kawthar	الكوثر	the name of a river in paradise, the banks of which are made of pearls
kitāb	كتاب	book

maghāzi	مغازي	literature that narrates the different excursions and skirmishes that the Prophet (ﷺ) and his Companions undertook
al-Masjid al-Aqṣâ	المسجد الأقصى	the 'Farthest Mosque', located in Jerusalem and mentioned in the Qur'an (17: 1)
matn (pl. *mutūn*)	متن	text or content of a hadith
muḥaddith (pl. *muḥaddithūn*)	محدِّث	scholar of Hadith
mursal	مرسَل	a category of hadith: a 'loose' hadith with a broken link in its chain of narration at the level of a Companion; reported by a tâbi'i as if it had been heard directly from the Prophet (ﷺ)
muṣannaf	مصنَّف	*lit.* arranged by chapter; a Hadith collection arranged in chapters by subject, such as Sahih Bukhari or Sahih Muslim
musnad	مُسنَد	a Hadith collection arranged by narrator rather than content
Naskh	نسخ	A calligraphic script used for the writing of Arabic and the basis for most modern printed texts
riwāyah (pl. *riwāyāt*)	رواية	transmission; version of a hadith
samā'	سَماع	a method by which a teacher reads his or her materials, either from memory or from a book, and the students listen or write
samā'āt	سماعات	records of transmission lines, starting with the compiler and ending with the scribe who wrote the manuscript by hand and received permission to transmit it
sanad (or *isnād*, pl. *asānīd*)	سند	chain of narrators supporting and proving the authenticity of the text of a tradition

sidrat al-muntahā	سِدرة المنتهى	a lote tree that marks the end of the seventh heaven; it is a boundary which no creation can pass
sīrah	سيرة	biography, *esp.* of Prophet Muhammad (ﷺ)
Sunnah	سنّة	the precedent, practice and collected sayings of Prophet Muhammad (ﷺ) that together with the Qur'an forms the basis of Islamic law
sūrah	سورة	chapter of the Qur'an
tābi'ūn (sg. *tābi'ī*)	التابعون	'Successors'; those who knew or met any of the Companions and transmitted hadiths from them
tafsīr	تفسير	exegesis: commentary, or explanation of the meanings (*usu.* of Qur'anic verses)
tārīkh	التاريخ	the most common Arabic word for 'history', in the sense of an ordered account of actual events
wahm	وهم	illusion, imagination
Zamzam	زمزم	the blessed spring of water that Allah caused to gush out at baby Ishmael's feet; located near the Kaaba

Index

A

B

C

D

E

F

G

H

I